GADAFFI

Also by George Tremlett

Caitlin (with Mrs. Dylan Thomas)
Clubmen
Dylan Thomas: In the Mercy of His Means
Homeless
Little Legs (with Roy Smith)
Living Cities
Rock Gold: The Music Millionaires

GADAFFI
THE DESERT MYSTIC

GEORGE TREMLETT

Carroll & Graf Publishers, Inc.
New York

Copyright © 1993 by George Tremlett

First Carroll & Graf edition 1993

Carroll & Graf Publishers, Inc.
260 Fifth Avenue
New York, NY 10001

Library of Congress Cataloging-in-Publication Data
Tremlett, George.
    Qadaffi : the desert mystic / George Tremlett.—1st Carroll &
Graf ed.
        p.   cm.
    Includes bibliographical references (p.   ) and index
    ISBN 0-88184-934-0 : $23.00
    1. Qaddafi, Muammar. 2. Presidents—Libya—Biography. I. Title.
DT236.T74   1993
961.204′2′092—dc20
[B]   93-27035
                                                                         CIP

Manufactured in the United States of America

Contents

ACKNOWLEDGMENTS

How, why, when, and in what circumstances this book came to be written is explained in the preface. Most of my research was conducted at my own expense over a six-year period. My only outside assistance was from the Libyans, who invited me to Tripoli in April 1990 to discuss the book, and the British Broadcasting Corporation, who paid my expenses when I set forth for Tripoli again in April 1992, only to find myself stranded in Malta with Gavin Dutton, a producer with the BBC Community Programme Unit, with whom I was planning to make a TV program similar in theme to this book. One group of Libyans invited us to board the S.S. *Toletela*, bound for Tripoli, while another group of Libyans threw us off the boat. This is also explained in the preface.

I have decided not to name any Libyan sources, however innocent, since Articles 175, 178, and 207 of the Libyan Penal Code provide for severe punishments, ranging from three years' imprisonment to the death penalty, against those who disseminate information about Libya's internal affairs. Likewise, I do not identify the British and American citizens working in Libya whom I have interviewed while researching this book.

All published sources are listed in the bibliography and acknowledged with gratitude.

I am also grateful to my good friend Tony Secunda, whom I have known for thirty years, for making this book happen by introducing me to the New York literary agent Mitch Rose and thereby to Carroll & Graf, its publishers; to Mitch, Kent E. Carroll, and Herman Graf for supporting the project; to the British Members of Parliament Tony Banks and Ron Brown, Tony for introducing me to Ron, and Ron for his assistance over several years when meeting the Libyans and traveling to Tripoli; to Jeremy Gibson, Giles Oakley, and Gavin Dutton of the BBC Community Programme Unit; to John Wright, author of *Libya: A Modern History*, who now works for the BBC, and to the Libyan Interests Section attached to the Saudi Arabian Embassy in London and the Libyan Interests Section at the Foreign Office in London for their background guidance. I thank them, one and all, while emphasizing, lest anyone doubt it, that all opinions expressed are mine, and mine alone.

PREFACE

Colonel Gadaffi stands accused of many crimes: fostering international terrorism; providing money, weapons, or shelter for Palestinian and Japanese Red Army hijackers operating throughout Europe and the Middle East; funding the Sandinistas in Nicaragua, opposition groups in central and western Africa, Marxist rebels in the Phillipines, and the Irish Republican Army in Northern Ireland. According to the United States government and the Central Intelligence Agency, Gadaffi murders his enemies at home, sends hit-men to assassinate Libyan dissidents living abroad, and helped plant the bomb that blew up Pan Am Flight 103 over Locherbie, Scotland, causing the deaths of 270 people. Less seriously, his critics claim that Gadaffi dresses up in women's clothes, takes his teddy bear when traveling abroad, and suffers from various forms of madness brought on by syphilis. Some days, his enemies say that Gadaffi is homosexual; at other times, they say no woman is safe in his company.

On a broader political level, each time Libya's oil wealth is used to buy banks, mines, hotels, or petroleum companies, Gadaffi is charged with plotting to disrupt the economies of European nations. When Libya builds a chemical plant as part of its long-term policy of becoming wholly self-sufficient, there is an immediate Western response. Nations already stockpiling their own weapons of mass destruction profess dismay that Gadaffi should want to make his own, i.e., he is a threat to world peace and they never are. Little evidence is ever produced to back these charges against

9

Gadaffi. The mere mention of his name is enough to get Western politicians reaching for their guns or talking about airstrikes. These knee-jerk reactions have been part of our daily media fare since soon after the Libyan revolution in September 1969, and especially since President Reagan entered the White House in 1981, and I tended to accept the Reagan view that Gadaffi was one of the Bad Guys threatening our security until I happened to be in Sicily during autumn 1985 and spring 1986.

My reasons for being there, staying on the outskirts of Catania not far from the U.S. airbase at Signorello, had nothing to do with Gadaffi, Libya, or world politics but stemmed from a lifelong interest in the poet Dylan Thomas. Soon after Thomas died in New York in 1953, his widow Caitlin met a Sicilian actor, Giuseppe Fazio, and has lived with him ever since, refusing to discuss her marriage to Thomas with any biographer. Realizing that she alone held the key to the warp and weft of Thomas's life, I spent eight years trying to persuade Caitlin to break her silence. She eventually agreed to write her memoirs with me, on condition that I went out to Sicily and stayed at their home. This is a rarer experience than one might think. Fear of the Mafia keeps many travelers away from Sicily. Tourists confine themselves to a few well-trodden routes. Wandering away from them one finds mountaintop towns and remote villages that are far more Arab than Italian in their language, customs, and attitudes; ancient communities bound by a Marian form of Catholicism. "It isn't quite like Europe," wrote D. H. Lawrence, staying there in 1920. "It is where Europe ends, finally. Beyond is Asia and Africa. . . ."

This is the southern Mediterranean, where the islands of Sicily and Malta and the ports of Libya changed hands constantly for over three thousand years. Like the Jews and Arabs, the Sicilians survive by bending to the wind, sustaining their way of living and their bloodline through centuries of foreign conquest. Life has been cheap, time means little, and they look to the past, treating modern states and their ever-changing laws with amused indifference.

Only by being here in 1985 and 1986, when the Americans were stepping up their military pressure upon Gadaffi, did I come to realize that the West was facing an enemy whose history and background lay centuries beyond its understanding; if, indeed, he is an enemy.

The Fazios have been here longer than anyone can remember, with Giuseppe thinking it more likely that he is descended from the Greeks than the Romans, who arrived a trifling two thousand years ago. Like all Sicilians, he looks east and south rather than to Rome, for Sicily only became part of the Italian state in 1860. In the 1930s, Fazio served in Libya with the Italian army. As we watched America's confrontation with Libya unfolding each night on local TV newscasts, he pointed out places on a Libyan map that he had visited, describing the people and landscape. Although unsympathetic toward Gadaffi, Fazio told me how the sea captains of the southern Mediterranean traded across these waters for centuries, and how Michele Papa, a Catanese businessman and lawyer, built up a local organization to develop commerce and friendship between Catania and Tripoli, with some three thousand members in Catania and their own mosque. It was Papa who introduced the Libyans to Billy Carter, brother of the U.S. President.

It must be remembered that, at the time of which I write, the U.S. Sixth Fleet was based in the southern Mediterranean. Two aircraft carriers patrolled the seas with up to forty support ships, supplied from Signorello but also linked to other U.S. military bases outside Palermo in the west of the island and in Greece, Turkey, Crete, Spain, and Germany.

Standing outside the Fazio home, I watched U.S. planes coming in to land. Some evenings Giuseppe took me down to Catania's deep-water harbor where ships of the U.S. Navy, like the *Yorktown*, bristled with antennae and satellite dishes. Reports of troop movements and bases being put on alert appeared each night on the local TV news. These were not the only military buildups since President Reagan and his Secretary of State Al Haig targeted Gadaffi in the early months of 1981, but there was a general feeling that something more was happening this time. The American government was looking for a fight, but first had to find a cause. Strange rumors began to circulate, all allegedly linked to the CIA. Military leave was canceled at Signorello after the CIA claimed to have uncovered a Gadaffi plot to release a plague of "killer flies" to spread disease and pestilence among his enemies. Then Gadaffi was said to be planning to let loose thousands of "killer dogs" with sticks of dynamite strapped to their bellies to terrorize the towns of the Mediterranean. These astonishing stories were cited as proof that the United States was facing a crazy, unpredictable foe, but were hardly credible reasons for the Sixth Fleet to commence a military attack upon Libya ... and, anyway, no "killer flies" or "killer dogs" were ever found.

Media fantasies like these, or "disinformation" as the intelligence experts call them, may have made sense thousands of miles away in the White House Operations Room where Col. Oliver North coordinated the anti-Gadaffi campaign on the President's behalf, "liaising" with Adm. William Poindexter, Caspar Weinberger, and Robert Macfarlane, but in Sicily, on the spot, traveling around the island, I sensed a deep unease.

That was in the autumn of 1985. The Sicilians felt vulnerable. So far as one could tell, few wanted their island to be part of Italy let alone used as a forward base in what some were already saying could be the start of a third world war, with the Russians and Arabs committed to support Libya under various treaties. Little of this filtered through to the newspapers of London and Washington, which tend to lean upon those reliable "government sources" at times like these. No one knew how Libya might react. Her defensive capacity had not been tested in all the years that Gadaffi dutifully set aside fifteen percent of the country's oil revenue to equip his army, navy, and air force with the best Russian, French, Swedish, and East German weapons, boats, planes, missiles, and even submarines that money could buy. Was Sicily within range of Libya's land-based missile sites? What missiles did they have; Russian, Chinese, French, or their own? Would they fire upon Signorello in revenge for any U.S. attack, perhaps hitting the city of Catania? There was fear in the air, something that citizens of any comparable American city might find hard to comprehend, for no foreign power has put mainland America under a threat like this, except, perhaps, Cuba in 1962. The Sicilians were asking, "What has all this got to do with us? Why does the government in Rome let the Americans come here? We have no disagreement with Gadaffi. Why should America put our lives at risk?"

America found its first pretext to launch an attack upon Libya on December 27, 1985. That day, pro-Palestinian terrorists attacked groups of innocent passengers at the airports in Rome and Vienna. Twenty people were killed, including five Americans, and another one hundred eleven were injured. It was an appalling crime, which the CIA immediately blamed on Libya. For months thereafter, President Reagan insisted that Gadaffi was responsible. This caused disquiet in Europe.

One of the terrorists was captured and interviewed on Italian television while in police custody. He spoke in English and with some authority, saying his group had no connection whatever with Libya, and the Italian police later confirmed that this was so. The Austrian Minister of the Interior went further and commented, "There is not the slightest evidence to implicate Libya." Later still the Italian and Austrian governments linked the terrorists to Syria, saying that the captured terrorist had given details of where in Syria the group was trained and that this had been independently verified. The Israeli Defense Minister Itzak Rabin agreed with their analysis.

Nevertheless, on January 1, 1986, President Reagan signed an executive order requiring all United States citizens to leave Libya by the end of the month ... and he expressed outrage when Gadaffi described the United States as the real terrorists in the Middle East, offering political asylum to any U.S. citizen afraid or unwilling to go back to the United States. Still insisting that the U.S. had "irrefutable evidence" that Libya was involved in the airport bombings, Reagan signed another executive order on January 7 imposing economic sanctions against Libya and making it a criminal offense for any American company or individual citizen to trade with Libya.

Although his intentions were kept secret at the time, the President also agreed at a meeting of the National Security Council that American ships and planes should be sent into the Gulf of Sirte with the deliberate intent of provoking a Libyan response. This decision was taken in the knowledge that Gadaffi had long claimed the gulf to be part of Libya's territorial waters, partly in the belief that there may be substantial oil reserves beneath its seabed. The National Security Council reasoned that if U.S. planes went into these waters, Gadaffi would send out Libyan planes to see what was happening—and this would give the U.S. forces an excuse to shoot them down. (These strange decisions are detailed in the Chronology on pages 255 to 258, and were examined at length both in the *Washington Post* on February 22, 1987, and in Tom Bowyer's 1987 BBC TV documentary "Twelve Minutes Over Tripoli," in which U.S. military personnel described their roles in setting their trap for Gadaffi. It was at this time that the very same White House officials also secretly agreed to commence arms shipments to Iran, setting in train the series of events that led to Irangate and the seizure of more Western hostages in Beirut.)

*   *   *

In March 1986, I returned to Sicily amid growing signs that a
U.S. attack upon Libya was drawing closer; there were even sugges-
tions that this might be a full-scale invasion. An intelligence satellite
positioned over Libya provided the White House with details of
Gadaffi's troop deployments. Phantom jets were flying in low over
the plains south of Catania. A third aircraft carrier joined the Sixth
Fleet, and there were more flights than ever in and out of Signorello. The pace was quickening. The sense of fear ran deeper.

Giuseppe Fazio again drove me down to Catania harbor and out
past the airbase. In the evenings we settled down to watch the
local Sicilian TV news. Most nights there was domestic news from
Libya: Gadaffi making a speech, visiting a hospital, inspecting a
factory production line, test-driving a tractor, riding his horse, welcoming visitors to his tent, and once, just once, relaxing with his
wife and children. This may have been propaganda, but the Libyans
seemed totally normal people. "Do you think I would live with this
man if he was as bad as the Americans say he is?" asked his wife.

One evening Gadaffi was interviewed by a local reporter. I cannot
give their exact words for Sicilian is only partly Italian with many
Greek, Arab, and Turkish phrases, and Gadaffi was answering in
Arabic, but it was easy enough to understand what he was saying,
with a little help from Giuseppe: "The Americans cannot be serious.
They say we are terrorists because we openly support the oppressed people of the world fighting for their freedom against colonial powers, but how could we terrorize anyone? Look at us. We
are a small country." More than what he said, it was the way
Gadaffi said it that intrigued me, for this was a Gadaffi different
from the one usually shown on Western television; charming, relaxed, calmly fatalistic. Dressed in a well-cut Italian jacket, slacks,
and an open-necked shirt, he was friendly and engaging with an
open smile. "If the Americans attack us, what can we do? We will
try to defend ourselves, but if we have to die we will die with
honor." His demeanor was curiously impressive. "That is how a
Bedouin would think. I may not like him, but he is a good Arab,"
said Giuseppe Fazio, emphasizing again that the people of the
southern Mediterranean have so much history running through
their veins.

There and then, that evening, I decided to write this book, without realizing how difficult it would prove.

* * *

A few days later, after a farrago of preliminary abuse from Washington, with President Reagan describing Libya as "an outlaw state" and Vice President Bush saying Gadaffi was "mad and unpredictable," the U.S. Sixth Fleet was sent in to the Gulf of Sirte under the command of Vice Adm. Frank Kelso. Senator William Proxmire was among the American politicians who joined in the chorus, arguing that "the great powers must defend their right to sail in open seas."

As a statement of strategic thinking, Proxmire's argument was unexceptional. But what, in this case, *is* an open sea?

The logistics are better understood if one looks at a map of Libya and the surrounding countries of the Mediterranean. Under international law, all nations may claim the sea as theirs within twelve miles of their coast. Gadaffi has gone further, calling the 32nd parallel, the line across the map south of Benghazi to Misurata, his "Line of Death," warning that any ships crossing it do so at their peril.

Geographically, one can see his point. This is, after all, a gulf, enclosed on three sides by Libyan coastline, and it is difficult to see why any other country would wish to send its ships into these waters. But there is far more to these claims than territorial pride; something that was not explained in the military briefings given by the U.S. State Department to justify America's use of military force.

For Libya, the Gulf of Sirte has strategic and economic importance. Nearly all Libya's oil and gas discoveries have been made in the Sirte Desert, inland from the gulf's southern coastline. Along this shore there are five ports whose names are largely unknown to the outside world—As Sidrah, Ras Lanuf, Bishr, Braygah, and As Zuwaylinah. They are not much to look at, being mainly oil and gas terminals with ancilliary engineering buildings, some docking facilities, and residential complexes where foreign workers live in compounds with their own golf and sailing clubs, soccer fields, tennis courts, swimming pools, and private beaches. So far as I know, no Western journalist has been allowed to go there, for these places are the heart, liver, and lungs of the Libyan economy. This is where Libya's wealth is earned. From here, oil and gas pipelines stretch up to 150 miles south to the desert wells at Zeitan, Mabruk, Bahi, Facha, Dahra, Hofra, Farrud, Dor, Kotla, Ora, Khuff, Meghili, Megid, Khatt, Buattifel, Samah, Beda, Bel Hedan, Ora, Harash, Waha, Jalu, Defa, Zaagut, Amal, Awila, and Nasr.

Libya's oil is exceptionally pure, low in sulfur content, and easy to refine. When foreign tankers come to collect either oil or gas, their crews rarely step ashore. The pipelines are connected to floating platforms a mile offshore. When a tanker arrives, a pilot goes out to it either by motorboat or helicopter and stays on board until the vessel has been loaded. This often requires seamanship and engineering skills of the highest order. Storms are frequent in the Gulf of Sirte. The platforms become unstable, and forcing crude oil or liquid gas down a mile of pipe into an empty ship that may be bobbing in the sea can cause an air bubble in the pipe or a sudden shift in the center of gravity on board the tanker. One engineer who has experienced these problems told me, "They're a bugger"—and it is hardly surprising that Colonel Gadaffi should be so anxious to protect what is, in effect, his economy's underbelly. He has other reasons, too. For many years Libya has been secretly shipping oil to Israel. One of the American engineers who works here gave me the names of two Israeli-owned companies whose tankers transport oil from Braygah to Israel, and identified the tankers. I have decided not to reveal the details or the source for reasons that will be explained later in this preface. When I asked him why, this American said: "Colonel Gadaffi is always pragmatic. He never lets politics interfere with trade." And he added that Israeli canned foods were openly on sale in Libyan supermarkets.

This, then, was the Gulf of Sirte that Vice Admiral Kelso and the U.S. Sixth Fleet entered on March 24, 1986 for what were variously described as "naval exercises" and "a demonstration of America's right to sail in open seas." Their real reason for being there only became clear ten months later when the *Washington Post* published details of the President's meeting with the National Security Council. At the time, Colonel Gadaffi had no inkling of America's intentions. Indeed, there was some speculation that night on Libyan and Italian television that the United States was about to seize Libya's oil fields.

American planes flew in low over the Libyan coast to test the radar installations. Some flew in behind normal passenger flights to see whether the radar systems could differentiate between domestic and military aircraft. Others went "fishing" to test the Libyans' responses. Two missiles were fired from a Libyan battery near the town of Sirte, only to have their guidance systems jammed from the *Yorktown*. Libyan Mirage jets, bought from France, were sent up to see what was happening—just as the strategists had expected—and that gave Kelso his excuse to open fire. So many claims and denials were made thereafter that one cannot be sure precisely what happened, but several (possibly three) Libyan planes were shot down. The radar station at Sirte was bombed. Four Libyan boats were sunk. The Americans insisted these were gunboats loaded with missiles; the Libyans said they were fishing boats. Whatever the truth, fifty Libyan bodies were picked up out of the water by a passing Spanish tanker. On Libyan television that night it was claimed that U.S. ships deliberately refused to pick up any of these men, even though they could be seen floundering in the water, struggling for their lives.

As an exercise in the arts of war, these maneuvers in the Gulf of Sirte were far from conclusive. Confusing figures were given by both sides. There seemed to be some reluctance on the part of the Americans to explain what happened. No one knew *why* American ships were there. When asked the direct question, had the U.S. Navy or Air Force entered Libyan waters or air space, U.S. spokesmen denied it.

And then came the bombing of La Belle Epoque, a discothèque in West Berlin frequented by off-duty American servicemen. On the night of April 5, 1986, a terrorist bomb exploded, killing an American serviceman and a Turk. Within hours President Reagan and British Prime Minister Margaret Thatcher were again claiming to have "irrefutable evidence" that Libya was responsible. This was immediately denied by Libya, but the White House went into overdrive, mobilizing American forces and warning Gadaffi that punishment was on its way. For over a week, the world's press speculated when this might occur, with European politicians and police chiefs insisting that there was no evidence to link the discothèque bombing to Libya. The United States produced copies of telexes allegedly sent between Tripoli and Libyan diplomats in Europe that could be interpreted as meaning that the Libyans had a role in the discothèque bombing, but were far from conclusive and capable of many other interpretations. Most of America's NATO allies refused to have any part in President Reagan's threatened airstrike. The French, German, Spanish, and Italian governments all denied American planes access to their airspace. The only support for the President's proposed action came from Mrs. Thatcher, anxious as always to project herself as the President's closest ally. Without consulting her Cabinet, Mrs. Thatcher told President Reagan that the U.S. planes earmarked for the airstrike could be stationed at the U.S. bases at Mildenhall and Lakenfield.

Early in the evening of Monday April 14, the F111 bombers took off from these two British bases, flying down toward Gibraltar, refueling in midair, before coming in low from the west for their bombing runs on Tripoli and Benghazi. Down below in the Mediterranean, Admiral Kelso again stationed his aircraft carriers off the Libyan coast with a supporting fleet of destroyers, cruisers, and nuclear submarines. Nearly two thousand U.S. Marines were armed and ready for action. Eleven squadrons of U.S. combat aircraft were standing by, their pilots ready to scramble and come in with air support in the event of a landing.

Clearly this was intended to be more than a retaliatory air strike ... but the Marines did not go into action, the fleet stood back from the coast, and the planes were held in reserve. In Tripoli, it was rumored that U.S. commandos were already operating inside the country, preparing to knock out the radio and TV stations, liaising with dissident officers and underground supporters of the National Front for the Salvation of Libya. Gadaffi was expected to fall that night, but he confounded them all.

The Americans chose several key military targets. Bombs fell on or near the Bureau for External Security, which maintains radio contact with the Libyan People's Bureaus in neighboring countries; the military barracks at Benghazi, a training camp for Palestinian guerrillas, Tripoli harbor, the coastal radar stations, the airports at Tripoli and Benghazi, and—most significantly—the Aziziyah barracks outside Tripoli.

Later that night, in briefings at the Pentagon, the U.S. government insisted that their purpose had been wholly military. They had to say this. It would be an indictable offense for an American president to assassinate a foreign head of state without the approval of Congress.

It is now known that assassination *was* the U.S. government's intention, although this was denied on the night. Gadaffi's home was the primary target. Seven bombs fell near the house within the grounds of the Aziziyah barracks. I have been there and seen the damage. Two bombs fell on his tennis court. One bomb fell near his front door, causing considerable damage. Flying shards of glass injured two of his sons and killed his adopted daughter Hana.

A dozen bombs also fell on the residential district of Bin Ashur, where many ministers and senior officials have their homes. One bomb severely damaged the French Embassy, destroying the house next door. Nearly a hundred people died in Bin Ashur, mostly innocent civilians, women and children, killed as they slept in their beds.

By then, I was back in London trying to establish contact with the Libyans having already discovered that no one can go to Libya without an invitation. For reasons that may become clear in this book, the Libyans distrust the outside world—especially Britain and the United States—although their diplomats are careful to stress that Libya has no quarrel with the British and American people, only with the policies pursued by their governments. Visas are issued only *after* a visit has been agreed. In practice, this means that the only foreigners to go there are overseas workers who apply for a job; salesmen with a product that the Libyans wish to buy; journalists invited for an expressly defined purpose, or politicians generally sympathetic to the revolution.

Through a friend in the Parliamentary Labour Party, Tony Banks, I arranged to meet Ron Brown, then M.P. for Leith, who acquired an unfortunate reputation by espousing Marxist theories, visiting Libya and Afghanistan, and making uncompromising speeches in the House of Commons. My friend warned me not to be put off by Brown's appearance, for his face had been disfigured in an industrial accident, and I soon found that his fiery rhetoric was deceiving. Away from Parliament and media temptations, he displayed a shrewd understanding of Libyan affairs and I could see why Gadaffi repeatedly invited him back to Tripoli for private meetings. He introduced me to the Libyans, described his sessions with Gadaffi, gave me much information about the country, and sought permission for me to go there. Arrangements were first made for me to fly to Tripoli in the autumn of 1986, and then again the following year. In August 1989, I was invited to attend celebrations to mark the twentieth anniversary of the revolution.

This invitation came with only two days' notice, which is how things tend to happen when one is dealing with the Libyans. When I said this would be difficult for me to manage with my children on holiday from school, the Libyans replied:

We are sorry, Mr. Tremlett. We didn't know you were married with children. Mr. Brown should have told us that. Our society is built upon the family, Mr. Tremlett, and we would not wish you to be apart from your family. Please bring your wife and children with you, as our guests. We will look after everything. A car will be sent to your home. Rooms will be booked overnight at a hotel near Heathrow Airport, and then you will fly to Frankfurt the following morning. All flights to Tripoli that day are fully booked so we will book you all into a hotel in Frankfurt for the night and then you can join us in Tripoli next day. . . . We will have rooms reserved for you in Tripoli. You and your wife will be comfortable. It is a very good, modern hotel.

For the next forty-eight hours we dashed around, buying new clothes, washing old ones, going to the doctor for cholera jabs and antimalaria tablets, persuading our children to bathe early and be ready for the car that was due to arrive at 11 A.M. on August 29. We waited and waited and waited, with the children first to get restless. The car never came. When I phoned to find out what had happened, my hosts were apologetic. "We're sorry, Mr. Tremlett. We had to give your seats to someone else . . . but don't worry. There's always tomorrow." This is something else that often happens when one is dealing with the Libyans.

The following April, 1990, I was invited again, this time on my own and at equally short notice, having by then spent four years talking through the possibility of writing a book that would be a study of Gadaffi, his personal background, the history of his country and its character, and the ways Libya has changed since the revolution. At one stage I was promised his personal cooperation and offered to learn Arabic or Italian. "That won't be necessary, Mr. Tremlett," came the reply. "Our Leader's English is good but he prefers to speak only in Arabic when being interviewed for foreign television. As a matter of honor he would speak to you in your language when you were a guest in our country. . . . There is only one thing we ask. Please stay long enough to travel around the country, meet our people, and see what we have achieved since the revolution. We would like you to stay at least six months. We will provide you with a car and a driver and you will be free to travel wherever you wish. Our Leader will give you every assistance. He has asked me to tell you that he hopes you will talk to his family and friends and also to our ministers so that you can form your own opinion of our society."

When I said that if my interviews with Gadaffi were tape-recorded, I would return with my final manuscript and go through it with him line by line, not to allow him any powers of censorship but as a reciprocal courtesy to ensure that the manuscript accurately reflected whatever he told me, I was told, "That won't be necessary, Mr. Tremlett. We would like you to feel free to form your own judgments. . . ."

In April 1990, I spent nearly a week in Tripoli discussing my proposed book in detail, meeting officials from various ministries and Libyan television, traveling around Tripoli, touring the National Museum, going around the streets and markets, and attending an evening of music and speeches arranged at Gadaffi's former home to mark the fourth anniversary of the American bombing. This is another aspect of the Libyans' character that needs explanation; they are constantly arranging musical celebrations or days of mourning to commemorate past events. These are always attended by vast numbers of people who listen carefully, applaud vigorously, eating iced cakes or drinking either orange squash or Pepsi Cola, for this is a Muslim country in which alcohol is forbidden. These gatherings continue late into the night, for the Libyans live by a different body clock. They avoid too much movement in the heat of the day, either resting or sleeping, and then socialize in the coolness of the night, often into the early hours of the morning. Every night I was there, I had a main meal at 2 or 3 A.M. Gadaffi follows this same pattern. It is the one part of the day that is not interrupted by prayers.

There was then another long silence, which I used to further research the climate, geography, and history of the region, and especially of the Sirte Desert, which was the traditional grazing ground of Gadaffi's tribe, the el Gadadfa. My next visit was drawing closer and was finally confirmed for April 1992. This time I was planning to also gather material for a BBC TV program. The Libyans knew that contracts had been signed. To avoid causing any embarrassment to the British government or to the BBC, the producer and I arranged to attend briefing sessions at the Foreign Office and the BBC External Affairs Department. There was a reason for our caution. Britain was on the eve of a general election, the United Nations sanctions against Libya were due to come into effect on April 15, and we did not want our TV program to be caught in any political crossfire.

Flight tickets were booked for April 15, long before it was known that sanctions would commence that day, so I contacted the Libyans to see if we should change our plans. "No, you will be all right, Mr. Tremlett. The sanctions do not come into force until midnight. . . . We are looking forward to seeing you again. We have booked you into a hotel here and made arrangements for you to meet all the people you need to see for your book."

By the time our plane arrived at Luqa Airport in Malta, where we were due to change flights, Gadaffi had decided to close Tripoli Airport. No more foreign planes were being allowed into Libya. All communications had been cut with the outside world. Gadaffi had declared another day of mourning, this time to commemorate those killed in the U.S. raid upon Tripoli six years earlier. For the next two weeks, I found myself stranded in Malta, phoning the Libyans daily, visiting their People's Bureau, the Libyan Arab Airways office, the Libyan Bureau for Cultural Affairs, and the shipping office that arranges the hydrofoil service between Valletta and Tripoli. One evening I spent five hours on a Libyan cargo ship while it was being loaded with bananas from Ecuador, bed linen from Calabria in Southern Italy, and Toyota trucks from Japan, only to be thrown off minutes before departure. The People's Committee on board ship would not accept the papers issued by the Libyan People's Bureau in Valletta, even though a senior Libyan diplomat from the Bureau came down to the ship to answer their questions. "We believe everything you tell us, Mr. Tremlett," said the committee's spokesman, flanked by his confreres, "but you are a writer—and we have been told to allow no more writers into the country." This is something else that one has to learn about Libya; each People's Committee can countermand another People's Committee, and they do so politely, without anyone losing his temper.

Night after night in Malta, I talked into the early hours with British, American, Tunisian, Greek, Italian, and Danish citizens who had all been on their way back to Libya when Gadaffi closed the airports. One group of eight engineers from Birmingham, working in Libya under a three-month contract, had been asked to stay on for another three months. However, rather than issue new visas the Libyan Immigration Department insists that all foreign nationals leave the country when their visas expire, and then reapply for fresh visas, producing all necessary documents. In practice, they have to fly to Malta for a few days, book into a hotel, and then apply to the People's Bureau, who then telex or fax their colleagues in Tripoli for authorization. These eight engineers went back to the People's Bureau every morning for a fortnight until their visas came through. Some days, there were queues outside the Bureau. No one ever dares speak out of turn.

If this sounds addled, I can only report that the hotels of Valletta were packed that fortnight with foreign nationals working in the Libyan oil and gas fields, or in the factories established with Libya's oil revenues. "They treat us like this to show that they're in charge," one of them told me, while another Briton said that he had been working near Benghazi for twelve years and still had to leave the country every three months to renew his visa. There were also eight Irish Catholic laborers staying at a nearby hotel, drinking themselves stupid every day. A Libyan escort doled out their drinking-money each morning and paid their hotel bill while they waited for the People's Bureau to issue new visas. In my innocence, I said I thought alcohol was contrary to the laws of Islam. "So it is," said my informant, "but we're in Malta now and the Libyans couldn't care less. Money means nothing to them. They're pragmatic. So what if the Christians want to kill themselves with booze! The Libyans think that's funny. It appeals to their sense of humor."

Slowly, since initially I had envisaged meeting Gadaffi and persuading him to explain his revolution, it dawned on me that in these six years trying to break through his barriers I had gathered an extraordinary archive of original material, anecdotes, and documents, relating to Libya and its leader; an archive collected in London, Sicily, Malta, and Tripoli, dating back before the Italian occupation, the Second World War, the British postwar administration, the battle for independence, the brief Sanusi monarchy, and Gadaffi's revolution, an archive that put Libya and Gadaffi in a new light.

There are no books currently available in the West with accurate up-to-date information about Libya, and yet here I was in Malta quietly interviewing the mainly British and American engineers and administrators who happily spend their working lives inside a country that they all agreed was a living madhouse. "The Libyans are lovely people," I was told,

> but they haven't a clue. . . . Without foreign workers, their whole economy would fall apart. They can't master modern technology,

which comes unnaturally to them. . . . They have spent hundreds of millions of dollars importing the finest industrial machinery that you will find anywhere in the world; the range of their equipment is astonishing, but a lot of it is either never used or left in packing cases because they don't know how to handle it. . . . They've got half-a-million Egyptians in there, working for them—and another seven hundred thousand Arabs from the Sudan, who are given all the dirty, shitty jobs that the Libyans don't want to touch. . . . The Libyans are wealthy, but they're in a mess. No one has ever taught them how to dispose of rubbish, so wherever you go there's dirt and filth and abandoned cars. . . . These guys are no threat to anyone, but they're too proud to admit it. . . . The truth is they need help."

These were eyewitnesses talking. People who had gone where no foreign journalist is allowed, into the oil and gas fields, and the shining new factories built by German, Japanese, and South Korean contractors to enable Libya to manufacture consumer goods. In theory, Libya should be producing its own rather than buying abroad . . . but, in fact, these factories are at low levels of efficiency, either because the machines are not working; have broken down and cannot be repaired, or lack trained personnel . . . factories where the future lies in a packing case, just as Libya's new planes, tanks, and missiles often stand idle in storage sheds because the country cannot produce enough trained technicians to operate their electronics.

Superficially, Libya appears a highly efficient modern state; the most prosperous in Africa. The oil and gas flowing through its desert pipelines have brought the country great wealth. This has been invested on a worldwide basis through LAFICO (the Libyan Arab Foreign Investment Company) to ensure that Libya remains wealthy once its oil and gas reserves are exhausted—although that date may be many years away. Geologists working there told me that Libya has thirty years' known reserves of oil at current rates of extraction (which is more than most countries). The Libyans are now drilling for oil in previously unexplored parts of the desert, and the geologists say there is a strong probability that they will find important new reserves. More significantly, Libya's gas reserves are worth far more than their oil and are expected to remain in production at present levels for at least two hundred years. The

Libyans are also investing substantially in a desalination plant. Originally this was to boost their water supply, but they have now discovered that the Mediterranean is rich in natural minerals with a thick crust of salts beneath its sea bed. Libya is even extracting small quantities of gold from seawater! Inside Libya, new towns, schools, and hospitals have been built for its people. Every Libyan has access to education and modern health care, as of right. Housing standards are high . . . and where once camels trekked for days between oases, Libyan Arab Airways shuttles its passengers by airbus between Ghat, Sebha, Houn, Kufra, and Ghedames and the main cities, Tripoli and Benghazi. Modern telecommunications systems installed by Plessey and Marconi bring together remoter areas in a way that was impossible thirty years ago. But all this remains largely unseen by the outside world, for the Libyans have chosen to reject both East and West, and particularly those consumer-based materialistic values by which America and Europe thrive. The Libyans have seen what tourism has done to Tunisia, Morocco, Spain, Italy, and Greece, with their coastlines wrecked by ugly concrete-block hotels and their towns given over to bars, nightclubs, and giftshops. "Why should we let that happen to us?" they ask, proudly telling you that thanks to their Leader the beautiful landscape of Cyrenaica with its mountain peaks and forests, the fishing villages, and the ancient cities of Leptis Magna and Sebratha are better-preserved than any comparable anywhere in the world.*

Instead, the Libyans remain largely isolated from the modern world, living simply by the Koran and the principles laid down in *The Green Book*, the pocket handbook that enshrines Gadaffi's

---

*Leptis Magna is a complete Roman city on the Mediterranean coast that was swallowed by sand after the fall of Rome, thus preserving for all time its ampitheaters, marketplace, forum, harbor, lighthouse, public baths, and the homes of an estimated one hundred thousand people. The older parts of the city were built by the Phoenicians three thousand years ago. The main building materials were marble and sandstone. "The centuries have turned it into a city of amber—from the patina which has spread over its stones," wrote Aubrey Menen, in *Cities in the Sand*. "Sometimes, when the sun is right, and when it is seen from the sea, it looks like a legendary city built of gold." Gadaffi has encouraged its restoration, largely so that Libyan children may appreciate their heritage, but it is virtually empty of visitors. If Gadaffi ever changed his mind, this could be one of the world's great tourist attractions—like the Pyramids of Egypt, the Great Wall of China, etc.

philosophy. There is no tourist literature, no books or brochures for visitors, no maps or street signs in any language but Arabic. Even postcards are hard to find, and always have Gadaffi's slogans on the back—AL FATAH WILL ALWAYS REMAIN THE PEOPLE'S PATH TO REVOLUTION or THE ULTIMATE AIM IN LIFE IS FOR MAN TO BE FREE AND HAPPY—THIS BEING THE MESSAGE WHICH THE GREEN BOOK CONVEYS TO PEOPLES OF THIS PLANET.

Visitors are invited only when the government has a point to make, and then provided with escorts from the Ministry of Information. Pretending to be helpful, the escorts carefully restrict the visitors' movements. A journalist asking to go somewhere inconvenient will be told that transport is unavailable or a sandstorm expected. The Libyans are too polite to openly refuse a request. Escorts have been known to accompany photographers on official photo-calls—and then confiscate their rolls of film. Protests serve no purpose. The Libyans begin talking in Arabic and ignore the visitor, who may expect a car to arrive suddenly to take him to the airport. It is no good trying to complain to some other level of authority, for all people are equal in Libya. Visitors soon discover there are no telephone directories. Phone calls have to be made through an operator. This communications system has been devised so that the whole country can be rendered incommunicado at the touch of a switch, enabling Gadaffi to thwart any attempted countercoup. The government is in total control. No one may own or operate a fax machine or a photocopier without a license. When they do cut themselves off from the outside world, as has happened several times while I have been researching this book, the Libyans are saying *bukra* (they will speak to you tomorrow) or *ba'de bukra* (the day after tomorrow), which is how they respond to most requests. Everything has to wait until the time is right; *In'ch'Allah* (until God wills it).

Earlier in this preface, it was mentioned how difficult this book turned out to be. The problem lay not so much in the subject matter as in this attitude that the Libyans have to the outside world. They seem paranoid, perhaps with reason. In one way or another, the West has supported at least nine attempts to assassinate Gadaffi, most notoriously trying to bomb him in his bed, but also through arming and training his enemies, and encouraging his rivals to prepare for his overthrow. This has left the Libyans suspicious of anyone who wants to write about them. It is a criminal offense to divulge any information about any aspect of the country's affairs to a foreigner. Early on in my researches, I was asking a prominent Libyan about the country's population, its birthrate, death rate, levels of infant mortality, incidence of disease, and also about its system of justice, the criminal code, the way the different courts adjudicate. In most Western countries, one would be able to find information like this in a public library, but it is not easy to discover reliable statistics relating to Libya—and I thought he might be able to help me. We were talking freely in a European hotel when his face clouded over. "I must be careful what I say or they might hang me," he said, which brought our conversation to an embarrassing end.

In a similar vein, Britons working in Libya told me they had heard of police calling to arrest people in the middle of the night, without warrants or explanation. Gadaffi claims such things do not happen, and in fairness it must be said that I was never able to establish where or when any such arrest might have occurred, but this was said—and Amnesty International has published lists of Libyan dissidents alleged to be held in detention without trial. So I have taken care not to identify those who helped me by answering my questions.

This book has an unusual structure, with chronological sections interspersed with narrative or descriptive chapters. This device enables me to separate fact from rumor, putting the Libyan revolution in a broader context, without allowing extraneous or repetitive detail to swamp my argument. Inevitably, there is some overlap, but such a technique allows me to expand, develop, and justify an unfamiliar case. I would like to have been more precise in some parts of the chronology, but the problem here has been that events in Libya are often not reported until days, weeks, or even years later. This is especially true of events which touch upon civil unrest or attempts to challenge Gadaffi's power. Reports like this tend to filter out through emigre organizations or intelligence agencies, and need to be treated with care. Also, throughout *Gadaffi,* I write of monetary figures interchangeably in dollars and pounds. To assist in your understanding of the text, the average exchange rate for the two currencies is as follows: in the 1950s, 2.8 dollars to the pound; in the 1960s 2.5 dollars to the pound; in the 1970s, 2.38 dollars to the pound. At the beginning of the 1980s, the exchange rate was approximately 2.15 dollars to the pound. It then went haywire in 1983 with a rate of 1.7 dollars to the pound. In 1984, the exchange rate was 1.25.

Lastly, may I emphasize that I am not pro-Libyan or anti-American, although I did receive some limited assistance from the Libyans, which is fully declared in this preface so that the reader may judge my bona fides. This book is written in a spirit of genuine independence and in a search for truth, with me having originally formed the view that the West misunderstood Gadaffi, overestimating his threats and underestimating both his achievements and also the intellectual nature of his revolution. If my opinion is correct, then it has to be said that this misapprehension is largely Gadaffi's fault for trying to live in isolation when barriers are coming down all over the world; nevertheless, it follows that Britain and the United States should reexamine their past attitude to Libya and seek to help Libya take her proper place within the community of nations. This will require humility on all sides, not least from Gadaffi.

—Laugharne
July 1993

Part I

Colonel Gadaffi and his countrymen see their revolution as the final stage in Libya's search for independence and a sense of national identity. To understand the revolution, and Gadaffi's achievements since, it is necessary to know what went before; what the Libyans felt they were fighting for—as well as what they were fighting against. This general area of North Africa has been known as Libya since ancient times. With so much of its landscape vast, arid desert, there was no need to define frontiers. Herodotus came here twenty-four hundred years ago, observing that its people could be broadly divided into two ethnic types—"Aethiopians" and Libyans. The former were the darker-skinned races of the south, living in what is now Sudan, Mali, Niger, and, yes, Ethiopia; the latter, the wandering Berber tribes of the deserts and coastal plains. And so they remained, sometimes falling to the Greeks or the Romans, at other times to the Turks or Italians, until the mid-twentieth century and the post–Second World War settlement. Then, with no particularly good maps to go by, the victors drew lines across the deserts, defining the boundaries, creating the new state of Libya by United Nations decree.

THE EVENTS LEADING
UP TO LIBYA'S
INDEPENDENCE

1837   After founding the Sanusi Order at Mount Abu Qubais, near Mecca, al Sayyid Muhammad bin Ali al Sanusi (the Grand Sanusi) begins his journey across North Africa (1841), reaching Tripoli (1842) and turning back east after hearing that the French were colonizing Algeria.

29

1843	Foundation of the mother lodge al Zawiya al Baida on the plateau of Cyrenaica, near the coast.
1846—1853	The Grand Sanusi returns to Mecca before deciding to consolidate in Cyrenaica, forming over seventy *zawiyas* (or lodges), across the coastal plateau, the steppes and deserts of Libya and western Egypt.
1856	The Grand Sanusi establishes an Islamic University at the uninhabited oasis of Jaghbub. All the Bedouin tribes are now under his spell—including the Gadadfa, whose grazing grounds were in the Sirte Desert. This was Gadaffi's tribe, who had been living here since the fifteenth century, when their ancestors were driven out of Andalusia.
1859	The Grand Sanusi dies at Jaghbub on September 7. A regency of ten sheikhs controls the order until his eldest son Sayyid Muhammad al Mahdi is old enough to succeed. Sayyid was born in a cave near the mother lodge at al Baida.
1895	Sayyid al Mahdi, the second Grand Sanusi, moves the order's "headquarters" to the southern oasis, Kufra, then almost unknown to the outside world.
1896	Sayyid al Mahdi dies a few months after his only brother. Sayyid's sons are minors. Leadership of the order passes to his brother's son Sayyid Ahmad al Sharif.
1911	Italian troops land in Tripoli and Cyrenaica, both part of the Turkish empire. Resistance comes from followers of the Sanusi. This conflict, the first Italo-Sanusi War, continues until 1917. Gadaffi's grandfather dies in this war.
1912	The Turks cede control of Tripolitania and Cyrenaica to the Italians under the Treaty of Ouchy (October 18). A fortnight later Italy and France formally recognize each other's positions in Libya and Morocco.
1915	Italy enters the First World War on the side of the Allies. Ahmad al Sharif aligns with Turkey then attacks the British with calamitious results. His Bedouin troops are overwhelmingly defeated. Ahmad al Sharif relinquishes leadership of the Sa-

nusi to his cousin al Sayyid Muhammad Idris (hereafter referred to as Idris). After a truce is declared, both Britain and Italy recognize Idris as Emir of parts of Cyrenaica; the first time a Sanusi leader has been seen as a political figure.

1918   Tripolitania declares its independence.

1921   Idris seeks to unite the country, but fails to respond to calls for help from Tripolitania when the Italians begin to reassert their authority.

1922   The Italians refuse to discuss uniting Tripolitania and Cyrenaica, being willing to discuss only the future of Tripolitania. In a desperate bid to retain independence, Tripolitania offers Idris the role of emir. He dithers for three and a half months, and when the Italians object, he goes into exile.

1923—1931   The second Italo-Sanusi War. Gadaffi's tribe joins the others against the Italians. The Bedouin are led by Sheikh Omar al Mukhtar. The war becomes exceptionally vicious with the Bedouin fighting a guerrilla campaign and the Italians reacting with mass executions, enforced concentration camps and innumerable acts of unspeakable cruelty, forcing the Bedouin into starvation by destroying herds and crops, and cementing up their wells. Gadaffi's father and uncle are both sentenced to death and reprieved. Gadaffi's father loses an eye.

1931   The Italians break the Bedouin resistance with the capture of Sheikh Omar al Mukhtar, whom they publicly hang before a crowd of twenty thousand captured Bedouin on September 16. His few remaining supporters try to escape to Egypt but are mostly killed. Gadaffi estimates that half the population died in this war.

1932   On January 24 the Italians declare that the war has been brought to a successful conclusion.

1933   The Italians revoke all agreements with the Sanusi and begin confiscating Bedouin lands without compensation. Traditional Bedouin grazing grounds are allocated to Italian settlers.

1936   The Italians conduct the first census of what is

now Libya. The total population of Tripolitania and Cyrenaica is said to be 848,610.

1937   Mussolini visits Libya to open the 1,140-mile highway along the coast between the borders of Tunis and Egypt, describing himself as "the protector of Islam." The first seven hundred Italian farmers settle in Cyrenaica.

1938   Between March and December, another twenty thousand Italian farmers settle in Cyrenaica under a program of state-directed migration that is robbing the Bedouin of their heritage.

1939   On January 1 Libya becomes integrated with Italy and is hereafter considered to be not a colony but an integral part of the Italian state.

Between January and December, another twenty thousand Italian farmers arrive to settle on land allocated to them in Cyrenaica. By 1942, it is variously estimated that the Italian population of Libya is from seventy thousand to over one hundred thousand.

The Second World War begins on September 3 with Britain declaring war on Germany after Hitler's attack upon Poland.

1940   After geological research by Professor Desio of Milan University, the Italians begin drilling for oil in the Sirte Desert. Drilling stops when the war reaches North Africa—but it is here in the Sirte basin that the great oil discoveries are made nearly thirty years later.

April   Idris offers support to the British, who visit him in Egypt, where he is living in exile.

June 10   Italy enters the Second World War in support of Germany. The British take up the offer from Idris. A Libyan Arab Army is formed with five battalions. All the officers are British.

June 28   The Italian Governor of Libya, Balbo, killed at Tobruk.

August 9   Libyans living in exile hold a conference in Egypt, with those from Tripolitania complaining that Idris is too close to the British.

1940/1942   The Desert War rages throughout North Africa, with the German Army under Rommel entering the fray and the British losing ground before the tide turns in 1942 with the Eighth Army's advance on the towns of the Sirte Desert and Rommel's retreat to Tripoli. The Allies win the decisive Battle of El Alamein in October/November. The British take Benghazi, the main town in Cyrenaica, on November 20.

1942   Muammar Gadaffi born—but he has no idea which month, and is not totally certain of the year; he was born in a goatskin Bedouin tent in the Sirte Desert.

1943   The British take Tripoli and thereafter assume full legislative, administrative, and judicial authority over Tripolitania and Cyrenaica under the Hague Convention.

1944   In January, a Free French brigade led by General Leclerc takes the Fezzan, thus bringing together the third region of what is now Libya. All Axis troops leave Libya.

July 28   Idris returns to Cyrenaica for the first time in twenty-two years.

1947   Britain signs a Peace Treaty with Italy on February 10 whereby Italy renounces all claim to land in Africa. Britain begins disbanding the Libyan Arab Army. Three battalions are demobilized; the other two become the nucleus of the Cyrenaica Defense Force, which comprises a thousand Arabs with British officers.

1948   The National Congress of Cyrenaica is formed under the presidency of Idris's brother, al Rida. The Congress recommends a federal constitution for an independent Libya under Idris, reserving the right to separate independence if Tripolitania rejects it.

June 1, 1949   Idris announces the independence of Cyrenaica. Britain immediately recognizes Idris as Emir of Cyrenaica.

September 16   Britain issues a Transitional Powers Proclamation, giving Idris authority to draw up a constitution.

October 11– November 1   A United Nations subcommittee considers the future of Libya.

November 21	The United Nations recommends that Libya should become an independent state by January 1, 1952.
December 24, 1951	Libya becomes an independent monarchy with a federal system of government and Idris its first king.

The Land of His Fathers

Libya only became important to the West with the onset of the Second World War. Until then, its existence was safely ignored. In her days of imperial expansion, Britain made no attempt to conquer North Africa, which was generally thought to be, and was, an unpleasant place to live. The climate was harsh, ravaged by sudden rainstorms, intense humid heat, and sandstorms; the landscape barren, beset by poisonous snakes and scorpions. The region as a whole was believed to possess no natural mineral resources. A vast desert separated the two main coastal towns, Tripoli and Benghazi, and other deserts lay between them and the much smaller towns in the south that had grown around oases. For centuries, travelers avoided Tripoli if they could. This was the Barbary Coast, and Tripoli was a haven for the pirates who terrorized the Mediterranean.

Only once did America have dealings with this land, and that was in 1800 when President Thomas Jefferson objected to the payment of tolls so that Christian fleets might use the Mediterranean. America had already paid two million dollars to Yussuf Karamanli, the Pasha of Tripoli, whose family had ruled the seas since 1711. The Pasha threatened to declare war upon the United States unless the tolls were paid. Jefferson sent in three frigates and a sloop to blockade the port, where many Christians were kept in captivity, either to go into slavery or be ransomed. One of these frigates, the *Philadelphia*, ran ashore on an uncharted reef. Captain Baimbridge was forced to surrender with 308 men, and they were all imprisoned for nineteen months until a small force of United States Marines went in to rescue them, whereupon the Pasha capitulated. This was the beginning of the end for the Barbary pirates, with other nations feeling able to challenge them as well. To this day these events are commemorated in the hymn of the United States Marines—

From the halls of Montezuma to the shores of Tripoli . . .

However, the North African coast continued to be an area that Europeans avoided, for its wealth came largely from piracy and slavery. Many lurid tales were told in the popular fiction of the time about unwary women being taken off to harems and white men into slavery. The nomadic Arab tribes of Bedouin and Tuaregs had a terrifying reputation, for it was they who brought Negro slaves up across the Sahara from central Africa for shipment to the East, the West Indies, and North America. Few enquired too deeply into their customs for the Bedouin murdered one hundred and fifty explorers and missionaries during the nineteenth century. Although the colonial powers suppressed piracy after Jefferson's epic confrontation, the slave trade continued well into the twentieth century.

The slave trade was concentrated largely on Tripoli, which had been a western outpost for many eastern civilizations. With a natural deep-sea harbor and a fertile coastal plain protected by low-lying hills, Tripoli has been continuously inhabited for at least three thousand years, conquered successively by the Phoenicians, the Carthaginians, Greeks, Romans, Goths, and Byzantines long before the modern world came into being, but it was still little more than a busy trading post until the Italians seized it from the Turks in 1911.

Under Mussolini, the Italians set out to restore the area now defined as Libya to the developed state that it had been only once before in its history. Under the Caesars, Libya was "the granary of Rome." For over two centuries, Roman engineers dug wells, laid down irrigation channels, and turned the desert into farmland, creating ten thousand farms and a highly developed system of agriculture. This all vanished under the dunes when their empire fell and the Saharan sandstorms swept up from the south. The Arab tribes made no attempt to conquer the elements, preferring a pastoral form of agriculture, wandering with their flocks of goats and sheep just ahead of the seasons.

Little changed in a thousand years until the Italians arrived, determined to evict the Bedouin and settle the coastal plains around Tripoli and Benghazi with immigrant farmers to once again meet the growing food needs of the Italian mainland. Largely unknown to the outside world, they crushed the Bedouin in the two cruelly oppressive Italo-Sanusi Wars of 1911–17 and 1923–1931. With the execution of the Bedouin leader Omar el Mukhtar, the Italians established their hold on the North African deserts. The commencement of the Second World War saw them firmly in control of twelve hundred miles of coastline and its desert hinterland. Only then did the Allies appreciate Libya's strategic importance.

Several explorers attempted to penetrate these remote deserts, notably Rosita Forbes, who reported in *The Secret of the Sahara* (1921) that even under the Italians slavery continued to flourish in the south. News of the Italian suppression of the Bedouin was revealed to the world by the Danish travel writer Knud Holmboe in his book *Desert Encounter* (1931), but the region was still largely unexplored when Brigadier Ralph Bagnold became the first European to travel by car from east to west, an adventure described in his book, *Libyan Sands: Travel in a Dead World* (1935).

When France collapsed in June 1940 and the Italians entered the Second World War, aligning themselves with Germany and declaring war upon Britain, the Allies suddenly realized Libya's importance to the Axis Powers. By stationing fighter aircraft along its coast they could control the Mediterranean sealanes and inflict untold damage upon Allied shipping. To their horror, the Allies discovered that they had no accurate maps.

General Sir Archibald Wavell, commanding the British forces based in Egypt, recalled Brigadier Bagnold, who was in retirement—and was told that the Allies had better get cracking. Bagnold confirmed that the Italians had laid down 1,750 miles of road across Libya, along the coast from east to west between the borders of Tunis and Egypt and down into the interior of the Sahara. If they chose to, the Axis armies could sweep across North Africa into Egypt just as he had done; even worse, they might release the sluices of the Aswan Dam and flood the plains of Egypt.

Suddenly, in the midst of a wider war, North Africa became a theater of the utmost importance. This perception did not last long.

Long-range aircraft and intercontinental ballistic missiles were to overtake the strategic thinking of World War II, but briefly, just briefly—for little more than thirty years—Libya was a key forward position for the Allied powers, who found themselves having to study its geography and history as they learned to master its terrain. Many books and films have been produced about the memorable desert war that followed, culminating in the Battle of El Alamein in November 1942, when the Eighth Army, commanded by Field Marshal Montgomery, roundly defeated the German and Italian forces led by Field Marshal Rommel, drove them back across the desert, finally winning this phase of the war in further battles in western Libya and Tunisia. In particular, I would recommend Fitzroy Maclean's *Eastern Approaches* (1949) and Virginia Cowles's *The Phantom Major: The Story of David Stirling and the S.A.S. Regiment* (1958), for what they tell us about the landscape and character of North Africa, which Stirling—who appears again later in this book—learned to penetrate through the use of his Long Range Desert Group, a mobile armored corps that traveled by night, striking behind enemy lines.

Gadaffi was born in a tent in the Sirte Desert some time during this conflict. He believes the year was 1942 and knows no more than that, not even the day or the month. His parents belonged to a wandering Bedouin *kabyle* or tribe, the Gadadfas, who had roamed across the Sirte Desert since the fifteenth century, following the rain, measuring their wealth in sheep and goats, seldom owning more than one or two camels. Later, Gadaffi learned that a tank battle raged beyond the walls of their tent as his mother was giving birth. He was quite literally born to the sound of gunfire with the ground shaking beneath his parents' home.

Although "Libya" has been mentioned as a place so far in this narrative, it should be remembered that "Libya" as a nation did not exist. And never had.

For thousands of years, North Africa was one sprawling landmass, known as the Maghreb to the Arabs, with no agreed territorial boundaries between the Atlantic and the Nile. A hundred million years ago this was a fertile land of mountains, rivers, forests, and steppes. By 3000 B.C., the rivers and marshes had dried but there are still three- to four-thousand-year-old olive trees and ancient cypress trees high in the mountains to the south, where ancient man left cave paintings eight thousand years ago; paintings of antelopes, giraffes, ostriches, leopards, lions, rhinos, and elephants with him as the hunter, which show that the landscape then was as green as the sub-Saharan game parks are today.

The climate probably changed when the isthmus joining Gibraltar to Morocco collapsed or eroded, letting in the Atlantic waters to fill the Mediterranean basin. This sea acts as a thermal vacuum, drawing cold winds down from Europe to meet the warmer winds of Africa, giving Libya the peculiar climate that has molded its history; violent storms, heavy rainfall, and flash floods interrupting long periods of intense humid heat, with fearsome sandstorms when the Ghibli sweeps up from the south, which it may at any time of year but more frequently in spring and late summer. The Ghibli may suddenly raise the temperature by ten or fifteen degrees, hurling sand into every crevice, blocking out the sun, destroying crops, and showering Libya's northern towns with a fine dustlike layer of sand. Occasionally these sand clouds sweep on over the Mediterranean, falling on Malta, Sicily, southern France, or Italy, where it is given a different name: the Sirocco.

When a sandstorm warning is given, all windows and doors are closed; shutters drawn, and yet the sand creeps in everywhere, stinging the eyes. Occasionally Western newspapers unfamiliar with this climatic feature show Gadaffi photographed with every inch of his body covered by layers of clothing, with goggles where his eyes should be. AS BARMY AS EVER ran a headline in the *Independent Magazine* (September 16, 1989), with a full-page color photograph of him dressed like this—but these are the precautions that every Libyan learns to take before traveling across the deserts when the Ghibli may be due, to protect his eyes and skin. The West knows little of the privations that are part of Libya's heritage. In this intense heat, the body can lose up to twenty-four pints of sweat in a day. Long before that, by the time the body has lost ten percent of its weight, the blood turns viscous, circulation slows, and death becomes inevitable. Ninety percent of all slaves taken across the desert perished. Sometimes whole caravans died. In 1805, a caravan comprising two thousand men and eighteen hundred camels perished to the south of here, traveling between Timbuktu and Taoudenni.

To the north of the country, along its Mediterranean frontage, and especially in the areas once known as Tripolitania and Cyrenaica, which are protected by low-lying mountains, Libya enjoys a mild, typically Mediterranean climate, with hot and humid summer days, and light evening breezes wafting in from the sea before the night turns cool. During late autumn, winter, and spring, temperatures are comfortable. Sometimes the air is so cold and wet in the eastern range of mountains where Cyrenaica protrudes into the Mediterranean that snow falls on the three-thousand-foot plateau, making its pine forests look as picturesque as those of Switzerland or Austria. This is another area where Libya could develop a tourist industry if it so chose, for the mountains slope down to the clear blue waters of the Mediterranean on one side and down to desert on the other: Mainland Greece is only four hundred miles beyond, with Crete midway.

These natural features—vast, arid deserts to the south, reaching right up and turning to steppes between Tripoli and Cyrenaica; sudden storms, and wild variations in temperature—have given Libya its character. Every fifth or sixth year, as though by some meteorological clock, the rains cease and then there is drought, followed by violent storms, heavy flooding, sudden fertility, a blaze of color as flowers and grasses bloom, and then plagues of locusts, disease, and famine. As many veterans of the Second World War will never forget, the northern deserts also suffer from millions of flies, scorpions, and many varieties of poisonous snakes, especially around Cyrenaica. Many are the sad stories told in Libyan folktales of families abandoning their land after a child tried to brush one of these creatures away.

With careful husbandry, the coastal plains can produce enough food for Libya to be self-sufficient. In most years, there are up to twenty inches of rain but there is no telling when the next disaster may fall. Not surprisingly, the population has always been small, with Libya taking its name from the Lebu, a wandering tribe that lived down by what is now the Egyptian border four or five thousand years ago. Like the Bedouin, they followed the seasons, wandering across the Maghreb, using sheep and goat hair to make wool, weaving clothes and carpets and trading in the oases. The Egyptians called them Libyans, and this was the name used by Herodotus who visited Libya in 450 B.C. when the Grecian empire was in its prime and Cyrenaica famous for its climate, temples, and wines.

The first race of settlers to arrive in Libya were the Phoenicians, who founded the cities of Tripoli, Leptis Magna, and Sebratha in the eighth century B.C. Together with Carthage in what is now Tunisia, this enclave formed the eastern end of the Phoenician empire. Historians disagree on the exact date of their settlement, for it is likely that the Phoenicians arrived from Tyre (Lebanon) to establish trading posts, which then grew gradually into cities. The Phoenicians ruled the southern Mediterranean for over two hundred years, never going far down into Africa beyond this coast, and were followed by the Carthaginians, who held sway until 146 B.C., when the Romans destroyed Carthage, initially allowing Berber tribesmen under the King of Numidia to sweep up from the south but later deciding to incorporate most of North Africa into the Roman province of Africa Nova.

With their usual efficiency, the Romans brought in engineers, builders, and administrators in the form of the Third Augusta Legion—a legion comprised a mobile corps of twelve thousand men, established in the Roman tradition with each soldier signed on for twenty-five years' service and a firm line of command. Each legion was led by the Roman equivalent of a general, supported by staff officers, quartermasters, and brigade commanders coordinating sixty subordinate units, each commanded by a centurion. The Third Augusta Legion controlled an area of roughly a million and a half square miles for the next 250 years, creating the towns and cities whose ruins now dominate Gadaffi's coastline.

Although its units fought when they had to, a legion was more than just a military force. In *The Great Sahara* (1964), James Wellard writes:

To a Roman commander, a battle was an engineering problem: clearing and leveling the ground, removing the debris, and preparing the site for rebuilding. So, in a sense, the Legion marched out of their camp en route to battle more like a company of engineers and road-builders than a division of fighting men. There was no comparison with a modern military unit on the move. The Romans, on the whole, moved much quicker. There was no waiting around for transport. The Legion marched its regulation twenty miles a day, twenty-five if accelerated, day in and day out. In the vanguard rode the cavalry scouts; behind them came the engineers and road-makers; next the artillerymen; then the commanding general with his staff, followed by the banners and trumpeters; then the infantrymen drawn up six abreast with a centurion in the rear of each company to keep discipline; then the baggage of the Legion carried by servants and beasts of burden; then the rearguard of mercenary troops; and finally a detachment of hand-picked cavalry troops. Cavalry units also rode reconnaissance on both flanks of the column. In the event of an attack by an enemy, the infantry formed a hollow square into which the baggage train was moved for safety. It was the function of the light infantry to attack the enemy from the flanks, pinning them against the wall of shields until the cavalry could get amongst them. No barbarian troops ever found a method of breaking this formation. . . .

The Third Augusta Legion was permanently based at Lambaesis, northwest of Tripoli, and from there controlled all the deserts, oases, and coastal towns from the Atlantic in the west to Egypt in the east, down to the edges of tropical Africa in what are now Niger, Chad, and Mali, constructing a chain of forts and defensive ramparts. Its soldiers were superbly disciplined, route-marching, exercising in formation, drilling in barrack-squares, running, jumping, swimming, "expected to swim a river, vault a ditch, and, on order to attack, to finish the last stretch between himself and the enemy at a run." Their fitness so impressed Emperor Hadrian that he issued the infantry and cavalry with a special order of the day, remarking upon their ability to hurl both a javelin and a shield simultaneously before engaging in hand-to-hand combat or to leap into a saddle in full combat uniform.*

The legion was sent to Lambaesis with a purpose that went far beyond the immediate military objective of bringing the tribal desert rulers under the authority of the Caesars. Rome was growing so fast that it needed more bread, fruit, and vegetables to feed its people. So that Africa Nova could provide this harvest, the legion was ordered to lay down roads, build aqueducts and bridges, restore and extend the towns and cities abandoned by the Greeks and the Carthaginians, repair their harbors, construct piers and

---

* The Romans' achievement is mentioned for one special reason; Gadaffi has frequently denied it ever happened, preferring to dwell on the Arabs' history in North Africa. No mention of Rome's long period of rule is made in many history books or in Libyan accounts of how their state came into being. The scale of Rome's expansion only became known between 1946 and 1949 when a French Air Force colonel, Jean Baradez, began surveying the Sahara from the air. It is no exaggeration to say that the remains of an empire lie almost untouched beneath Libya's sands.

warehouses, and build forums, temples, libraries, and ampitheaters; shops, houses, and public baths.

Wellard agues convincingly that Rome's achievement far exceeded its conquest of Germany, France, or Britain, for the legion turned

one of the most backward areas into one of the most civilized and prosperous provinces of the Empire—a region which was to produce emperors, soldiers, saints, philosophers, and writers until it was destroyed by the Arabs and returned to its pristine state of barbarism . . . a land of splendid cities, villages, and farms was largely the achievement of the Third Augusta Legion . . . they pushed the desert back to a line which had never been attained before or since . . . [building] hundreds of cities, thousands of miles of roads, the frontier forts and farmhouses . . . the Romans had at least 2.5 million acres of what is now full desert colonized and under cultivation in South Algeria alone. If we assume, as the evidence suggests, that the Romans followed the same practice of building roads, forts, and irrigation networks in Morocco, Tunisia, and Libya, as in Algeria, the total area exploited under the Empire and now abandoned would be 10 million acres at the lowest estimate.

By channeling rainfall through aqueducts, wadis, subterranean gulleys, and both natural and manmade storage tanks of rock, the Romans kept and stored enough water to raise crops of oats, wheat, and barley, which all ripen early in the Libyan sun. They established orchards and vineyards, bottling wine for the imperial court in Rome, but the population began to shrink with Rome's decline, the towns and cities slowly diminishing as the sands began to return until the Vandals surged down from Germany into northern Africa in A.D. 429, destroying all before them with the support of the Berbers, who had long resented Roman occupation. The Vandals used the coastal ports as a base for piracy until they, too, fell to the sword a century later when Justinian sought to establish a Christian empire in the Roman mold, ruling from Constantinople.

In oases far from the coast, where Roman wells provided a water supply, their farming methods continued for several centuries, only to finally end in the seventh century when the Arabs arrived from the east, driven by their newfound faith in Islam, the religion born in the deserts of the Hejaz (now part of Saudi Arabia) and revealed to the Prophet Mohammed (A.D. c. 570–632). His book the Koran lays down a formal pattern for daily life that all Muslims follow to this day.

The first Muslims were required to fight for their faith, to carry its message out into the world, either through converting every conquered territory to Islam or by putting to death all nonbelievers. The first Arab armies, led by Omar Ibn al As, conquered Cyrenaica in A.D. 642 and then Tripolitania and the Fezzan in A.D. 644–645. Further waves of immigration followed in the ninth century and, more importantly, the eleventh, when the Bani Salim and Bani Hilal tribes settled in Libya, bringing with them the language and customs of Arabia and a total belief in the Koran. This book lays down a code of civil and criminal law, forbidding theft or violence, prohibiting drugs and alcohol, requiring all Muslims to keep their bodies pure for God. They are told how they may live their lives, under what circumstances they may marry and bring up their children, when they may divorce, and the penalties for committing adultery or fornication.

The language of the Koran is poetic, its message pure and absolute, defining how a people with few possessions may find God through a life of simplicity. With these parameters to guide them, the Arabs had no need for the Phoenician, Greek, and Roman ruins that lay all around them. Neither had they any need for the Roman irrigation systems. The aqueducts and storage tanks fell into disuse, though many Roman wells are still being used to this day. The Roman field system was abandoned, since the Arabs—or, as we might now call their descendants, the Bedouin—might grow a quick catch-crop of oats and barley, but in the main preferred a pastoral life, depending largely upon their flocks of sheep and goats for meat, milk, and cheese, and taking special pride in their camels.

To Western eyes, a camel is a quaint creature—a horse designed by a committee, as one humorist said—but to the Bedouin from whom Gadaffi was descended, and in whose traditions he was reared, a camel is prized. They will curse the camel's nasty temper, obstinate character, and tendency to fleas ("May the fleas of a thousand camels infest your armpits" is an old Arab curse), but train him to race or ride into battle. At other times, he is their beast of burden while the female provides milk twelve months a year, converting even the dirtiest water and roughest pasture into a highly nutritional milk. The Bedouin will drink this milk straight from the udder, if need be (and often by choice), for then it is warm, frothy, and salty. The meat is also prized. British and American workers employed in Tripoli are startled when they see their first camel slaughtered. There are no secret abbatoirs here. The camel's legs are trussed outside the butcher's shop; the head is then strapped back toward the hump with cords, and its neck slit with a knife so that the blood spurts forward in an arc, proving to any spectator that the blood is pure. News of a freshly slaughtered camel brings people rushing to the butcher, for the main joints are rather like beef, but stronger flavored, and every part of the camel's entrails is eaten, with raw camel's liver, rubbed in salt, considered a delicacy. No part of the camel is wasted. The hoofs are ground down into a powder used in baking, and even the camel's urine has a use. Just as American boxers at one time healed their wounds with horse urine, so the Bedouin bathe cuts and injuries with camel urine and use it to wash their eyes; the women use it to wash their hair.

These customs have continued for a thousand years, for although Libya was seized fourteen times by successive foreign powers with long periods of Turkish, Egyptian, and Spanish rule, and although it was held by the Knights of Malta for two decades in the mid-sixteenth century, it remained a land largely occupied by wandering Bedouin. Whoever might be caliph or pasha, and from wheresoever his authority might flow, this part of North Africa committed itself to Islam, with its people offering just one commodity to the outside world: the Negro slave.

Exploitation of black labor was the contribution of the Arabs to mankind," wrote James Wellard.

It was they who organized the vast traffic in human merchandise out of Africa to the Atlantic and the Mediterranean ports. . . . The slave trade [was] the corner-stone of the Saharan economy for a thousand years. It made the desert an exceedingly busy place, with tens of thousands of men and animals crawling every day across the immense wasteland, since by the 18th century the demand for Negro slaves had become insatiable in almost every corner of the globe. Who else was to work the salt mines in the Sahara Desert itself, who the sugar plantations in Barbados, who the cotton fields in Virginia, who the American, British, French, Portuguese, Spanish, and Turkish mines and factories, if not the docile African Negro? The Arabs had the answer to the world's economic problem.

Whichever empire nominally controlled the Mediterranean coast, the Sahara slave routes remained open. Conflicts were constant between the desert tribes and foreign forces based in Tripoli, often resulting in pitched battles and hand-to-hand slaughter, but the promise of riches and yet more wealth eased the path for the caravans. An estimated twelve million Negro slaves were seized in the lands bordering the Niger River—the countries known today as Chad, Niger, and Mali—with the northern route to Tripoli preferred by the Arab traders. Only ten percent of their slaves survived the journey, for the slaves walked mostly in chains in intense heat with not enough water or food. For centuries, this route was littered with human bones; the bodies were left where they fell, picked clean by vultures and whitened by the desert sun.

The first Europeans to cross the deserts were three Britons, Maj. Dixon Denham, Lt. Hugh Clapperton, and Walter Oudney, who made the journey from Tripoli to Lake Chad in 1822. Denham reported:

About sunset, we halted near a well within half a mile of Meshroo. Round this spot were lying more than one hundred skeletons, some of them even with the skin still remaining attached to the bones—not even a little sand thrown over them. The Arabs laughed heartily at my expression of horror and said, "They are only blacks, nam boo" [Damn their fathers] and began knocking about their limbs with the butt end of their firelocks, saying, "This was a woman! This was a youngster!"

In trying to form a judgment on Gadaffi's Libya, and the attitude its leaders have to the Western World, one should never think of slavery as some remote historical phenomenon that ceased nearly 130 years ago, as it did in the United States. Slavery is part of the modern culture of Libya, with all the attitudes this statement implies, for it continued to be an essential part of the desert economy until at least the Second World War and may still be practiced in remoter parts of central Africa that are seldom visited by Western man. After her journey down into the Libyan Desert in 1920, Rosita Forbes reported in *The Secret of the Sahara: Kufara* (1921) that,

There is a large market in Jof twice a week, to which people come from as far away as Hawari and Tolab to barter pigeons, eggs, fowls, girbas, and foodstuffs. Slaves are not now sold in the public square on Mondays and Thursdays, but many a human bargain is arranged in the shuttered houses around it. For 100 mejidies one can buy a man and for 200 a woman, but young girls of fourteen and fifteen fetch up to 250 mejidies (nearly £50). "These be high prices" said Zouia despondently. "But the people of Barca have bought many slaves lately and there are fewer caravans." We learned that the Tuaregs of the west have regular slave farms, where they bred and sold human beings as we do cattle. "You can see sixty slaves in one farm," said our guardian sheikh. . . . Deep in conversation we skirted the rough, rocky ground to the south of the broad belt of Jof palms and came to Talakh, at the end of the emerald maze where Sayyid Ahmed owns many gardens. A whole colony of slaves dwelt in clusters of *tukels* within neat palm-leaf fences, and there were some biggish houses of sand bricks, on whose flat roofs masses of dates were drying in the sun. . . .

When Knud Holmboe traveled across North Africa in 1930, he heard that there was still a weekly slave market being held at Kufra every Thursday and met the only European known to have escaped from there alive. A traffic in slaves continued long afterward in this part of the world. The trade was not formally abolished in Saudi Arabia until 1963 nor in Mauretania until 1980.

In Libya itself, it is by no means clear when slavery ended. Slavery and piracy continued to be the basic trades of the desert and the North African coast throughout the first period of Turkish rule between 1551 and 1711, under the Karamanli dynasty from 1711 to 1835, and again under the Turks during their second period from 1835 until 1911 when the Italians invaded, taking possession of Libya the following year. Throughout each phase of foreign rule, even under the Italians and the British, Libya remained wild and untamed, its landscape governed by its climate, its people sharing a faith in Islam that gave them their only certainties. The Bedouin never owned land or property in the sense that the West understands these things; it was theirs through right of ancient conquest and through continuous occupation in much the same way that North America belonged to the Sioux or the Cherokee. Even under

Mussolini, slavery continued in some parts of the country although he saw the North African coast as "the fourth Italian shore," described the Mediterranean as "our great Italian lake," and sought to diminish the Bedouin hold.

Whatever one may think of Fascism, there can be no doubting the scale of Mussolini's development in North Africa, achieved though it was through a campaign of systematic brutality directed against the Bedouin. Mussolini first drove them out of their traditional grazing grounds, and then encouraged and finally drove Italian farmers to settle the fertile plains around Tripoli and Cyrenaica. Civil administrations were established in both regions, supported by a civil service and a formal structure of law and land registration. Over a hundred thousand Italians migrated from the mainland, converting the pastoral steppes into farms and orchards. In the area around Tripoli, the Italians planted two and a half million olive trees, believing from their experience in Sicily and southern Italy that olives would thrive. They did.

The Italians also planted enough wheat to produce an annual crop of 150,000 tons, only to discover that drought would cut this back to a tenth in a bad year. However, since fresh vegetables ripen twenty or thirty days earlier in Libya than elsewhere in the Mediterranean, they plantered early crops of tomatoes, potatoes, and carrots and orchards of almonds, figs, peaches, and soft fruits plus 300,000 citrus trees, mainly oranges and tangerines. The Bedouin had never shown much interest in fishing, since fish was not part of their usual diet, but off the coast in the warm waters of the southern Mediterranean the Italians found plentiful supplies of tuna and sardines and a rich crop of sponge.

Italian investment went far beyond basic farming. Electricity-generating stations were built at Tripoli, Misurata, Homs, and Benghazi; houses constructed for the immigrant workers, and 1,750 miles of metalled road laid down, with Mussolini himself opening the 1,140-mile coastal road between the Egyptian and Tunisian frontiers in 1937.

The Bedouin saw these Italian investments as an attempt to destroy their traditional culture. They preferred a simple life, as defined by the Koran and defended by the Sanusi, their religious leaders. As part of their suppression, the Italians closed Sanusi lodges, prohibited their teaching, and drove Sheikh Idris into exile.

In 1930, Knud Holmboe visited the Sheikh in Alexandria where Idris maintained that the Sanusi

only aim at piety and nobility of heart . . . by excluding everything but God from our thoughts, by moderation, and by abstaining from all enjoyments which do not bring us nearer God. . . . The man who follows our teaching becomes healthy in body and mind. The Italians are interested in making the entire population of Cyrenaica degenerate, as in so many places in the world of Islam. If that happens the Italian civilization can advance more rapidly. So long as our teaching rules it will not happen.

When Holmboe asked why not, Idris continued:

Our teaching is not intolerant towards any other form of Islam or towards any other religion. It is simplicity itself: the body must be strengthened by a healthy and abstemious life, so that it becomes a worthy dwelling for the soul. You are not permitted to enjoy any narcotics, not even tobacco. You must be a slave of nothing save God, that is, you must be the master of circumstances. The civilization which the Italians want to introduce into Cyrenaica makes us the slaves of circumstances: therefore we must fight against it. . . . [Their policy] makes external splendor and power the ruling factor in the judgment of a person or nation, and it despises the inner development. . . . Do you know why the Italians are using Eritrean troops? Because the Eritreans are Christians. The Italians have created a religious war in Cyrenaica.

A King Without a Kingdom

G adaffi was only eight years old when Libya became an independent nation for the first time in its history. The story of how this happened, creating the situation that brought him to power, is no less extraordinary than his own. Ignored for almost fifteen hundred years, seized by the Italians and then wrested from them during the Second World War, Libya was a problem to the postwar Allies, none of whom wanted to see it become part of any rival colonial empire.

None of the Allies wanted it for themselves, for Libya looked as unpromising as ever, with the major part of its landmass uninhabitable and only the coastal areas around Tripoli and Cyrenaica able to contain sufficient population to support any form of government. For all the Italians' endeavors to develop its agriculture, Libya remained a miserably deficient country with over ninety-four percent illiteracy, forty percent infant mortality, low life expectancy, and an average per capita income of only ten pounds per annum. Although the Libyans had been fighting for their independence, there were not enough educated Libyans to administer a civil service, set up financial institutions, operate a legal system, provide officers for a police force, staff an army, navy, or air force, or provide teachers in its schools. This was one of the poorest regions in the world

In his *General Economic Appraisal of Libya*, prepared for the United Nations in 1951, J. Lindberg says, "The average income per head is only slightly higher than in India and markedly lower than in most Middle Eastern areas." During years of normal rainfall, catch-crops of wheat and barley might be grown during the brief spring growing season plus olives, citrus fruits, almonds, grapes, and some root vegetables, but when the rains did not come, as so often they did not, these crops failed and there would not be enough rough grazing for their sheep and goats, although camels might last five or six weeks without water. At times like these, the Bedouin were reduced to a diet of camel's milk and dates, which grew plentifully, with over three million date palms growing wild, each producing around a hundred pounds of dates a year; dates of every variety of texture and succulence, for there are 140 different types. The Bedouin could survive on a date-based diet, but only just and in conditions of hardship. In good years, the Libyans might export sheep and goats to Malta or Sicily and there was always a market for their esparto grass, (a very dry and fiberous grass used in rope making) which grew wild, but other than that Libya's industry mainly lay in traditional handicrafts. Its prospects seemed grim.

The Allies realized that, if granted independence, Libya might always be a debtor nation, depending upon others for food in times of drought or famine. There were strategic advantages in Libya's poverty, for the Allies could offer its government financial assistance in return for permission to maintain military bases along its Mediterranean frontage, thereby continuing to control the sealanes and keeping Britain and the United States within striking distance of all potential sources of conflict in the Middle East.

This could have been secured without conceding independence, but the Allies were also aware of Libya's regional and tribal tensions. Approximately seventy percent of the population lived in the west, centered around Tripoli; a quarter in the eastern region of Cyrenaica, and another twentieth in the sparsely populated southern oases of the Fezzan. These divisions were at the heart of the Allies' problem, for the west was strongly pro-Italian; the east were led by the Sanusi (who had committed themselves to Britain), while the French were dominant in the southern oases, which were closer to Algeria than Tripoli.

During the War, the British Foreign Secretary Sir Anthony Eden made it clear that Britain did not wish to see the Italians regaining authority once the war was over. On January 8, 1942, Eden told the House of Commons

I take this opportunity to express the warm appreciation of His Majesty's Government for the contribution which Sayyid Idris al

Sanusi and his followers have made and are making to the British war effort. We welcome their association with His Majesty's forces in the task of defeating the common enemies. His Majesty's Government is determined that at the end of the war the Sanusis in Cyrenaica will in no circumstances again fall under Italian domination.

This objective was achieved by allowing the Sanusi to assume authority over the whole of Libya, with Sayyid Idris al Sanusi (Idris) being recognized first as Emir of Cyrenaica and then as Libya's first monarch, King Idris. Sure enough, the King allowed the British to maintain the bases established during the Second World War, with the United States permitted to build up its base at Wheelus Field until this became the largest military base outside mainland America, with ten thousand Americans living within its perimeters, establishing radio communications with every part of the Middle East, and spending over $100 million to make it a self-equipped town, with better facilities than any other part of Libya, an airfield up to international airport standards, well-stocked shops, clubs, and sports facilities, and modern housing. It all looked very good on paper but caused deep resentment among the Libyans. The West had rewarded the Sanusis' loyalty by creating a king without a kingdom.

Libya meant little to Britain or America, neither of whom had many ties with North Africa. Britain colonized south and west Africa, but its interest in the north was limited to Egypt, where it had a long-established commercial and military presence. Three generations of Englishmen went out to staff Egypt's civil service and financial institutions or to serve in the army. Britain's overriding concern was to ensure that the Suez Canal remained open, since this provided the shortest route between Britain and her overseas dominions in Asia, West Africa, and Australasia. With this political objective always in mind, Britain continued to be a power in the region after Egypt became a monarchy in 1922, only withdrawing her forces in 1936, and even then maintaining a major base close to the Canal.

Being separated from Egypt by desert, Cyrenaica never became part of this overall strategy. The only time Britain took any interest in Cyrenaica was in 1908, before the First World War, when the Foreign Office considered recommending Cyrenaica rather than

Palestine as a permanent home for the Jews. This idea was abandoned in the belief that Cyrenaica, hemmed in as it is by sea, mountains, and desert, would never be able to accommodate more than 300,000 immigrants.

Had the British possessed historical roots in Cyrenaica, they would have realized that the Sanusi were primarily a religious order founded in 1837 by al Sayyid Muhammad bin Ali al Sanusi, known to his followers as the Grand Sanusi. A Sufi Muslim born in Algeria, the Grand Sanusi studied in Morocco and the Heijaz (Saudi Arabia), joining at least three other orders before deciding to start his own in which he urged the faithful to return to the basic philosophy revealed by God to the prophet Mohammad and contained within the Koran.

The Grand Sanusi acquired a loyal following and, faced with the opposition of the authorities there, he decided to return to his native land, accompanied by his disciples. They spent some months in Cairo and then continued their journey across the desert, resting at the Siwa oasis before moving on to Tripoli and thence to Quabis. There, the Grand Sanusi heard that the French were colonizing Algeria.

Rather than establish a new community under French rule, he turned around, returned to Tripoli, and then crossed the Sirte Desert to Cyrenaica, establishing a *zawiya*, or lodge, at al Baida on the central plateau, not far from the ancient ruins of Cyrene. This became the mother lodge for the order, the Sanusiya or Sanusi, a fellowship of brothers trained to go out into the desert as missionaries, urging the Bedouin to return to the principles of their faith. Wherever they found a response, the Sanusi would establish another *zawiya*, usually in an oasis and always near a well. Initially, a *zawiya* might be just one low-lying stone building, but soon they would expand, with extensions, and then more buildings and perhaps a mosque.

"Like the Christian monasteries of Europe in the Dark Ages, Sanusi lodges served many purposes besides catering for religious needs," wrote Evans-Pritchard in *The Sanusi of Cyrenaica* (1949).

They were schools, caravanserai, commercial centers, social centers, forts, courts of law, banks, storehouses, poor houses, sanctuary, and burial grounds, besides being channels through which ran a generous stream of God's blessing. They were centers of culture and security in a wild country and amid a fierce people, and they were stable points in a country where all else was constantly on the move. A Bedouin camp might be anywhere. A *zawiya* was fixed to the earth and its community with it. . . . The chief benefits the lodges conferred on the Bedouin were . . . that they and their children might learn from scholarly and pious men the faith and precepts of Islam, that they might have the opportunity to worship in a mosque, and that by charity to their lodges they might earn recompense hereafter.

Each lodge had its Shaikh who represented the Head of the Order. He arbitrated between the Bedouin, led the tribesmen to holy war, acted as intermediary between the tribe or section and the Turkish administration, dispensed hospitality to travelers, supervised the collection of tithe, directed cultivation of grain and care of stock, dispatched surplus revenues to the Headquarters of the Order, acted as prayer-leader on Fridays, and assisted in preaching and teaching. There were besides a number of other functionaries among the Brothers: the Shaikh's deputy, the *imam* to lead the daily prayers and to teach the Koran and canon law, the *mu'allim* to teach reading, writing, and arithmetic in the *zawiya* school, and perhaps a special *muadhhin* to call the faithful to prayer, though any of the Brothers could do that. . . . In course of time the tendency for the Shaikhship of a lodge to be regarded as hereditary became very marked, it being understood that if there was a suitable candidate from the family already established in the lodge he would be appointed, a view with which the later Heads of the Order concurred. Thus we find charge of a *zawiya* continuing in the hands of a single family to the point at which Muhammad Yahiya bin al Sanusi bin 'Umar al Ashhab was appointed by Sayyid Ahmad al Sharif to succeed his father as Shaikh of Msus at the age of sixteen. Some of these families sent their roots so deep that not only did they obtain what amounted to hereditary rights to a particular lodge, but controlled several lodges. . . . The Shaikh of a lodge brought up his family in it and his sons had no other home than the lodge and no other friends than the Bedouin around it and the families of Shaikhs in nearby lodges.

The Bedouin responded eagerly to the Grand Sanusi's teachings, which gave their limited lives a sense of meaning and purpose. Forced to live frugally, their horizons bounded by deserts, mountains, and sun, the Bedouin understood a philosophy that required them to worship only one God and live by a moral code that defined all aspects of their personal behavior.

The Sanusiya established forty-five *zawiyas* across Cyrenaica, and one of these was to cater for Gadaffi's tribe the Gadadfas, whose *zawiya* was at Sirte on the coast. Fifteen more *zawiyas* were founded in Tripolitania, fourteen in the Fezzan, and nearly eighty in what are now Saudi Arabia, Egypt, Nigeria, and the Sudan. Each *zawiya* was a self-supporting resident community, where the wandering Bedouin could hear the brothers reciting daily verses from the Koran and take their children to receive a limited religious education.

Nearly all the Bedouin of Cyrenaica and the Sirte Desert followed the Sanusi, looking to them for religious leadership, helping them at harvest time, and bringing meat, milk, butter, or honey to help with the economy of the *zawiya*, but this is not to say—as first the Italians and then the British apparently believed—that the Sanusi were the leading tribe in Cyrenaica. Strictly speaking, they were not a tribe at all. There were nine basic tribes in the east, with each of them broken down into sections, or families, but numbering in total twenty to thirty thousand men, women, and children, bound by webs of intricate hereditary and family ties. A Bedouin tribe traveling across the desert knew precisely who owned which well and to whom they should pay respect; an outsider would not.

Sanusi teachings complemented this tribal system but never replaced it. The Bedouin had their own customs. They respected sanctity in others, traditionally honoring *marabouts*, the holy men or hermits who wandered the deserts alone, dispensing wisdom. When a *marabout* died, the Bedouin would erect a shrine in his memory, for mysticism was also part of their culture. In due time, the Sanusi exercised a unifying influence upon the Bedouin, but only that, for the Bedouin remained essentially a nomadic people. Some lived on the plateau all the year round, but the majority, nearly three-quarters of the Bedouin population, were nomads— including the Gadadfas—and migrated south each December when the rainy season began, returning to the plateau in May. Their lands both north and south were as clearly defined as those of the native North American tribes.

"There are many advantages in this annual move to the south," observed Evans-Pritchard.

Rain falls and the grasses spring up in advance of the plateau, and grazing is more abundant and of a better quality. On the other hand, the grasses of the plateau and its southern slopes are still green when the desert grasses, except in specially favored depressions, are withered . . . the Bedouin thus give their animals the best grazing at all seasons of the year. Sheep mostly lamb round about November, which is the month in which new grasses spring up in the *barr*, so that the move southwards gives the sheep the richest grazing at a time when they need it most; and the warmer conditions prevailing in the south suit the lambs. . . . There are no water problems at this time of year. Sheep, goats, and camels do not have to be watered from the time the first rains make grass till the end of April or early in May: even horses do not drink until well into April or early May. This fact is important, because it means that the prolific pastures can be grazed by all without dispute, since the wells, which belong to tribal sections or families, are not drawn on. . . . To the south of the Tariq Aziza, generally speaking, there is no ownership in land—there are no *hudud*, boundaries, as the Arabs say—and anyone may cultivate or graze where he pleases, but there is strict ownership in wells. . . . The water of the southern wells is essential for the Bedouin who own the country and who live in it all the year round, and their rights are respected by those who graze there. . . . The animals grazed in the southern steppe are mostly sheep and camels. The Bedouin say, "Cattle and goats do not migrate; camels and sheep do." Camels are essential to no-madic life as it is impossible to move camp without them, and the richer Bedouin are in camels the more frequently they move, seeking richer pastures.

When the Italians landed in 1911, seizing Libya from the Turks, they may not have appreciated the depth of Bedouin culture and certainly made little allowance for their religion. The Bedouin coexisted with the Turks, for both belonged to Islam, but even under them there had been a growing demand for independence as there was in Egypt. This accelerated under the Italians, for the Bedouin thought they posed a threat to their faith.

Gadaffi's grandfather died in the first Italo-Sanusi War (1911–17). This began with Bedouin resistance to the Italians, and then broadened when Italy entered the First World War, siding with the Allies. On the principle that my-enemy's-friend-is-my-enemy, the Sanusi attacked British positions in the western desert of Egypt. They were easily repulsed; a truce was signed; and older generation of

Sanusi leaders replaced, and Idris recognized as the new Sanusi leader. This gave him a political role.

"The terms were very favorable to the Sanusi," Evans-Pritchard commented.

> The status quo was preserved, the Italians being left in control of those parts of Cyrenaica in which they had established themselves—the coastal towns and a few inland posts—and the Sanusiya Order retaining the rest of the country. Idris had saved the organization of the Order his grandfather had founded in Cyrenaica, and though he was not formally recognized as more than the Head of a religious Order he was, in fact and of necessity, treated as though he were ... the secular ruler of an independent people.

Thereafter, Cyrenaica was peaceful until Mussolini rose to power. It was then that the real conflict began, the one known to the Italians as The Second Italo-Sanusi War (1923–31), for Mussolini was determined to make Italy a colonial power, invoking the spirit of Imperial Rome in support of his aims. This second conflict slowly turned into a horribly bloody, murderous war between Christian and Arab, fought largely unnoticed by Europe or the United States. Fascism was then in its early days. Neither Hitler nor Franco had risen to power in Germany or Spain, and many Europeans looked upon Mussolini as a social reformer determined to build good roads, provide affordable cars for the people, and make sure the trains ran on time. Tired of war, exhausted by their losses on the Western Front, the Western powers felt no sense of danger.

This second Italo-Sanusi War cannot be described in conventional military terms. There were few battles, but hardly a day went by without the Bedouin or the Italians attacking each other. Gadaffi's father and uncle fought in this war. His father lost an eye, and both were captured, sentenced to death, and then reprieved.

In the early months, the Bedouin moved openly across the steppes with their families and flocks, but as the fighting intensified the women and children either went into exile in Egypt or surrendered, taking refuge in the Italian concentration camps where they lived in rags and desperation. The Italians never knew who was living in these camps unless they caught someone smuggling out food, weapons, or information to their menfolk, in which case the penalty was death.

Similarly, the Italians never knew who they were fighting, for the tribes coalesced beneath the Sanusi banner when that was convenient, and then plotted against each other if their tribal interests were threatened. Evans-Pritchard wrote:

> Among the collaborationists, the *mtalyanin*, the Italianized as the Patriots called them, there was every degree of participation from passivity, the refraining from taking an active part in the resistance, to full cooperation with the Italian Army as spies, guides, informers, and administrative officials; but even those guilty of the worst complicity could, especially when some personal tie was involved, do the guerrillas a good turn.
>
> Many poor Bedouin near the towns joined the Italian forces as one kind or other of irregulars, police and friendlies, as laborers and camelmen, and it was found that these, while drawing Italian pay and rations, did not hesitate to assist the Patriots when an opportunity offered itself. Desertions to the enemy with full equipment were frequent. Italian rifles and ammunition and even pay were often handed over to the guerrillas. After an engagement the ground was left strewn with live ammunition for the guerrillas to glean. . . .

The native population of Cyrenaica was no more than 200,000, but three-quarters of them were the nomadic Bedouin, still abiding by the same cultural traditions brought from Saudi Arabia over a thousand years before. They still lived within tribal and subtribal family groups with only a limited command structure and a faith in Islam, more particularly that taught by the Sanusi, holding them together.

> Whether the Bedouin fought in the name of the Sultan or the Sanusi, or just fought, they always realized, from the first days of the struggle, that the issue was their right to live by their own laws in their own land . . . with the destruction of the Sanusi, the war still went on in the name of religion. It then became simply a war of Muslims to defend their faith against a Christian power. Deep love of home and deep love of God nourished each other. In fighting for their lands and herds the Bedouin were fortified by the knowledge that they fought also for their faith.

The Sanusi were admired by the Bedouin for their scholarship and sanctity, but were not expected to provide military leadership. In the first conflict with the Italians, the Sanusi leader Sayyid Ahmad al Sharif collaborated with the enemy, "lowering the prestige of the Sanusi family in the eyes of the Bedouin by drunkenness and debauchery, for he led openly a scandalous life in the company of Italian officers" (Evans-Pritchard, p. 129). In this second conflict, his brother Idris willingly went into exile at the first hint of conflict and failed to set foot inside his country again for over twenty years. The Bedouin

> knew that the descendants of the Grand Sanusi had been brought up in the oases to a sedentary and bookish life and not in the hard way of their own children and that they were unsuited to the frugal and exhausting life of a guerrilla.... In the eyes of the Bedouin they lacked in full measure the manly qualities of courage and endurance that Bedouin demand in their own folk.

Instead, leadership came from Sheikh Omar el Mukhtar who is revered now in Libya as the real hero of their revolution, hailed by all—from Gadaffi down—as the father of their revolution.

Virtually unknown to the outside world, Omar el Mukhtar was a teacher already in his sixties when the second Italo-Sanusi War began; Evans-Pritchard describes him as "a simple man, religious, courageous, contemptuous of worldly honors and success, and with singular tenacity and powers of physical endurance." He was to become, in Libyan eyes, a leader as symbolic as Che Guevara or Fidel Castro in our own times; or any of the great founders of the Western World.

Omar el Mukhtar abandoned his life of scholarship and took to the hills with just a few men, leading the Bedouin against the Italians for over nine years, organizing them on tribal lines, although he also brought in recruits from other tribes and volunteers from Sudan and Tripolitania. Each unit had its own commander and a *gadi* to look after religious and legal affairs, ensuring that the Bedouin followed Sanusi teaching, observing their prayers five times a day as laid down in the Koran. His was real, physical leadership, for Omar el Mukhtar risked his own life repeatedly, thereby becoming an almost mythical figure, a sort of Robin Hood, which is how the Bedouin regard him to this day.

The Italians saw Omar el Mukhtar as a rebel leader—and

wrongly assumed that the Sanusi banners that his men carried meant they were all members of one united army. They were not. The banners meant they were fighting for their faith. From one day to the next, the Italians could never anticipate whence the next Bedouin attack might come, for this was a war of constant skirmishes, with the Bedouin suddenly attacking by horse or camel, or creeping across the steppes by night. Even in the final year, when the scale of fighting was much reduced, there were 210 skirmishes (or *conflitti*, as the Italians called them), and 53 engagements (*combattimenti*)—and at no time were the Italians faced by more than a few hundred men. It was as difficult a war for the Italians to fight as those fought later by the Americans in Vietnam and other parts of Southeast Asia, for the Bedouin were defending terrain to which they belonged and understood, and which their enemy did not. Used to traveling by night, the Bedouin slept by day with their tents merging into the folds and hollows of the steppes.

> Text-book strategy does not apply to an enemy who wanders at will over a country with which he is familiar from birth, among a friendly people ready to provide him with exact intelligence, and in small mobile bands; and whose strategy is little more than the guerrilla imperative—strike suddenly, strike incessantly, strike hard, get out quick. . . . The Italians were fighting a people, not an army, and a people can only be defeated by total imprisonment or extermination. (Evans-Pritchard)

The Bedouin knew better than to engage in open battle with a superior force. Instead, they took possession of Cyrenaica as dusk fell, engaging their enemy by day only when they had the benefit of surprise attack. By night, the Bedouin would crawl under the barbed wire surrounding the Italian camps, slit a few throats, leave the soldiers' genitals in their mouths, and depart as silently as they came—a tactic that was greatly feared by the Italians, who retaliated not only by bringing in Christian troops from Eritrea but also by raiding Bedouin positions with such ferocity that the war came close to genocide. Once a Bedouin camp had been identified, the Italians would bring in planes, tanks, and heavy guns, "slaughtering man and beast indiscriminately and destroying the grain stores, leaving no doubt that their purpose was to kill as many of the

Bedouin as possible, striking terror into the hearts of the shepherd folk of Cyrenaica."

The Italians found themselves tied down militarily, having to employ large numbers of troops while the Bedouin were as careful as ever not to engage in face-to-face conflict. Wars for independence are often cruel, but this became something deeper, with the Italians cementing up Bedouin wells to starve their flocks, deprive them of food, and drive them into submission. Reduced to rags and starving, the Bedouin would still not surrender—and when captured knew they faced execution. Some of the Italian atrocities were witnessed by the Danish writer Knud Holmboe, who described the Eritreans burning three Bedouin alive, Bedouin women being taken off to brothels, poison gas and machine guns being used against the tribesmen, soldiers driving Arabs from their mosques, and the constant, often daily, executions staged in Derna, Benghazi, and Cyrene. Holmboe commented,

> During the terror of the French Revolution an average of three people were executed daily in France, which roughly gives twelve hundred a year. During the time I was in Cyrenaica thirty executions took place daily, which means that about twelve thousand Arabs were executed yearly, not counting those killed in the war or the imported Eritreans on the Italian side. The land swam in blood.

In Benghazi, Holmboe watched Eritrean troops parading in brand-new parade uniforms on the day new recruits were given rifles. General Graziani, who led the Italian forces said:

> Boys, today you have received your rifles, the rifles you are going to use in defense of the Italy which we all love and for the futherance of her might and honor if this is needed. Remember, in whatever you are doing, that you are Italians, Romans, and remember that your forebears were once in this country. You are Romans fighting against barbarians. Be kind to them, but always be their superiors. Remember that you are Romans.

And to the Negro Christian soldiers from Eritrea, whom he had led in other campaigns, Graziani continued:

You are fighting in order that the Italian eagle shall spread its wings anew over the old Roman Libya. . . . I know that you will be victorious together with us Italians, who profess the same religion as you. Let us cry "Evviva" for Italy and her colony of Eritrea.

Holmboe noticed that while the Eritreans danced and sang, the Arabs watched in silence. Later still as he traveled across Cyrenaica, welcomed warmly by the Arabs as a convert to their faith, he met Bedouin warriors, and in the Italian camps saw others walk calmly to the gallows, invariably facing death with courage. He was in no doubt that the Libyans were fighting for their independence.

This murderous war could only end one way. The Italians had grown to detest the Bedouin. As Evans-Pritchard puts it:

Long years of campaigning against guerrilla bands had irritated them more than governments are usually irritated by Bedouin and made them increasingly flamboyant and brutal. . . . Because they lived in tents without most of the goods the peasant, and even more the townsman, regard as signs of civilization, the Italians spoke of them as barbarians, little better than beasts, and treated them accordingly.

By now, the Italians knew that Omar el Mukhtar would never give in; they also realized that his followers would fight to their last drop of blood so long as he continued to live among them, so the Italians hunted him down like a dog, bringing in over twenty thousand men to seal off the areas of Cyrenaica where the Bedouin lived, fencing off the concentration camps with barbed wire so that the captured Bedouin lost all contact with their tribes, and then systematically laying the landscape bare until the Bedouin had been driven back, step by step, into a corner of the plateau. Through sheer force of numbers, the end was inevitable. In a skirmish near the tomb of Sidi Rafa, Omar el Mukhtar fell beneath his horse on September 11, 1931, was pinned down by the animal's weight and captured. Five days later, still suffering from his wounds, he was publicly hanged with over twenty thousand captured Bedouin forced to watch his execution.

With the Bedouin crushed, the Italians proceeded to confiscate their land, barring them from their grazing grounds and seizing the Sanusi lodges. The Italians promised to respect Islamic law and custom, to allow Islamic schools to stay open, and even to rebuild the mosques and shrines damaged in the war, but Cyrenaica and Tripolitania were to become part of Italy—not colonies but provinces—with the landscape transformed through a program of building modern roads and railways, factories, schools, hospitals, clinics, and Fascist clubs. There were to be no more tribal grazing grounds. All wells would be taken into public ownership, and the Arabs had to accept a subordinate social status within their own land to the immigrant settlers.

Had the Second World War not intervened, this program might have succeeded, for the Arab population of Cyrenaica had been decimated during the second Italo-Sanusi War. Gadaffi claims that the population was halved, with another twenty thousand Libyans emigrating to Egypt rather than live under Italian domination. The Italians literally cleared the landscape like the Third Augusta Legion of old. By early 1937, over seven hundred Italian farmers had settled in Cyrenaica. The following year, over twenty thousand arrived.

> The farms had been prepared and the houses built in advance and furnished down to the last pot and pan. Each farm was part of a village and attached to a center comprising all that a paternal state considered necessary for the bodies, minds, and souls of its citizens: a clinic, a granary, a school, a Fascist club, administrative offices, and a church and a priest's house. . . . Northern Cyrenaica had become in population and in appearance, as well as in law, part of Italy. Benghazi and Derna had become modern Italian towns that might well have been on the shores of Sicily or southern Italy. Modern roads cut through the plateau and for mile after mile were lined with Italian farmhouses and every few miles bisected Italian villages. . . . (Evans-Pritchard).

The aim was to have an Italian immigrant population of 100,000 by 1942, rising to 500,000 within twenty-five years.

Given their suffering at the hand of the Italians, in war and in occupation, it is scarcely surprising that the remaining Bedouin welcomed Britain's attack upon Italian positions in Libya; neither is it all that startling that Britain should respond warmly when Idris offered his support to the Allied war effort. In war, help is welcome no matter whence it comes. But was Sir Anthony Eden wise to reciprocate with such a commitment when Idris remained far from the sound of battle, at his home in Egypt, a would-be king whose legitimacy lay in the gift of a foreign power, and whose leadership of the newly created (and British-staffed) Libyan Arab Army could never be more than titular?

Part II

HAVING CREATED THE NEW STATE
AND MADE IDRIS ITS KING,
BRITAIN PROCEEDS TO SHORE HIM
UP, PROVIDING HIM WITH INCOME
IN RETURN FOR MILITARY BASES
(IN CONJUNCTION WITH THE
UNITED STATES), AND EQUIPPING
TWO ARMIES—ONE TO PROTECT
THE COUNTRY, AND THE OTHER TO
GUARD THE KING.

THE EVENTS LEADING UP
TO THE REVOLUTION

1952

February	19	The first General Election. The National Congress Party wins sweeping victory in Tripolitania where it is opposed to the government. Riots break out. The King bans the party.
March	28	Libya joins the Arab League.
July	23	The monarchy is overthrown in the neighboring state of Egypt. Nasser emerges as the strongman in the military coup, becoming Prime Minister in 1954 and President in 1956.

1953

| July | 29 | Britain signs a twenty-year friendship treaty with Libya, securing its military bases in return for an annual subvention of £3,750,000. |

65

| August | 22 | Police suppress anti-British riots in Tobruk, where the British have established a submarine base. |

1954

June		First oil-prospecting licenses granted to a French company in the Fezzan.
July		United Nations helps Libya conduct its first Census since 1936, establishing the population at 746,064 in Tripolitania, 291,328 in Cyrenaica, and 54,438 in the Fezzan.
September	9	The United States signs a seventeen-year agreement with Libya enabling the U.S. to stay at its Wheelus Field airbase, where it spends $100 million equipping the base and installing jet runways for Phantom squadrons. Ten thousand U.S. servicemen are based here, the largest U.S. base outside America. In return, the U.S. gives Libya 2 million a year.
October	18	The Libyan Senate approves the U.S. treaty after dismissing President Omar Mansour Kikha, who opposes the deal.
November	5	Ibrahim el Shalhi, Minister of Palace Affairs, assassinated by a nephew of the Queen. The King exiles seven members of the royal family to the oasis at Hun and decrees that the royal family be reduced to include only himself, the Queen, their children, and the Crown Prince, his brother. The assassin Sherif Muhieddin Sanusi is later executed and his body displayed in public as a warning to others.

1955

| July | 29 | Crown Prince Mohammad Rida el Mahdi el Sanusi dies, leaving his son Sayyid Siddiq as heir. |
| August | 10 | France agrees to withdraw her forces by the end of November 1956, but is allowed to continue using airfields at Sebha, Ghat, and Ghadames. |

November		United States and Britain agree to equip one Libyan army battalion. Libya also accepts military aid from Egypt.
November		American Esso Standard receives an oil prospecting concession. A limited find made the following month.
December	16	Libya admitted to the United Nations.

1956

January		A Russian diplomatic mission visits Libya. Gadaffi begins attending a secondary school at Sebha.
June		Libyan Prime Minister bin Halim visits London. Britain agrees to provide the nucleus of an air force and navy, and arms and equipment for an army of ten thousand men. Britain also agrees to train Libyan officers.
July	26	President Nasser of Egypt nationalizes the Suez Canal.
August		A telecommunications system installed in Libya, with all calls to Europe channeled through London.
October	29	An Israeli force invades Sinai with support from Britain and France. The British and French bomb Egyptian airfields prior to an amphibious landing. Egypt accuses Libya of allowing British planes to use Libyan airfields to attack Egypt. This leads to public protests in Libya.
November		King Idris decrees that the Crown Prince be replaced by his own younger brother Hassan al Rida.

1957

January		Libya establishes telecommunications links with the United States, Canada, Cuba, and Mexico.
March	15	United States Vice President Richard Nixon visits Libya after attending the Ghana Independence celebrations.
April		Libya opens its first pilot radio station; by

the end of this year this is broadcasting nationwide.

1958

July   14   Britain expands its military bases in Libya after the monarchy is overthrown in Iraq.

1959

April   12   Esso-Libya announces a major oil find at Zelten, one hundred miles from the coast. This is the start of the Libyan oil boom.

Still at school in Sebha, Gadaffi forms a secret society, the Free officers, basing themselves on Nasser's group in Egypt, which had a similar name.

1960

March   President Kennedy approves a secret report from the National Security Council, authorizing the CIA to make contact with rebel factions in Libya, and making contingency plans for intervention with Britain and France if Idris is overthrown. The Allies are now aware that the king is vulnerable.

August   The neighboring state of Chad receives its independence from France as a republic and not as a monarchy.

1961

September   12   First cargo of Zelten crude loaded on the Esso tanker *Canterbury* at Braygah, bound for Britain.

Gadaffi organizes a series of protests in Sebha in support of President Patrice Lumumba, who is overthrown in the Congo and later murdered. The Free Officers also protest in support of Nasser and against Britain.

October   5   Gadaffi's biggest demonstration yet; a crowd of four thousand gathers supporting Nasser and demanding Arab Unity. Gadaffi is later singled out as the main troublemaker and questioned by Sayf al Nasr, head of Sebha's leading family, who suggests disciplinary action.

October   29   On Sayf al Nasr's recommendation, Gadaffi expelled from Sebha and all schools in the Fezzan. However, the Free Officers continue to meet—and he establishes a new group in Misurata where he moves to continue his education. He urges both groups to follow the Koran, praying five times a day and avoiding alcohol, women, and gambling.

1962
November   Britain begins equipping the Libyan navy, although it never amounted to more than a hundred men during King Idris's reign.

1963
April   27   The federal system of government abolished by royal decree, establishing Libya as a unitary state with one center of government and ten administrative regions.

Gadaffi becomes a trainee officer at the military academy in Benghazi. Later in the year, its commandant is assassinated. Many years later it was claimed (but never verified) that Gadaffi shot him. The academy was attached to the university where Gadaffi spent three years (1963–66) reading for a degree in history in the faculty of arts.

August   Formation of a Libyan air force, trained and equipped by the British. Its strength is no more than two hundred men under King Idris.

December   Armand Hammer begins negotiating a long-term oil deal. In return for oil concessions, he agrees to help the Libyans irrigate Kufra oasis, build a fertilizer plant, and divert natural gas—and privately agrees to pay the Minister of Labour and Omar el Shalhi three percent each per barrel of crude oil.

1964

January	13	Student riots in Benghazi, where Gadaffi is now a student.
January	16	Eight students killed in four days of rioting in Benghazi. The students are demanding evacuation of U.S. and British bases. The King's security force attacks them with bayonets. Libyan Parliament calls for Western withdrawal
January	21	Prime Minister Fekini demands removal of Mahmud Buquwaytin, chief of the internal security force and brother-in-law to the el Shalhi brothers. The king refuses. Fekini resighs.
January/ March		After weeks of protests the King announces that he will abdicate, and then changes his mind "in response to public opinion."
August	22	New Prime Minister Mahmud Muntasir tells Parliament that Britain and the U.S. have agreed to evacuate their bases when their treaties expire.
October		General election. On nomination day, the security forces arrest antigovernment candidates. After more unrest, the King dissolves the new Parliament.

During this period, Gadaffi was at the military academy in Benghazi and had already formed the Free Unionist Officers, insisting upon strict observance of the Koran. On one occasion, Gadaffi is said to have summarily executed a fellow-officer in the rifle butts at the Military Academy for homosexuality, but this story has never been confirmed.

1965

May	Another general election. To minimize opposition, the King reduces the Parliamentary constituencies from 103 to 91.
	Widespread rioting. Five oil fields bombed.

1966

Armand Hammer secures further oil concession by agreeing to fund an agricultural development program.

Gadaffi sent to Britain for ten months to study radio and electronic communications with the Royal Army Signals Corps at Beaconsfield, Buckinghamshire, and Bovington, Dorset. He is later able to use the skills he has learned to develop a code and maintain radio contact with Free Officers stationed around Libya. The group agree to take up overseas training to prepare for a coup. Mustafa el Kharrubi and Suleiman Mahmoud both study at the San Antonio School of Languages, Texas, and the Signals School in New Jersey.

The Sarir oil field comes on stream, shipping through Beirut. Nelson Bunker Hunt estimates its reserves at seven billion to nine billion barrels.

1967

May/June

More student riots as the Arabs prepare for war with Israel. Libya suspends oil shipments to the United States for twenty-seven days.

June   5

A mob attacks the British embassy in Benghazi as the war begins. Libyan volunteers join the Egyptian army. Widely believed in Libya that the U.S. used Wheelus Field to provide support for the Israelis who triumphed in what became known as the Six Day War, defeating the Egyptian, Syrian, and Jordanian forces and occupying the Gaza Strip, the Golan Heights, the West Bank, and the Arab sector of Jerusalem.

June   17

The National Security Council warns President Lyndon Johnson that King Idris is likely to be overthrown, and that this "would put Nasser on easy street with oil."

June	19—	Libya suspends oil production after widespread rioting and calls for a general strike.
July	3	
October	8	Two Libyan airmen try to commandeer a plane to use against Israel in the Arab cause. They are jailed for six years. Many Libyans who supported the war stay out of the country, mostly in Egypt, returning in 1969 after the revolution.

1968

A £300 million defense package agreed with Britain whereby Libya is supplied with Thunderbird and Rapier missiles, radar defenses, and Chieftain tanks. Gadaffi later claims that bribes totaling £40 million were paid by the British to secure these contracts.

Rebels in the Muslim north of Chad attempt to seize power. France sends in sixteen hundred troops to support the government, whose support largely comes from the Christian south.

1969

March	12	Gadaffi calls off his first attempt to seize power when he discovers that his coup would clash with a concert in Benghazi staged by the Egyptian singer Umm Khaltoum to raise funds for the Palestinian group al Fatah. Members of his Free Officers group are sent to Britain for training, which further weakens his preparations. Gadaffi returns home to Sirte and is injured in a car crash.
March	15	The authorities know something is afoot. A warrant is issued for Gadaffi's arrest and his Free Officers put under surveillance.... But the warrant is never served. Learning of this a year later, Gadaffi says God must have intervened.
March	18	Although he is on holiday, the Free Officers call Gadaffi back to Tripoli, by now aware they are being watched.

March	24	The revolution postponed again when the King moves to Tobruk, fearing for his safety. At Tobruk, he is close to the British naval base and knows that the British would help him leave the country in the event of a coup.
May	25	A military coup in the neighboring state of Sudan, led by General Numeiry.
June/ August		King Idris seeks medical treatment in Turkey and Greece accompanied by Queen Fatima and Omar el Shalhi. Widely rumored that el Shalhi and his brother Rida are planning a coup, possibly with the King's complicity to avoid the Crown Prince's succession. [It was the Shalhis's father who was assassinated in 1954.]
July		Gadaffi drop plans to stage the revolution on August 13 when most senior officers are due to attend a military conference in Benghazi, having learned that his Free Officers are under even closer surveillance.
August	4	King Idris announces from Turkey that he is planning to abdicate.
August —September	19 11	The Russian Fleet begins a major exercise off Cyrenaica, testing antisubmarine defenses near the British submarine base at Tobruk, giving rise to rumors that the Russians are supporting one coup attempt while the CIA is believed to be supporting the el Shalhi brothers. In fact, there is a third coup being planned—Gadaffi's.
September	1	GADAFFI SEIZES POWER IN AN OVERNIGHT COUP. Only one person killed. The Free Officers arrest the King's leading supporters, take control of the main barracks and the radio station—and meet hardly any resistance.

The House of Cards

Monarchies have seldom been founded by other than strong and ambitious men. The fascination of Shakespeare's historical plays or Machiavelli's *The Prince* lies in our realization that their heroes were murderous conspirators or upstart bastards who mortgaged every principle, sacrificing family or friends in pursuit of power. Through sheer force of personality, these princes cast an imprint upon their age, molding nations, leading them to battle, and so improving life for the common man that their merits seemed to outweigh their sins. That could not be said of Idris, first and only King of Libya. He was a weak, dithering, insignificant man who acquired his throne by ingratiating himself to the British in their darkest hour.

At the time Idris offered them his support, many external observers thought Hitler was winning the war, not least the United States Ambassador to London, Joseph Kennedy. In 1938, Germany annexed Austria and then swallowed Sudetenland under the terms of the Munich Agreement before occupying Czechoslovakia and then invading Poland in September 1939, the event that precipitated the Anglo-French declaration of war. Within months, German forces swept through Finland, Denmark, and Norway and then across Belgium and Holland before France fell in June 1940. The United States had not yet entered the war, and Britain was standing alone, facing invasion from Germany, when the Italians launched their attack upon British positions in Egypt.

If friendships are best forged in hours of need, Idris displayed impeccable timing in choosing that moment to make his offer—but there was nowhere else he could go. The Italians had forced him out of Libya twenty years ealier, and if they now conquered Egypt the Sanusi leader would have had to flee somewhere else. All he could offer was titular leadership, for he was neither a military man nor a politician with a constituency, but even that was a boon to the British—who proceeded to form a Libyan Arab Army. This comprised five battalions of Arabs, largely Bedouin living in exile or those who had stayed in Libya since the defeat of Omar el Mukhtar and were eager to seize any chance of throwing the Italians out of their country. This army was staffed by British officers with Idris as its nominal chief. It may not have been a magnificent fighting force in the modern military mold, but the Arabs scared the living daylights out of the Italians, happily employing once more the same nighttime, cutthroat guerrilla tactics against their hated enemy.

Initially the North African campaign, went well for the British, with Wavell's forces capturing 113,000 Italian soldiers and airmen. The tide turned against the Allies with the arrival of the German Afrika Corps under the command of Rommel. Thinking he already had North Africa under control, Wavell dispatched part of his army to Greece to resist any German advance through the Balkans and found himself without enough troops to halt Rommel's advance. Wavell's successor Auchinleck launched an Allied counteroffensive against Rommel late in 1941, but, too, was forced to withdraw. For the best part of a year the Allied forces were in disarray, defending themselves as best they could—and often brilliantly—by employing the Libyan Arab Army and David Stirling's newly formed Long Range Desert Group to mount unorthodox raids on German bases and supply lines. This tied the Germans down while the Allies regrouped, preparing for what proved to be the decisive battle of El Alamein. There, the newly appointed commander of the Allied Eighth Army Field Marshal Montgomery forced the Germans back on their heels, retreating across the North African desert while another Anglo-U.S. force under Dwight Eisenhower advanced from the west. On May 13, 1943, the Germano-Italian forces surrendered, 248,000 of their troops were captured, and Britain found itself in temporary charge of Libya. It was time for Idris to go back home.

The British military administration faced the same problems that had long confronted anyone seeking to unify North Africa. Here was a vast land mass that appeared virtually uninhabitable to a European. It was mostly desert and steppes with just the two main coastal pockets and the oases. The total population of Libya was little more than one million with only the population in Cyrenaica looking to the Sanusi for any kind of leadership, and that more spiritual than secular. With eighty percent of the population either nomadic or seminomadic, and only six percent of the total population able to read or write, Libya was a country almost totally bereft of skills. Commentators disagreed on one statistic; some said two Libyans had been to college; others thought the figure should have been four. Whoever was right, Libya was a land forced to rely upon others to run its most basic services. Even justice was dispensed by foreigners. Long after independence, the Libyan Supreme Court comprised two Egyptians, one Briton, and one American.

To make matters worse, there was an underlying bitter resentment between the Arabs who had been dispossessed under Mussolini and the forty-five thousand Italians who stayed on in Libya throughout and after the war, occupying farms and running the shops, offices, and small-scale factories that made Tripoli tick. These Italian immigrants were now settled and multiplying, entering their second generation, a sizable Catholic minority in an Arab land.

Britain continued to govern most of Libya under the terms of the 1907 Hague Convention until eight years after the Second World War ended. Resolving its future was one of those messy problems that had no easy answer, with so many conflicting tribal and regional loyalties. France was in control of the Fezzan, having sent in troops from Algeria under the leadership of General Leclerc, so any settlement had to depend upon Britain and France deciding boundaries, and then the four major powers—the United States, Russia, France, and Britain—resolving Libya's future form of government.

The issue was raised at both the Allied postwar conferences—at Potsdam and San Francisco—without a formula being settled. The matter was then referred to the Council of Foreign Ministers, who also failed to find an answer at their meetings in London in September 1945 and April 1946. Russia was advocating a form of Soviet trusteeship over Tripolitania; France thought this part of the country could return to Italy, which had invested $159 million in Libya before the war, laying down a basic infrastructure and providing farms for its immigrants. There was some suspicion on the part of the British that France was seeking to strengthen her position in North Africa, being already the main colonial power in central, west, and northwest Africa—Algeria, Tunis, Mauretania, Mali, and Chad. As the haggling continued, Russia sided with France on the form of trusteeship that might be introduced—and this disturbed Britain and the United States, who did not want anyone else left in control of the Mediterranean sealanes. At one stage, Britain seemed ready to give up Tripolitania on condition that it could decide the future of Cyrenaica—and in the middle of the difficult negotiations the Sanusi were quietly encouraged to stake their claim.

Idris was advised to return to Cyrenaica and promised British support. He proceeded to abolish all political parties, demanding that Cyrenaica be ceded to his authority, and went on to establish the National Congress of Cyrenaica under the presidency of his brother al Rida. This was formed on January 10, 1948—and two days later the National Congress of Cyrenaica recommended that Libya should become an independent federal state with Idris at its head. The other regions were told that if they did not like the idea, the National Congress reserved the right for Cyrenaica to go it alone.

These naked maneuverings continued while the Council of Ministers went on searching for a solution. A Commission of Investigation was sent to Libya in March 1948 to study conditions within the country. By the time its report was considered by the Council of Ministers on September 13, 1948, it was clear that the British and Idris were playing for time. By that date, it was too late for a detailed report to be put before the General Assembly of the United Nations, which was due to meet two days later—so the matter was delayed again, this time until the following April.

Next, a United Nations subcommittee was formed to go back over all the arguments and consider any new representations that might be made. This subcommittee comprised delegates from Australia, Britain, Brazil, Chile, Denmark, Egypt, Ethiopia, France, India, Iraq, Mexico, Poland, Russia, South Africa, and the United States. On May 13, 1949, the subcommittee agreed to a proposal put forward by the British and Italian foreign ministers that Tripolitania, Cyrenaica, and the Fezzan should be governed by Trustees appointed by the British, French, and Italians for a period of ten years, after which Libya would become independent.

There then followed six months of mind-boggling amendment and counteramendment, meetings canceled and rearranged, the Soviet bloc first voting one way and then another, the Catholic countries from South America also voting en bloc to help the Italians keep their hold in Africa, and the Italians themselves carefully stepping from side to side in their own negotiations, hoping a toehold in Libya might strengthen their claim to reestablish some form of influence in their other former territories, Eritrea, Somalia, and Ethiopia.

This was power politics at its worst. Twice, resolutions submitted to the General Assembly of the United Nations were referred back to reconstituted subcommittees, who heard new evidence and thought anew. At one stage, all hope of Libya achieving early independence seemed lost—until the delegate from the island of Haiti, Emile Saint-Lot, changed his mind, casting his vote for independence. By that one vote, Libya avoided trusteeship—and on November 21, 1949, the General Assembly agreed that Libya could become independent within one year and no later than January 1, 1952. But the British were one jump ahead. On June 1, 1949, before any of this had been resolved, the British government formally recognized Idris as Emir of Cyrenaica, acknowledged him as head of a government with full responsibility for its own internal affairs, promising full support to the principle of self-government for Cyrenaica, whatever the United Nations might decide for Libya as a whole.

The British were merely repaying a debt, but with such a headstart and their help at every juncture Idris was able to turn the next stage of the United Nations' deliberations to his advantage. A transitional National Constituent Assembly was established to oversee the evolution of the new state, working hand in palm with a U.N. Commissioner, Adrian Pelt from Holland, and a ten-member Advisory Council on Libya.

Idris did what all politicians like to do when outnumbered by their opponents: He rigged the voting. With British support, Idris suggested that Libya should opt for a federal constitution with a national constituent assembly—with each of the three regions equally represented. Thus, the Fezzan with only five percent of the population and Cyrenaica with only twenty percent were both given twenty seats in the new Assembly, with the same number allotted to Tripolitania, where seventy-five percent of any would-be electorate lived. Just to make sure that democracy did not triumph even over this obstacle, the King reserved the right to choose the twenty members from Cyrenaica himself—with his ally Sayf al Nasr having the same right of choice in the Fezzan. In Tripolitania, the Grand Mufti was given the impossible task of choosing among all the different factions, but that was hardly the King's concern.

Had time been on their side, or if the United Nations General Assembly had been more purposeful, the would-be political leaders of Tripolitania might have tried to force the King's hand; but they knew that if this opportunity for independence was not seized, something worse might be suggested in its place. Idris and the British had their way, with the United States remaining silent. The independent state of Libya was proclaimed on December 24, 1951, responsible for its own defense and foreign policy—a monarchy created by United Nations decree. First, there was a king without a kingdom. Now, there was a state without enough educated citizens to fill the seats of a motor car. A state that had neither the manpower to defend itself nor the means to feed its people.

In deciding to piece together the events that brought Gadaffi to power, the thought has always lain at the back of my mind that a sophisticated readership in the United States or Britain might find it hard to believe that the West was, in effect, his midwife. The events already described are strange enough, and they appear in hardly any of the books written about Libya, especially those produced under the Gadaffi regime, which seek to expunge British and American influence just as they disavow the ancient Romans. Instead, Gadaffi's tame historians clothe each and every tiny branch of the Libyan state's development with rhetoric or philosophy. It was never as simple as that.

The British, Italian, German, and American armies rode away from the battlefields of North Africa leaving the detritus of war behind them. Abandoned tanks, shot-down planes, crippled jeeps, blown-up trucks, vast barbed-wire fences, empty buildings, pillboxes and mangled heaps of rusting iron were left scattered across a landscape strewn with minefields and unexploded bombs. The Allied bequest to the newly born monarchy was the largest junkyard in the history of mankind.

Returning to their grazing lands, the Bedouin faced a constant threat of death. They could not walk upon the surface of their own land for fear of treading upon an unexploded mine, and feared for the safety of their children. This is another of the deep grievances that Libya has against the West. Between 1940 and 1983, they claim that 1,956 Libyans were killed by exploding mines with another 1,777 injured. Even today, five people die on average each year in similar explosions. These deaths tend to occur in the Sirte and Libyan deserts, nearer the coast, for it was here that the Allied and Axis powers fought their great tank battles—and here that people tend to wander—for this is where Libya's largest reserves of oil have been found.

Gadaffi has particular reason for sharing his countrymen's resentment. As a child, playing in the sands near his parents' tent, he, too, was injured by a landmine which left him with leg wounds that trouble him to this day.

There was another strange twist to this aspect of Libya's emergence as an independent state. Before oil brought riches, Libya's greatest post war fortunes were made by peddling junk. The Bedouin went out into the desert, risking life and limb, gathering up metal waste left by the departing armies. They sold it to scrap metal merchants in the West for an estimated $150 million at a time when Libya's national budget was less than $30 million a year.

It was the King's peculiar misfortune to ascend his throne at the very moment in history when monarchies were crumbling all around him. The Middle East was a seething hotbed, fueled by military coups, frequent assassinations, and Islamic fervor. As part of the postwar shake-out, monarchies were replaced by communism in Albania, Bulgaria, and Romania. Constant unrest in Algeria led to an eight-year war of independence, starting in 1954. Sixteen years of martial law in Iran were followed by riots, arrests, and assassinations long before the demise of the Shah. Coups were frequent in Syria. King Hussein managed to survive one assassination attempt after another in Jordan, but the monarchies fell in Egypt (1952) and in Iraq (1958).

With all the wisdom of hindsight, one can see that King Idris never stood a chance, especially with events in Egypt producing a boldly charismatic figure in Col. Gamal Abdel Nasser, who was to become Gadaffi's inspiration.

At the time of the King's enthronement, the young Muammar Gadaffi was nine years old, living with his parents in a tent in the Sirte Desert, still unable to read or write, like all other members of his family. Theirs was a simple life with few possessions, just cooking utensils, the communal bowls from which the family ate together at mealtimes, their hand-woven carpets to lay on the sand or provide decoration as wall-hangings, and their faith in Islam.

Gadaffi deflects all questions about his early or family background with the dismissive phrase "trivial details," but it is easy enough to piece together a description of the way they lived for it had barely changed in centuries.

As the third hereditary head of the Sanusi Order, as the Bedouin religious leader, as the man who successfully ended their involvement in the First World War and gave them nominal leadership in the Second, and as the Emir who presided over their transition to independence, King Idris was well placed to become the natural and accepted leader of his people and the founder of a dynasty. Had he led them forward seeking to improve their condition, the monarchy might have survived; but he lacked the qualities that founding monarchs must possess. Faced with hard choices, he could never make up his mind.

This basic weakness of character was known well before his elevation. Evans Pritchard, who met Idris in Egypt in the thirties, came to know him better when appointed political Officer to the British Military Administration in November 1942. When Evans Pritchard finished his study *The Sanusi of Cyrenaica* in April 1948, he recalled that Idris could have become Emir after the First World War, but fled rather than take any risks, having siphoned off money to Egypt to keep himself in comfort in exile.

At the time of his flight he was thirty-three years of age. He gave the impression of being tall and rather portly, very unlike the slight and delicate figure he presents today. Nurtured, as were all the Sanusi family, in piety and learning in oasis retreats and accustomed to a refined and sedentary life, he has never been a man of action or of a hardy constitution. . . . He early showed that his talents lay in diplomacy rather than in the field. It is evident from the part he played in the events leading up to the truce and during the period of the truce that he is astute and a man of sound political judgment. That he is often vacillating and evasive cannot be denied, and even though these characteristics may sometimes have been a wise response of the weak negotiating with the strong, and may often have served him well in the difficult circumstances in which he took over direction of the

Sanusi Order from Sayyid Ahmad, they seem to be weaknesses to which he is temperamentally prone and to have become an aversion to directness in either thought or action. Italian writers, who are, with some justification, scathing in their comments on most members of the Sanusi family, speak of Sayyid Idris with respect. They admit that he is intelligent, religious, and gifted with a profound moral sense and political intuition. He is firm in decisions once he has taken them and keeps his promises. . . .

His grandfather had been an ascetic in his devotion to God, but by the time spiritual leadership of the Sanusi reached Idris this third generation had grown into a large, straggling family with conventionally Arab features in one line and a dark Negro complexion in the other. Surrounded by teachers and acolytes, clerks and slaves, the branches were spread between the oases of Jaghbub and Kufra,

which produced little but dates, and had to be supplied from the lodges in the coastal region. Supplies were sent by caravan partly in local produce, such as skins, wool, grain, butter, honey, and meat, and partly in money or imported goods: rice, tea, sugar, and cloth. These gifts were *sadaqa*, freewill gifts, though if a lodge did not send them, its Shaikh was reminded of his obligations . . .

Inevitably, in circumstances such as these, Sanusi standards slipped. The Bedouin continued to tithe income to their spiritual leaders, but the money and goods that they sent were not always used for the good of the order. The Sanusi became adept at creaming off money for themselves. Corruption ran through the family like a vein. This might not have been noticed had they continued to while away their lives in remote oases, but with the ascendancy of the King these venal little men were put in charge of public exchequers, government departments, and his embryonic army, navy, and air force. They became his ministers and his courtiers, important figures in the politics of the region, for Libya was still potentially a battlefield in any future war.

Handed his kingdom upon a plate, Idris kept his side of an unspoken bargain, duly agreeing to a twenty-year friendship treaty whereby Britain maintained its bases, paying an annual subvention to the Libyan Government of £3.75 million and also agreeing to help with the country's economic development. Likewise, the Americans signed a seventeen-year agreement whereby they, too, paid an annual subvention ($2 million) as rent for their Wheelus Field airbase. Together, these two rents represented seventy-two percent of Libya's gross annual budget. Financially, the kingdom's future seemed secure—but only because of these two agreements. Otherwise the Sanusi monarchy was little more than a house of cards. At its apex sat the King, who held power through the gift of foreign governments. Beneath him were ministers, appointed on the basis of family relationship or tribal affiliation, presiding over ministries staffed by foreigners because there were not enough educated Libyans to operate telephones, man desks, or keep the cashbooks. The schools were largely run by Egyptians, teaching Egyptian history from Egyptian textbooks. The army, navy, and air force—all piddling little outfits presenting no real threat to anyone—wore British uniforms, carried British weapons, and were led by British officers. Farms and businesses were still run by the Italian settlers.

Wherever one looked, the future seemed bleak. The Royal Institute of International Affairs viewed this landscape in *Libya: A Brief Political and Economic Survey* (1956) and concluded,

The situation in Libya can only be described as fundamentally unstable. Besides the differences between Tripolitania and Cyrenaica, there exists a cleavage of opinion between those in authority and the man-in-the-street. While the King has always been well disposed toward the West, and particularly to Great Britain, Egyptian influence has permeated deeply in Cyrenaica as well as in Tripolitania where there exists a strongly xenophobic attitude toward the West. Moreover, there are further deep divisions in the Palace which are likely to lead to trouble when the matter of the succession arises on the death of King Idris. . . . Characterized by an adverse climate and inhospitable terrain, Libya suffers above all from two handicaps: scanty natural resources and violent fluctuations in income caused by crop failure. Known mineral or power resources are virtually nonexistent. . . . There are no permanent rivers and only a few springs or seasonal torrents, though underground water resources exist in parts of Tripolitania and the Fezzan. . . . The present high death rate, especially the excessive infant mortality, are ascribed mainly to malnutrition

and poor living conditions. The population is sparse in relation
to Libya's total area, but not in relation to available natural resources. In drought years visible and disguised unemployment
may reach eighty percent of the labor force, which in itself is
small compared with the total population. There is also a high
proportion of partially or totally unemployable people.... Little
plant, equipment, or housing exists outside the Italian sector, and
the improvement of water supplies is a basic requirement both
for agriculture and the welfare of the population. Funds are required for better irrigation, flood control, grazing land, and live-
stock breeds, for reforestation, tools, and seeds, new plantations,
packing and freezing plant for meat, fish, and vegetables, transport facilities, schools, housing, and sanitation.... In the absence
of important new discoveries the best that anyone hopes for is
that by the end of perhaps twenty years Libya may gain viability
at a reasonable living standard, provided always that in the mean-
time she continues to receive financial and technical assistance
from abroad....

King Idris may have been weak, but he was not stupid. Having
spent most of his adult life outside his country, he was sufficiently
detached to realize where the weaknesses might lie in Libya's new
autonomy. Having promised free elections to a democratic parliament, Idris swiftly banned the National Congress Party when it
won sweeping support in Tripolitania on an antigovernment ticket
and then went on to expel known troublemakers, i.e., communists
and other left-wingers, from the country. When students at the
newly opened university in Benghazi started to protest, the King's
security forces went in with bayonets. Eight students were killed.

Throughout his reign, Idris realized that any challenge to his
authority was likely to come either from within his own family or
from the army.

On November 5, 1954, his most trusted personal adviser, Ibrahim
el Shalhi, Minister of Palace Affairs, was murdered by a nephew
of the Queen. Realizing this Shakespearean crime foretold an attempt upon his life, the King exiled seven members of his family
to the oasis at Hun and decreed that hereafter the royal family
would be reduced in size to comprise just himself, the Queen, their
children, and his brother the Crown Prince. This bumbling attempt
to hang on to the throne fooled no one, for the King was by then
sixty-five years old and he and Queen Fatima had no children; their

only baby died in childhood. So the crown would pass to his brother, who was only one year younger than he was. The assassin, Sherif Muhieddin Sanusi, was publicly hanged and his body left hanging from the gallows in the center of Tripoli as a warning to others.

It was widely known that the Queen's side of the family had their own reasons for wanting to be rid of Ibrahim el Shalhi, for the el Shalhi family were virtually running the country in the King's name and might make their own bid for the throne on the King's demise. That possibility remained viable when Idris appointed one of Ibrahim's sons to succeed him as Minister of Palace Affairs, later putting the other son in charge of the army.

Within months, Crown Prince Mohammad Rida el Mahdi el Sanusi was found to be mortally ill—leaving his son Sayyid Siddiq as the natural successor. This caused panic in the royal household, with the King first persuading Parliament that Sayyid's younger brother al Hasan Rida would be a better choice . . . and then himself at the age of sixty-six entering into a second marriage, which was possible under Islamic law, in the hope of siring an infant son who might one day inherit the throne after a period of regency. The king's marriage to Alia Abdel Kader Lamloun, daughter of a rich Egyptian merchant, was solemnized in the presence of Colonel Nasser.

By such extraordinary decisions, King Idris managed to humiliate his first wife Queen Fatima, enrage her family, alienate both his brother's eldest son and other family members in that line, and reveal himself to the Arab world as a vain, capricious, weak old man clinging to power for all the wrong reasons.

The King's fundamental analysis was, of course, correct. There were militant officers at all ranks in his new army, and although the King tried to ward them off by building up his own private army, the Cyrenaica Defense Force (which was based upon two surviving battalions from the wartime Libyan Arab Army), the odds were stacking against him, not suddenly but steadily throughout his reign. Having given them better pay, tanks, helicopters, armored corps, and the best British weapons he could buy, the King thought the Cyrenaica Defense Force would stand by him to the end. He was wrong again. The house of cards had virtually nothing holding it together, not even loyalty.

The Wrong Side at Suez

As the King's authority crumbled, an air of desperation set in within the Libyan capital. Western diplomats reported back to their governments in London and Washington that sooner or later the King would have to go. His position was becoming more and more untenable. Throughout his reign, King Idris presided over an anarchic shambles, dissolving parliaments, dismissing prime ministers and cabinets, trying to placate both the Arabs and the West (who at that time seemed irreconcilable), and surrounding himself with bodyguards.

Realizing that an assassin's bullet might be fired at any time, he abandoned his palace and gave it to "the people," i.e., the palace became the main building for the new university at Benghazi while the King and Queen moved to a newly built palace, designed by a British architect and constructed by a British firm. He had the new palace erected close to the British submarine base at Tobruk, in the belief that the British would save them if the country rose up against him. The King knew that he governed without the consent of the people.

Under the terms of the 1951 federal constitution, King Idris was the head of a hereditary monarchy but, as he happened to have no natural heirs, he had the right to nominate his own successor. Had he produced an infant heir, the constitution provided for the appointment of a regency. If he failed to choose a successor, or died without doing so, the constitution required both Houses of Parliament to appoint a new king. The constitution also gave King

86

Idris power to appoint and dismiss prime ministers and all other ministers, although they were in theory answerable to the House of Representatives for government policy and could also be dismissed, either individually or collectively, if the House passed a motion of no confidence against one or all of them. In the House of Representatives, each deputy had a constituency with an electorate of approximately twenty thousand people. Initially, until 1963, only men could vote. There were thirty-five seats for Tripolitania, fifteen for Cyrenaica, and five for the Fezzan. In the upper house, the Senate, half the twenty-four members were appointed personally by the King and half elected by legislative councils in the three provinces, Tripolitania, Cyrenaica, and the Fezzan, which had delegated local government powers.

The existence of upper and lower houses, with devolved power in the regions, should have been enough to provide the checks and balances essential to any form of government, but at no time was there a general consensus within the state as to the general direction a Libyan government might take. Having concluded long-term military agreements with the United States and Britain, the King sought vainly to establish his country's independence by visiting Egypt or welcoming delegations from the Eastern bloc. Neither gesture could dispel his image as a Western puppet; he was trapped by his past and the ways power was shifting in the Middle East.

His first Prime Minister, Mahmud al Muntasir, oversaw the transitional arrangements for the creation of the new state and the negotiations with Britain, which provoked violent demonstrations on the streets of Tripoli even at the start of the King's reign. Muntasir's premiership came to grief over the question of who should appoint the *walis*, regional governors. The King insisted that this was his right; the Prime Minister thought the government ought to decide, and the regional authorities wanted to choose their own nominees. The premiership lasted just over two years. Muntasir's successor, Muhammad al Saqizli, survived seven weeks before he, too, resigned over similar issues after the King abolished the legislative council of Tripolitania for criticizing their *wali*. The president of the legislative council appealed to the supreme court, which decided that the King's decree was unconstitutional—which Idris took as a personal insult for which he blamed his Prime Minister.

The third Prime Minister, Mustafa bin Halim, was appointed in April 1954 and survived with some skill, steering Libya into membership of the Arab League and the United Nations. It was he who signed the Wheelus Field airbase agreement with the United States on September 9, 1954, and also negotiated a friendship treaty with France in return for French withdrawal from the Fezzan, similar treaties with Tunisia and Italy, and the commencement of formal diplomatic relations with the Soviet Union. Bin Halim's government survived thirty-seven months, but there were frequent cabinet reshuffles and his relationship with Idris was far from easy. Bin Halim had to bear the brunt of widespread criticism for allowing Egyptian weapons to be channeled through the Fezzan to supply the rebels in Algeria who were fighting for independence from the French, and far more serious criticism, including student riots and violence on the streets, when he appeared to support Britain at the time of the Anglo-French invasion of Suez in 1956. Although this was denied at the time, there is little doubt that British planes operated from Libyan bases, with the result that bin Halim was seen as the supporter of a Christian state's aggression against an Arab neighbor, Egypt. He did not survive many weeks after that.

The fourth Prime Minister, Abdul Majid Kubar, held office from May 1957 to October 1960, and was also seen as a conspirator with the British, allowing them to use their Libyan bases in an attempt to thwart the Iraqi coup in July/August 1958. Eventually, Kubar's government collapsed after allegations that building contracts had been given without proper approval. Kubar tried to avoid a motion of no confidence in the House of Representatives by asking the King to dissolve Parliament, but when the King demurred Kubar resigned rather than make a personal explanation to the House.

The fifth Prime Minister, Muhammad bin Othman bin Said, was appointed in October 1960, but found himself faced with the same problems that had bedeviled his predecessors; the regional governments wanted more autonomy while the King wished to surrender power to no one. The ordinary day-to-day business became almost impossible when the King, by now seeking conspirators concealed behind every date palm, removed the royal court to Bayda, the new palace near Tobruk, insisting thereafter that the government should travel to him whenever consultation was needed. This was an unhelpful stipulation. Bayda was on the coast in Cyrenaica, approximately a thousand miles from Tripoli. After little more than two years in office, bin Said resigned, ostensibly for health reasons.

The sixth Prime Minister, Dr. Mohieddine Fekini, survived for ten eventful months during which he was able to abolish the troublesome federal system of government, make Libya a unitary state, and give all adult women the right to vote. His period of office between March 1963 and January 1964 coincided with widespread student demonstrations demanding that the Palestinians be allowed to return to their land. As Dr. Henri Habib explains so clearly in *Libya Past and Present,*

On January 22, 1964, there were demonstrations in the major Libyan cities in support of the Arab cause in Palestine. A number of students were fired upon in Benghazi. The Prime Minister asked the King for the resignation of Bukuwaytin, brother-in-law of el Shalhi ... and Commander of the powerful Cyrenaica Defense Force, which was responsible for shooting the students. The King refused to ask for Bukuwaytin's resignation, and instead the Prime Minister resigned. ...

This appalling shambles then degenerated still further, with the now seventy-five-year-old King hanging on to his throne by keeping as far away as he could from his people, guarded all the time by the Cyrenaica Defense Corps while he remained hidden away in his new palace, only occasionally visiting Tripoli, and approving harsh punishments for those who took part in strikes or public protests.

As his seventh Prime Minister, the King recalled Mahmud al Muntasir on January 24. There were immediate public demonstrations in favor of the ousted Prime Minister Fekini. Muntasir successfully persuaded the King that the British and the Americans would have to be asked to vacate their bases when the treaties expired, for he could see that it was their presence that was causing unrest—but this concession came too late to stem the groundswell of opposition to the King who, characteristically, offered to abdicate in the middle of the crisis, and then changed his mind. A general election was held in October 1964, the fourth in twelve years. On nomination day, the King's forces went around the country arresting opposition candidates. With unrest gathering momentum week by week, the King again dissolved Parliament after only three months, and Muntasir resigned.

Libya was becoming ungovernable. Each new general election—the fifth was held in May 1965—provoked a new wave of riots with the people believing, correctly, that the King was trying to rig the electoral system in his favor. Five oil fields were bombed in these latest elections. Prime Ministers now came and went without effect. In his last four years upon the throne, King Idris appointed four more—Hussein Mazek (March 21, 1965 to June 28, 1967), Abdul Qadir Badri (June to October 1967), Abdul Hamid Bakkush (October 1967 to September 1968), and Wannis Qadhafi (September 1968 to September 1969). All of them had an impossible task, for the Middle East was seething with resentment against the West for supporting Israel. And there was now another new ingredient in the equations: oil.

The conflict over the Suez Canal in 1956 left many questions in the Middle East unresolved. Although militarily defeated, Colonel Nasser emerged a hero in Arab eyes, the one Arab leader prepared to defend his people against what the Arabs saw as Israeli aggression, aided and abetted by Britain and the United States.

The rights and wrongs of his dispute with the West are peripheral to this book; his significance is central, for Nasser used a new tool to communicate with his supports in the Arab world: radio.

The principal issue in the 1956 conflict was Nasser's seizure of the Suez Canal. Designed by the French engineer Ferdinand de Lesseps, the canal ran for 103 miles between Port Said in the north and Suez in the south, connecting the Mediterranean to the Red Sea. Its completion in 1869 opened up Asia to the West, enabling Britain to ship soldiers, goods, and bureaucrats to its colonies in the East. Disraeli bought control of the Suez Canal Company for Britain from the Khedive of Egypt in 1875. Thereafter, even when the canal was opened to ships of all nations, the British tended to look upon it as their own personal fiefdom, the main vein connecting the far-flung limbs of this empire.

Stung by Britain's refusal to help him build a new dam across the Nile at Aswan, Nasser seized the canal in July 1956. He timed this move carefully, waiting until Britain withdrew its troops from the Canal Zone under the terms of the 1954 Anglo-Egyptian Treaty. In that treaty, Nasser agreed to keep the canal open to international shipping. This was important to the West, for seventy percent of the ships passing through the canal belonged to member nations of NATO (the North Atlantic Treaty Organization), and they were becoming increasingly dependent upon it for oil supplies from the Persian Gulf.

Most governments thought Nasser would keep the canal open, but the recently appointed British prime minister, Sir Anthony

Eden, saw Nasser's action as the first step toward dictatorship in the Middle East; an action that had to be nipped in the bud lest Nasser become a latter-day Hitler. This was not the way the issue was seen in the United States, nor was it a viewpoint that commanded total support in Britain, either within his own Conservative Party or within Parliament as a whole, but Eden was adamant. And one aspect of history was on his side. He had correctly foreseen Hitler's rise in Germany, putting his career on the line rather than participate in appeasement, and standing by Churchill's side throughout the Second World War. In a highly emotional broadcast to the nation, Eden said: "The pattern is familiar to many of us, my friends. We all know this is how Fascist governments behave and we all remember, only too well, what the cost can be in giving in to Fascism. . . . Our quarrel is not with Egypt, it is with Nasser."

The French also had an investment in the canal, and colluded with the British. They secretly agreed that if Israel invaded Egypt, Britain and France would then issue an ultimatum to Israel and Egypt calling upon them to withdraw from the area around the canal, before sending in an Anglo-French military force that would seize the canal on the pretext that it was keeping the route open for international shipping and acting as a buffer between the combatants. This wheeze impressed no one.

Israel went into battle on October 29. The Anglo-French ultimatum was issued the next day—and Britain and France went ahead with their invasion, only to find themselves reviled by the United Nations and even publicly rebuked by the U.S. government and their wartime comrade in arms, President Dwight Eisenhower, and Secretary of State John Foster Dulles. Overnight, military conflict turned into a financial crisis that sent the British pound plunging on the international market. It was at this moment that the U.S. Secretary of the Treasury phoned Rab Butler, Britain's Lord Privy Seal, telling him bluntly: "The President cannot help you unless you conform to the United Nations resolution about withdrawal. If you do that, we here will help you save the pound."

And so two leading powers, Britain and France—who had presided over the birth of Libya, deciding its boundaries between them—were forced into a humiliating retreat, leaving Nasser firmly in control of the canal. The Arab world saw this as a victory for Nasser, even though Israel came out of the conflict territorially stronger, occupying the Gaza Strip and the Sinai Peninsula, which gave her access to the Red Sea. With the Western powers supporting Israel and the Soviet bloc drawing closer to the Arabs, there were growing fears that any future conflict might develop into a Third World War.

The Palestinian cause lay close to Gadaffi's heart. As a teenager he followed this unfolding drama by radio, listening to the Voice of Arabs broadcasts coming from across the desert in Egypt. In the West, it is assumed that Gadaffi must therefore be anti-Jewish. This is not necessarily so. Arabs and Jews lived side by side in Tripoli and the towns of Cyrenaica for centuries, freely practicing their religions, but numerically the Muslims outnumbered the Jews.

The Arab hostility to Israel was largely political. When the new state of Israel was created in 1948, the United Nations intended Palestine to be divided into three separate states—one Jewish, one Arab, and the third centered on Jerusalem but governed by international agreement so that Christians, Muslims, and Jews could all worship freely at their shrines in the Holy City. This did not happen. When Israel's independence was proclaimed and Britain withdrew its troops, the new state was immediately invaded by Arab forces from Egypt, Iraq, Syria, Transjordan, and Lebanon. In repelling them, Israel annexed the territory intended for the new Arab state of Palestine, forcing the Arabs there into refugee camps, where they have lived ever since.

This Palestinian issue may not have been central to the Suez Crisis in 1956, but it was to the younger and more radical Arabs in Libya who were angered when they heard that British and possibly French planes had been operating from Libyan bases. Though still in his mid-teens, Gadaffi shared that anger.

By the time Egypt sought to resolve its territorial dispute with Israel, another factor entered the equation: oil. Rapid industrial growth in the twentieth century made the developing nations increasingly oil dependent, with the U.S.—the world's most advanced economy—owning only ten percent of the world's known reserves.

Rather late in the day, having surrendered their colonial rights in the region, the West discovered that the Islamic states, which they had tended to ignore and even despise on religious, cultural, and philosophic grounds since the time of the Crusades, now possessed roughly two-thirds of the world's known oil reserves.

In the earlier stages of exploration, the region's oil deposits were thought to be concentrated farther east, beneath and surrounding the Persian Gulf, where prospecting had continued, off and on, since the 1890s, with major finds in Iran before the First World War and then later in Iraq, where one of the world's largest fields was discovered at Kirkuk in 1927. After the discovery of oil on Bahrain Island in 1932, prospecting began in Saudi Arabia and continued without much success until the Abqaiq and Abu Hadriya fields were found in 1940 and then the massive field at Ghawar in 1948. Another large oil deposit was found at Burgan in Kuwait in 1937, but its full potential remained unrealized until production resumed after the Second World War when two more major fields were discovered at Magwa (1951) and Ahmadi (1952).

Even as late as the 1956 Suez conflict, the West thought it knew who to respect or protect in the Middle East. The Saud family of Saudi Arabia controlled almost half the region's known reserves of nearly three hundred billion barrels; the Sabah family of Kuwait held another quarter, while a fifth lay in the hands of the pro-Western Shah of Iran, and under a tenth, the King of Iraq. The heads of four ruling families were thus controlling nearly all the West's future oil supplies from the Middle East.

Suddenly this picture changed. Oil was discovered first in Algeria in 1956 and then in Libya in 1959, suggesting that Europe might be able to receive its future oil not by shipping it through the Suez Canal but by carrying it across the Mediterranean, thereby dramatically reducing the transport costs and helping them to live without Colonel Nasser.

During the Italian occupation, Professor Desio of Milan University suggested there might be oil deposits below the Sirte Desert, where there is a natural rock basin varying in depth between 50,000 and 110,000 feet. The British Petroleum Company's handbook *Our Industry* describes this as

a Mesozoic-Tertiary feature with considerable thicknesses of marine clastic and carbonate sediments. The productive structures may be described in general terms as basement or Lower Paleozoic horst blocks, with draped Mesozoic or Tertiary sediments overlying. Reservoirs are most commonly carbonates with shale providing the cap-rock.... In certain parts of the Sirte Basin, particularly in the southeast, the reservoir is a sandstone of Cretaceous (as for example the Sarir field) or Cambrian age, overlain by thick marine Cretaceous shales. The west of the country is essentially one large Paleozoic basin, with a southern Mourzouk or Fezzan Basin separated from its northerly extension by the Jebel Fezzan basement uplift.

Put in simple everyday language, this means that there is a natural basin beneath the desert into which the oil filters through porous rock, the oil being the end matter of the forests and grasslands that once characterized what is now the Sirte Desert. The Italians began drilling in 1940 but abandoned their search when war broke out in North Africa. During the immediate postwar years, while the future of Libya was still undecided, Professor Desio's geological researches lay forgotten. According to the United Nations survey of Libya's postindependence potential, the most substantial mineral resources at its command were the salt flats of Cyrenaica. These were thought to be worthy of development since their salt had long been used locally for tanning leather. Apart from salt, Libya's other mineral wealth was believed to be only small quantities of gypsum, limestone, sulfur, chalk, and natron. In 1955, the Libyan Government established a Petroleum Commission that issued concessions for oil exploration across a third of Libya's landmass. Eighty percent of these concessions were granted to American companies with fifteen percent to the British and five percent to the French. When the Royal Institute of International Affairs published its survey in 1957 it was reported that:

The only test well so far drilled was in the northwest corner of Cyrenaica; it was a failure but exploration in the region continues. A marine survey is also being carried out along the coast of Tripolitania. The focus of interest, however, now lies in the Libyan-Algerian frontier area, since the Compagnie de Recherches et d'Exploration des Petroles au Sahara made a promising oil strike in the winter of 1955/56 on the Algerian side of the border. Libya's oil potential is as yet unknown, but even in the absence of worthwhile oil discoveries, the present period of exploration is bringing considerable benefit to the economy through the local expenditure of oil companies. By the end of 1956 their annual rate of expenditure had reached 8 to 10 million British pounds, of which some thirty to forty percent is estimated to have been spent on local labor, accommodation, supplies, and services.

They were all wrong, the professor was right—oil was found beneath the Sirte Desert. The discovery was made at Zelten by Esso-Libya, who announced their find on April 12, 1959. The test well had been sunk only one hundred miles from the coast, which meant that Esso-Libya had few problems constructing a pipeline across the desert to the deep-sea port at Braygah. Production commenced on September 12, 1961, when the first shipment of Zelten Crude was loaded on board the Esso tanker *Canterbury*, bound for Britain. This was, the authors of the British Petroleum handbook observed, "the shortest and most successful search for oil in the history of oil exploration." Even more significantly, Zelten Crude— and all other oil from the Sirte Basin—proved to be of far higher quality than the crude oils of the Persian Gulf. Virtually sulfur-free and with few other impurities, it could be refined at low cost—and there was a market waiting for it just across the Mediterranean in Italy, France, and Spain, which meant the producers could also minimize their transportation costs.

Curiously, both the Zelten field and most of the other major Libyan oil discoveries were made either close to or within the traditional grazing grounds of Gadaffi's tribe, who had lived in the Sirte Desert, just south of the Mediterranean coastal towns of Sirte and Baharia, since arriving there from Andalusia in the fifteenth century. The el Gadadfa were not to know it, but their tents were perched above a rock basin that was approximately 590 million years old, one of the earliest examples of its kind, and possibly the first to naturally fossilize the earliest forms of sea life and natural land vegetation in North Africa, converting it into one of the richest deposits of oil to be found anywhere in the world.

Oilmen flocked to Libya after the Zelten find, with their geologists quick to realize its significance. This became one of the most extraordinary oil rushes of all time, with major producers—among them Mobil, British Petroleum, Chevron, Hunt, Amoseas, Pan American, Occidental, and Aquitaine—all finding oil. By 1969, the Sirte Basin was producing 3,110,000 barrels per day, i.e., an annual output of approximately 1,135 million barrels. Reserves then were estimated at 30 million barrels. Within these ten years, Libya became the world's fourth largest oil producer.

Even though Libyan crude was of higher quality, easier to extract, cheaper to refine, and saleable at low cost to a nearby market, the oil companies offered the Libyan government no better royalties than they paid to any other government—and the government was too inexperienced to realize the strength of its position. To what extent bribery was a part of these transactions one cannot say with certainty, but it was no secret to the oilmen that the government and the royal court were profoundly corrupt; Armand Hammer later admitted securing his concession by paying an extra three cents per barrel to the Minister for Palace Affairs, Omar el Shalhi. The money was paid into a Swiss bank in Geneva, where el Shalhi established a private fortune estimated at over 25 million dollars, a sum that enabled him to set up home there when King Idris was deposed.

Little of this newfound wealth made its way to the Libyan people. Most of them were as poor as ever, still mostly nomadic or seminomadic, scratching a living from the sands, racked by occasional droughts and famines, with forty percent of their babies dying in infancy and only a short life ahead of those who reached maturity. But some now possessed the other innovation of the modern age: radio.

Every night, the Egyptian radio station Voice of the Arabs broadcast its potent message of freedom from tyranny and the defeat of imperialism across the deserts. Sitting in their goatskin tents, even the poorest Bedouin could now hear what was happening in the outside world, of the Arabs' conflict with Israel, of what was seen as the West's interference in Middle East affairs, and of the downfall of other corrupt regimes in the region—

> raise your heads from the imperialist boots, for the age of tyranny is past. Raise the heads that are bowed in Iraq, in Jordan, and on the frontiers of Palestine. Raise your head, my brother in North Africa. The sun of freedom is rising over Egypt and the whole of the Nile Valley will soon be flooded by its rays. Raise your heads to the skies.

It was heady stuff for the impoverished Bedouin, who had endured Italian occupation, the battles of the Second World War, British administration, the maneuverings of a corrupt and incompetent government, and the sight of British and American servicemen enjoying a standard of living conspicuously higher than theirs. One person listened with particular intensity, memorizing Colonel Nasser's speeches by heart, learning a sense of regional geography and history much as some Western teenagers learned of rock 'n' roll by twiddling the knobs on their parents' radio sets to find programs broadcast from down south. The Voice of the Arabs broadcasts began in 1953 with the downfall of King Farouk in Egypt, and then gathered momentum the following year when Colonel Nasser succeeded General Neguib, reaching a peak of virulence against the West at the time of the Suez conflict and then continuing unabated, rabid and breathless, as the Arabs prepared for what they saw as an inevitable war with Israel.

As oil production increased in the Sirte Desert, with five new ports on the coast to accommodate the flow, the tenor of the Voice of the Arabs broadcasts started to change. America, Britain, and France were warned to keep out of any future Middle East conflict—or the Arabs would cut off their oil supplies. If that happened, where would Libya stand under King Idris? Would he support his Arab brothers or provide shelter for the West? Would he cease supplying the West with oil to strengthen the Arab boycott or be the one producer to blunt its effectiveness?

Gadaffi was now working his way up through the army, having been at the forefront of student rebellions, both at school and also at the new university in Benghazi. Modeling themselves on Colonel Nasser's Free Officers, he and a group of similarly radical young students had formed their own cells at school, the university, and inside the military academy at Benghazi, keeping in touch with each other through short-wave radio and coded messages.

More than any other man in Libya, Gadaffi recognized that radio was the key to controlling the country. A radio system could be direct and personal. Across a vast landscape of almost 700,000 square miles, one man could talk to another by radio, orders could be given and received, plans coordinated, plots constructed. British officers were still staffing the Libyan Army, teaching the Libyans the skills of military management, and any young Libyan could go overseas for more intensive courses if thought worthy of training or promotion. When his chance came, Gadaffi volunteered to go to Britain to study with the Royal Corps of Signals. And it was there, visiting London during a period of leave, that he saw something which convinced him that Libya was heading for a revolution.

A Son of the Desert

Gadaffi spent nine months in Britain in 1966 studying radio, electronics, and telecommunications. Even then, age twenty-four or twenty-five, he foresaw a Libyan revolution, although not necessarily with himself as its leader. Since his student days Gadaffi had gathered around himself a group of like-minded friends who shared his view that Libya needed a different form of government based on Islamic beliefs and a particularly Islamic sense of equality, without a hereditary monarchy at its head.

How Gadaffi managed to maneuver himself into the Libyan army has never been explained. When interviewed, he is vague, avoiding questions about his early life, providing few personal details and talking about the revolution in such broad terms that it sounds a much more substantial military event than it actually was. He talks of "the people" and their historic role, making the revolution appear more like a popular uprising than an opportunistic coup by a tiny group of young and inexperienced army officers. One cannot deny his skill in choosing the right moment, when the King was about to abdicate and the government was divided, but how did Gadaffi gather fellow-conspirators around him? Why were they willing to risk their lives in a dangerous challenge to the state's authority that would surely have ended in arrest and execution had they failed?

And what persuaded the army to admit Gadaffi to their ranks in the first place, when he was a known student radical, expelled from Sebha and forced into a form of internal exile in his teens?

It is possible that someone, somewhere, thought a spell of army discipline would cure Gadaffi's rebelliousness, but the more likely explanation is that the Libyan army was so inexperienced that its officers let him sign up without bothering to check his background. In a word, they were lax.

When considering Gadaffi's rise to power, one should remember that Libya was still an impoverished country that had only recently achieved independence. It had never had its own army, government, civil service, or police force, let alone such sophistications as a navy, an air force, or health services. Even the famous deep-sea harbor at Tobruk, which was fought over during the Second World War and subsequently held by Britain as an important submarine base, was little more than a coastal indentation surrounded by sand dunes and a few low-rise buildings that looked insignificant to the untrained eye.

After independence, a British Military Mission stayed behind in Libya to help the King establish his army. This did not include the Cyrenaica Defense Force, the mobile corps largely employing horses and camels, that Idris kept in being for his own personal protection, gradually equipping them with more modern armory, i.e., Land Rovers, armored vehicles, small tanks, trucks, and rifles. In 1957, the British helped the King establish a military academy at Benghazi. This was intended to be Libya's equivalent of West Point or Sandhurst, although the comparison is strained, for both these distinguished American and British military training institutions are nearly two hundred years old and enshrine within their corporate culture a sense of military tradition and discipline passed down through generations. Benghazi had none of this. The academy was formed from scratch, thousands of miles from the nearest similar institution, with nothing to compare itself against. The academy's enrollment figures are not known but, by comparison, the first Libyan university opened nearby in Benghazi just over a year earlier, on December 15, 1955, with a total student intake of thirty-one and eleven teachers. Since it was sharing facilities with the university, the academy probably commenced with even fewer numbers. Gadaffi was in the academy's seventh intake in 1963.

The British Military Mission comprised a total of fifty-four officers and NCOs, deployed at bases throughout Libya, eventually bringing the strength of the Libyan army up to around five thousand men by the time of the revolution. The number of trainee Libyan officers studying at the academy may have reached the low hundreds by the time Gadaffi arrived there, but was quite possibly less. A British officer, Colonel Ted Lough, ran the academy and was aware of growing unrest. "I noticed a wind blowing from the East," he said later. "A lot of cadets were pro-Nasser, anti-Western, and particularly anti-American." Lough has claimed that Gadaffi was the academy's most backward cadet*, insisting that he was one of only two percent that failed their examinations. He has also suggested that Gadaffi was an uncooperative student, who was "probably not as stupid as I thought at the time. Part of his problem was that he wouldn't learn English. I didn't like him and he made life difficult for my officers and men because he went out of his way to be rude to them."**

Lough has also been quoted as saying that Gadaffi was "inherently cruel," relating that he and an unidentified NCO knew of an incident where Gadaffi executed a fellow recruit for homosexual behavior and of other occasions where Gadaffi was responsible for the "mistreatment" of others.

At Sebha, Misurata, and Benghazi, Gadaffi is said to have established "cells" who called themselves the Free Unionist Officers, with two of the words echoing Colonel Nasser's Free Officers, and "Unionist" added to denote their commitment to Arab unity, if need be to the point of dropping national boundaries to form one Arab state or federation of states. This has been one of the great themes of Gadaffi's life, his dream that one day the Arabs would unite under an Islamic form of government, covering the whole of North Africa and the Middle East. At different times, Gadaffi has offered to unite Libya with Egypt, Syria, Iraq, and Tunisia, in various combinations, saying they could all share in Libyan oil. Sometimes he

---

*The Lough quote comes from *Qaddafi and the Libyan Revolution* by David Blundy and Andrew Lycett (1987), a book that I have treated warily, having realized from which newspapers and intelligence sources much of their information came. This is one of the great difficulties in writing about Gadaffi. So much "disinformation" has been planted in the press in order to discredit Gadaffi, and then repeated elsewhere, that an author has to be extra careful.

**In assessing this second quotation, it should be remembered that Gadaffi actually has a good command of English, which he tends to conceal, insisting that an interpreter is on hand to translate his Arabic. If there was an undercurrent of anti-Western feeling (which would be no surprise, for the West was seen as pro-Israel), Gadaffi's "rudeness" was probably his way of expressing opposition to the British officers. It is impossible to establish the truth of the other allegations. The author doubts them.

carries other leaders with him, but these schemes invariably collapse amid much ill-feeling (see Chronology sections).

The nature of Gadaffi's "cells" is also confusing, for they appear to have had no formal structure, owing their origin to his student days at Sebha where a teacher told him of the "cells" organized by Colonel Nasser. Although Gadaffi has occasionally mentioned other revolutionary leaders, there is little evidence that he was ever convinced by Marxism or Trotskyism, or inspired by Fidel Castro or Che Guevara; from the very earliest days, he has stressed that Islam was the Libyan revolution's motivating force, scorning communism (though that has not stopped him buying military hardware from the Eastern bloc). It has been claimed that a separate "cell" was established in each intake year at the military academy, with a separate "cell" in each civilian year at the university, but none of this has been documented, and I suspect that the Free Unionist Officers were substantially less numerous than Gadaffi proclaims. Insofar as they had any underlying theory or ideology, this was almost certainly linked to Gadaffi's perception of Colonel Nasser as the leader of the Arab world. His devotion to Nasser came close to hero worship.

If the Free Unionist Officers had one quality in common, it was a puritanical zeal. They were not joyless, for Gadaffi's personal friends insist he is privately charming, sensitive to the feelings of others, always the first to visit anyone ill in the hospital, impishly humorous and without affectation, but the officers were powerfully motivated, with Gadaffi insisting from the very beginning that they must all make the daily observances required of every Muslim.

No matter where they were or what business they might be engaged upon, the Free Unionist Officers prayed five times a day, first engaging in the ritual *Wudu*, washing all exposed parts of their bodies, and then reciting prayers at sunrise (*el Subr*), at midday (*el Dorr*), midafternoon (*el Asr*), sunset (*el Moghreb*), and finally at bedtime (*el Aschia*), always facing the holy city of Mecca with their hands supplicated, foreheads touching the ground. This was not as onerous as it might sound, for the prayer times are concentrated during daytime hours, and with night falling swiftly and early in North Africa the evenings are free for Muslims to meet socially, dine together, hold political meetings, or enjoy their family life. This is often the most comfortable time of day, with the temperature down and a cool night breeze. The Free Unionist Officers would meet to discuss their religious ideals as well as their political aims, expressing their belief as always in their one God, Allah, and his prophet Mohammad; committing themselves to observe the annual Muslim fast during the month of Ramadan*, to pay one-fortieth of all their income to the poor, and to make a pilgrimage (*haji*) to Mecca at least once during their lives, during the first half of the last month of the Islamic year.

In all these religious practices, the Free Unionist Officers were adhering to the teachings of the Koran, the book of verses (*sura*) in which the prophet Mohammad defined the manner and purpose of prayer and the ideals by which a Muslim should live to achieve the state of peace (*es-salam*) through worship that would bring him closer to God. Gadaffi argued that they should all follow the Prophet, keeping their bodies and minds healthy through regular exercise, never touching alcohol or narcotics, avoiding bad language or gambling, and at all times showing proper respect for women.

During the sixties, Britain posted six thousand soldiers, seamen, and airmen to Libya, mainly to man British bases but also, initially, to help train a Libyan officer elite for the newly formed Libyan army, navy, and air force. Any local Libyan recruits who displayed aptitude or ambition were encouraged to seek further training by going to specialist colleges in Britain or the United States. The Free Unionist Officers, still operating covertly, saw this as an opportunity that could be turned to their own advantage. Gadaffi organized them in such a way that individual cells operated separately from each other and the cells he had formed in Sebha and Misurata (see page 117). When the opportunity arose to acquire specialist skills, the Free Unionist Officers drew lots to decide who should apply to go on particular courses to ensure that each brought different skills to the group. Gadaffi chose (or was chosen) to study

---

*Ramadan is the ninth month of the Muslim year, with all Muslims required to fast daily from dawn to dusk. The fast continues until the next new moon becomes visible. Muslims believe that only God can decide this moment. Modern diaries may say when Ramadan begins and ends, but most Libyans prefer to wait until they are told that the fast is over. Gadaffi himself appears on television to make this announcement, which he says will be followed by a three-day public holiday. When Western workers ask their Arab friends why they do not know the date of the end of Ramadan, they explain that Allah is all-powerful—and until they see the new moon they cannot be sure Allah will not change his mind.

advanced communications in Britain, while Mustafa el Kharrubi
and Suleiman Mahmoud went off to the San Antonio School of
Languages in Texas and the Signals School in New Jersey.

Gadaffi spent four months at the Royal Army Signals Corps at
Beaconsfield, Buckinghamshire, where he found the greenery of
the surrounding countryside startling after his life in the Sirte Desert (it is something he frequently mentions to this day), before
moving on to a more intensive course at the Bovington army camp
in Dorset. During periods of leave, he traveled to London with
friends, window shopping and visiting the locations that appeal to
every tourist—the Tower of London, Buckingham Palace, Big Ben,
and the House of Commons. He was a striking figure, striding out
in long, flowing white robes; one that I remember clearly, for there
were few Bedouin that year in Piccadilly, which was near where I
happened to be working.

These were the swinging sixties. Briefly, London became the
rock 'n' roll capital of the world. The Beatles and the Rolling Stones
were out on the town, homosexuality had been decriminalized, the
gambling laws reformed, and fortunes were being made and more
usually lost on the gambling tables by oil-rich Arabs from the Gulf
states. The newspapers were full of stories about professional gam-
blers flying in from Las Vegas and New Jersey to find a seat at
the tables. One night a friend invited Gadaffi to visit a gambling
casino in Mayfair, not to wager—for this would be a serious sin
for a Muslim—but to see for himself how such places were furnished and managed, and how people behaved playing games like
blackjack and roulette. Gadaffi was horrified—for he recognized a
senior executive from Occidental, a man well known on the streets
of Tripoli, and saw him calmly lose tens of thousands of pounds
on the tables, only to then walk away nonchalantly as though nothing had happened. "That's when we think our leader knew that a
revolution had to come," I was told in Tripoli.

Hitherto, Gadaffi led a life of unusual innocence. He was born
to the sound of tankfire, but by the time he was one year old, war
had ceased in North Africa, and silence returned to the desert. The
soldiers departed, the defeated to prison camps, the victorious to
campaign through Sicily and up through Italy. Life went on as
before in the Bedouin tents.

A man must sire sons, that is the Arab tradition—for it is the
men who go out into the world to defend their land and home and

find food for their family, while the women stay within, barred from any contact with any man outside its walls. Nearing sixty, Gadaffi's father Mohammad Abdel Salam ben Hamed ben Mohammad Gadaffi feared he might never sire a son, so leaving no one to protect his wife in her old age and guard the honor of his three daughters. And then, to great rejoicing, was born the son for whom the old man longed—the boy given the name Muammar, literally "he who builds up," a name chosen in honor of one of the sacred men of Islam, Sidi Muammar.

From his earliest childhood, Muammar—or as I have called him throughout, Gadaffi—grew up surrounded by women, for a Bedouin encampment is something more than just a tent.

When the Libyan Bedouin first became exposed to the modern world during the Italian occupation, Italian writers tended to portray them as a primitive, degenerate people, dressed in rags; a race that had failed to progress and was now refusing to submit to Catholicism and the omnipotence of the government in Rome. This image may have been tempered a little by English writers like Thesiger, Lawrence, and St. John Philby, describing the Arab tribes of Iraq and Saudi Arabia, but there still remains an ignorance of Bedouin tribal customs and traditions.

The Gadadfas were one of five tribes occupying the Sirte Desert, dividing the grazing land among them, always using the same wells. Sirte is not the kind of desert one usually sees in films like *Lawrence of Arabia* or the glossy picturebooks produced by Time-Life; it is a vast, arid, open steppe littered with rocks and stones, in some places riven by rocky escarpments overlooking the wadis, the ancient riverbeds rich in fertile soil that may flood during the rainy season and at other times provide good grazing. These wadis cut across the Sirte Basin toward the coast.

"The steppe characterizes most of this countryside," wrote Mohammad Murabet in *Tripolitania: The Land and Its People* (1951).

It is made up of short grass, now gray, now green, or even black when seen from a distance, with scanty leafage; inured against the climate, it hastily completes its cycle during the most favorable part of the year, usually from January to April. This grass grows thickest near the coast, on high ground where there are depressions and where the soil is muddy; it grows sparsely on slopes, where the sand is not firm, or where the soil is too compact or stony.

The steppe, even though generally uniform, offers some variety, with grass whose growth is less stunted and which lives all the year round, and with low shrubs. These are steppes of maritime origin, once under the sea, in which grow tufts of large leaves that spring from the gigantic sea onion, the whitish ears of innumerable asphodels that flower between February and March, the green shrubs of the artemisia, including sagebrush and wormwood. Other steppes have low, thorny shrubs of the Caycotome family (*gandul*) with their brilliant yellow flowers, or are perfumed with the aroma of anise (*guzzah*). Steppes which show indications of ancient crops of cereals are filled with anthemis, chrysanthemum, marigold, garden-rocket, mignonette, poppies; on the higher tips of the Jebel there are ranunculus with large yellow flowers and squills; in the cultivated areas, tulips, gladioli ... among the sandy dunes, glistening white in the sun, are the large bushes of desert broom, with its white and yellow flowers, the tall green bushes of the Calligonum (*harta*) and the thorny bushes of Aristida pungens (*sbot, drin*), whose seeds during famines vie with barley in giving nourishment to the Nomads. The last of these is a plant which camel-drivers gather on their journeys, and is a favorite food of camels. All this plant life indicates a surprisingly humid soil in spite of the aridity of the surface and the lack of rain....

This, then, was the landscape of Gadaffi's childhood. Previous chapters have told how the Romans turned this land through irrigation into "the granary of Rome"; how their towns and cities sank into the sands; how other conquering armies came and went, never knowing what riches lay beneath its surface. This was never a barren landscape, but one steeped in memories, rich with colors and natural perfumes; a landscape that might suddenly burst into flower after showers of rain, providing unexpected food for the Bedouin and fodder for their animals. By being born in a tent in the desert, Gadaffi was not a deprived or impoverished child, but one born to a people who had learned to adapt to the landscape they knew, traveling south when the climate became too dry to live near oases and to harvest the dates that formed a vital part of their diet.

A small tribe might consist of four or five tents, or maybe a dozen, which could be quickly dismantled, folded, laden on camels, and taken on to the next pasture. Each tent would be home for part of the family unit, an aunt and uncle or cousins, perhaps with their own children. When migrating, they would all travel together, women and babies and the frail perhaps traveling by camel, the fit and able walking alongside.

Even the tents were different from our usual images; quite unlike the tepees of the North American Indians, for these are wide, low-lying tents, made of goatskins stretched tight by tentpoles, sometimes with a double membrane of carpet or skins to provide extra warmth in the cold nights or winter. In summer, the side flaps could be lifted to provide a cross-current of air, keeping them cool in the heat of the day. They were often attractive within, brightly decorated in primary colors, with floor carpets and hanging carpets separating the tents into different compartments—comparable with a kitchen, or a living room or separate bedrooms, with not a trace of sand or dust for the carpets, mattresses, and bedding rolls would warmly enclose the occupants, sitting around a fire of heated stones. Each tribe would make its own carpets, gathering the wool from their Barbary sheep and weaving their own intricate, often traditional designs. As a tribe had to travel light, there would be few other furnishings than the cooking pots, kettles, and large open dishes from which the family would eat communally, sitting cross-legged and taking their food with their right hand, as ordained by the Koran. These were a simple, honest, faithful people whose belief in Allah gave them certainty.

The Italian writer Mirella Bianco, who visited the Gadadfas' encampment while Gadaffi's parents were still alive, described other aspects of their life in *Gadaffi: Voice from the Desert* (1974), quoting his schoolfriend Mufta Ali,

> If one wants to understand Gadaffi one must always keep in mind the essential: he is a son of the desert. It was in the desert that he learned his first lesson, much more than at any school. It was the desert which taught him patience, endurance, generosity, and faith in God; and it is in the desert that he learned self-sufficiency, facing up to such difficulties as its storms, its immense distances, and the privations it inflicts. . . .

Subsequent studies of Gadaffi's career draw heavily on Mirella Bianco's book, for she met Gadaffi, his family, and some of his closest friends at a time when the Libyans were far more open, before Gadaffi became involved in what the West calls "terrorism"—or the West began trying to topple his regime, either through attempted assassination, or by training and funding Libyan "exiles" in the hope that they might mount a counterrevolution. This reliance upon one source, like the dependence of many Western journalists upon the CIA for their background material, has its drawbacks. Bianco is often sketchy, for the people she interviewed were clearly reluctant to say anything that might upset their leader, who dislikes discussing his private life. When writers find themselves caught like this, generalities may harden up too firmly and errors occur. Thus Bianco, or possibly her translator, describes Gadaffi's early days as if he were taught in a Western school, using words and phrases familiar to any local government education officers watching their charges progress from nursery to primary and then on to secondary school, gaining all the necessary certificates and school reports en route. This was not his situation at all.

As a child of the Bedouin tents, Gadaffi's earliest days were spent guarding the family's goats and sheep, drawing buckets of water at their wells, shooing away jackals, but his parents could see that he possessed an inner seriousness, seldom playing children's games with his cousins, lost within his own thoughts, listening to the legends told around the fire at night while a kettle simmered on a fire of twigs, camel dung, and heated stones, waiting for yet another cup of green tea. They always thought he seemed older than his years.

"I did not want him to continue in our sort of life," his father told Mirella Bianco, when the old man was eighty-seven years old, nearing the end of an exceptionally long life for a Bedouin, and proud of his son's accomplishments.

> You see, there were six of us and none of us knew our letters. He had to study, the only son. . . . So, on one of my trips to the Fezzan, where I would often go to sell or buy animals, I brought a teacher back with me, to teach him the Koran. How old was he then? Seven, eight maybe. And how quickly he learned. He would follow his teacher like a shadow. His cousins also took lessons, sometimes in the shade of the tent, but whenever they could they played truant. . . .

The teacher, what we might call a private tutor, was almost certainly one of the Sanusi brethren, or Sausiya, for the Gadadfa—or the al Qadhadfa, as some historians spell the name—were committed followers; the very people whom the Sanusi sought to teach, traveling across the desert, strengthening the appeal of Islam and bringing the Bedouin closer to their God. "Muammar learned fast," said his father. "He was a very pious little boy. He never forgot his prayers. As for me, I began to think he would have to go to school ... when he was nine, or maybe ten years old, I sent him to the Sirte school. It was indeed a sacrifice ... we were so poor."

Once again, the aging father, old enough to be a grandfather or even a generation beyond, guided Gadaffi's hand, taking him thirty miles across the desert to Sirte, then a small but ancient town standing on a low-lying hillside, overlooking the Mediterranean. This was one of the Sanusi's furthest outposts, a *zawiya* serving their followers in the Sirte Desert; farther west from here the tribes had been more resistant to their teaching.

Every week for about five years, Gadaffi walked alone across the desert to attend this school, reciting verses from the Koran as he walked, sometimes, no doubt, traveling by camel or donkey when a neighboring tribesman offered to help him on his way; mostly alone, but never lonely, for the desert is only desolate to those who do not know it. To those who do, there is always something to see; partridge rising, hares running, a Bedouin shepherd guarding his flock; the wind from the east may be turning south, a sign that a sandstorm may be on its way.

Gadaffi always walked back home on Thursdays to be with his family for Friday prayers, Friday having a similar place in the Islamic week to Sunday for Christians. On Saturday morning he would walk back to the *zawiya*. Mufta Ali told Mirella Bianco:

There were three or four of us Bedouin at the school, and we were held in utter contempt. We were so poor that we often had nothing to eat at break ... we felt ourselves to be outsiders in some way, and I believe that had it not been for Gadaffi we would have been ashamed of our origin. But he was proud of it. "We are equal to anyone else," he would say. "And we can learn as well as anyone," ... and he made up for the disadvantage of having come to school comparatively late because of his poverty.

Though still a child, he seemed to possess some extraordinary gift, a sort of innate authority, which made him a natural leader. All the pupils took their problems to Muammar, and often he helped them with their work, especially with mathematics, which he was tremendously keen on. Moreover, despite his evident poverty he had a bearing which made him look almost elegant. He was always tidy, always clean, and later when I would perhaps meet him even right out in the desert, he was always well-groomed. In his own tent, he looks like a prince.

At the age of fourteen, Gadaffi moved to a school for older pupils in Sebha, down in the Fezzan to the south of Sirte. Some authors claim that his father took the whole family there to take up a job as a caretaker in a block of flats, but this seems unlikely, for there were no blocks of flats in Sebha and Gadaffi's family continued to live in their tent in the Sirte Desert long after the revolution.

Sehba is now one of Libya's larger towns, but then, in the mid-fifties, it was another important area to the Sanusi, a fortified desert town that had grown around an oasis with a thriving market since the days of the slave trade. Now it is a regional center of government with its own airport, military airfield, and army barracks, but it remains remote, situated in the most arid region of Libya, the Fezzan, roughly a thousand kilometers from the coast, surrounded by hundreds of square miles of desert, broken only by occasional oases and clusters of date palms*. There was an ancient connection between the Gadadfas and Sebha, for the tribes of Sirte migrate south each year in time to harvest the date crop, upon which the Bedouin depend in times of hardship.

When Gadaffi arrived at Sebha, his character was already clearly defined. He was the eldest in his class, religious, soft-spoken yet assured, with an unusual capacity for companionship. The friends he made here became friends for life, forming the nucleus of the Free Unionist Officers and then later—after the overthrow of the monarchy—of the Revolutionary Command Council, which took control of the country. One particular friend, Abdul Salam Jalloud, has remained at his side since Sebha, the second most powerful man in Libya, and often the person to handle the detailed implementation of a policy or program after Gadaffi has defined its broad objectives; it is a relationship that has lasted nearly forty years.

---

*These are approximately 140 different varieties of date, with each palm tree producing a crop each year of between eighty and one hundred pounds or more. Gadaffi likes to eat them freshly picked, when they are most delicious with a sweet-tasting flesh. When he holds formal meetings, a bowl of fresh dates will often be placed on his desk. Traditionally, the Bedouin also made a drink, *legby*, by extracting juice from the new growth at the top of the palm tree.

"Gadaffi was above all an exceptionally gifted and conscientious pupil," according to Abdel Wafi el Ghadi, one of Gadaffi's teachers who later became the school's headmaster.

He was a solitary at heart. He had few friends. Jalloud was one. The two of them were inseparable. He liked to keep to the society of his friends to thrash out his ideas with them; he could expand only with those in whom he had confidence. Gadaffi was very mature for his age. All his teachers noticed him, of course, for it was impossible not to notice him. He was so different from the other pupils, but even when he began his activities as an agitator, organizing political demonstrations, with or without authorization by the school, I don't think any of us really took him seriously. I wonder whether any of his best friends, for all that they followed him so blindly, really believed that one day he would overthrow the regime.... We thought of him as a dreamer, a hothead; in any case, we did not imagine that his dreams could come true.

That was 1956, the year of Suez, and the young teenage militants had much to be angry about. Down in the Fezzan neither the Italians nor the British administration had ever counted for much, clinging as they did to the Mediterranean shoreline while the Fezzan oases were closer to southern Algeria, coming directly under the influence of the French Foreign Legion. That undoubtedly had its effect upon Gadaffi, for he developed a particular interest in the French Revolution, which he often cites in speeches, although he also saw France as a colonial power, suppressing the independence movement in Algeria and retaining far too great a presence in the Congo.

When some new cause took their fancy, Gadaffi and Jalloud would lead their fellow students through the streets of Sebha to protest outside the French Consulate, but their main inspiration was what to them was Nasser's heroic stand against Western imperialism. Here, too, the Voice of the Arabs was listened to nightly, with the students brandishing portraits of Nasser and distributing banned Egyptian pamphlets as they called for the elimination of Israel, and the overthrow of "Western puppet regimes" in Iraq, Jordan, and in the end, inevitably, their own country, Libya.

"We turned a blind eye ... and even sometimes advised them to keep the things hidden," said Abdel Wafi el Ghadi, but he was forever influencing the others, haranguing them from the top of the garden wall. When they went out into the streets ... his friends carried a little stool with them so that Gadaffi could stand upon it and deliver his speech. They demonstrated over Lumumba's death, over the explosion of the French atomic bomb in the Sahara, over the Algerian revolution; any occasion would do. At the time when the union between Syria and Egypt broke down, the authorities began to think they had had enough, for, on that occasion, not only were demonstrations expressly forbidden, but Gadaffi really went too far. . . . Since his early adolescence his personality appeared to be so uncommon that, although none of us had realized the extent of his underground activities, we found it natural, eventually, that he should achieve his aims ... his main qualities [are] intelligence—quite out of the ordinary, there is no doubt about that—and courage; then a sobriety which borders on asceticism, and a very deep, a very real, religious feeling.

Another teacher, an Egyptian, Mahmoud Efay, told David Blundy and Andrew Lycett that he recalled Gadaffi approaching him after a lesson with a note asking three questions, "What is a pyramid organization and which is the best manner to organize such a structure? Does the possibility of organizing a revolution in Libya exist? If a revolution were to be carried out in Libya would Egypt come to the assistance of the Libyan people?" Efay says he assured the young student that all revolutions needed to have the support of the military, and it was always difficult for those who were leading a revolution to keep their followers in line, no matter what the formal structure of command.

Gadaffi's classmates saw another side of this commitment—organizing ability, dedication, a willingness to work exceptionally long hours. One of his Free Unionist Officers, Captain Rifi Ali Sherif, who later became the first Secretary General to the Revolutionary Command Council, moved to Sebha in 1960 and joined the same class as Gadaffi and Jalloud:

Gadaffi organized quite a number of student demonstrations within the school. I still remember the first one I took part in. It was on the death of Lumumba. It was Gadaffi who made the decisions and organized everything. At night, while the others slept he would prepare the text of his speeches, write his pamphlets, and cut out his banners and placards. . . . Two or three days after the demonstration he organized another demonstration inside the school, in the courtyard. Perched up on the wall, he was haranguing us all. The police turned out in force to listen to him and they were properly dumbfounded. . . . We had blind faith in Gadaffi. He was different from everyone else. For all his poverty there was a certain air about him, setting him apart from the others. One just could not ignore him.

Another of his intimate friends, Sherif Hussein, who was lucky enough to own a little radio, enabled us to listen regularly to the Voice of the Arabs, and of course there were books and other publications which Muammar gave out to us all. Goodness knows how, he had got hold of a copy of Nasser's *Philosophy of the Revolution*. He treasured it, made all of us read it in turn . . . and we knew it by heart. He got on well with one of our teachers, Mustafa Mohammad el Malek, who was on good terms with an official in Information, and Gadaffi managed through him to get newspapers and news from Cairo, and he passed everything on to us. So we became followers both of his ideas and of the man himself. None of us ever doubted that sooner or later he would achieve his aims.

Inevitably, Gadaffi's political protests brought him into conflict with the regional authorities in Sebha. In September 1961, Gadaffi organized two anti-French demonstrations—against their alleged complicity in the murder of Congo Prime Minister Patrice Lumumba (which was probably the demonstration referred to earlier in this chapter), and in protest against the testing of a French nuclear bomb in the Sahara, where it was feared that the radioactive fallout would damage the wandering Berber, Bedouin, and Tuareg tribesmen. Each demonstration was becoming a little more noisy than the last, and on October 5, Gadaffi organized his most impressive yet—despite an order from the regional authority specifically banning it.

This time, Gadaffi's protests were directed dangerously close to home. He led a procession through the streets of Sebha. By the time the demonstrators reached the town square, the crowd had grown to over four thousand, nearly half the town's population. As usual, his followers brought a stool for him to stand on, and Gadaffi then harangued them all with a fiery speech abusing Syria for failing to work more closely with Egypt, and then attacking the

Western imperialists—Britain and the United States—for position-
ing forces on Libyan soil and colluding with King Idris. There is
no record of exactly what Gadaffi said, but he clearly went too far.
Pro-Egyptian banners were waved in the crowd. Photographs of
Nasser were handed around together with inflammatory leaflets,
and Gadaffi wound up his speech by urging the members of the
crowd to dip into their pockets to pay for a telegram of support to
the Egyptian leader. The police moved in to break up the demonstration. Fighting began, windows were broken, and twenty students were arrested.

Still only nineteen years old, Gadaffi had become too prominent
for his own good. The police went around his school, interviewing
his classmates, persuading them to sign statements, before arranging for Gadaffi to be formally arraigned before the Wali (governor)
of the Fezzan, Sayf al Nasr, the most powerful man in the region
with direct access to the King. This was a crucial moment in Gadaffi's early career. Looking back, one can see that Gadaffi could
have been stopped in his tracks, had the Wali dealt with him severely. As it was, Sayf al Nasr reprimanded Gadaffi, ordered that he
be expelled from Sebha and forbidden to attend any other school in
the Fezzan.

The incident is described cursorily in Western accounts of Gadaffi's rise to power, probably through lack of information from
inside Libya, but a more revealing commentary appears in *Libya
Past and Present* (1979), written by Dr. Henry Habib and published
by Aedam, a publishing house with offices in Tripoli and Malta
that has published various works concerning Gadaffi's politics,
mainly for distribution in the Arab world. Dr. Habib, who graduated
from the American University in Beirut and then studied in the
United States at Princeton and Fordham, became a professor in
political science after completing his Ph.D. at McGill University in
Montreal. Dr. Habib is generally sympathetic to the Libyans and
was given access to an unpublished account of the episode that
Gadaffi had written himself, and so was able to add the extra detail
that shows how perilously close Gadaffi came to exposure. Habib
turns Gadaffi's memoir into a third-person narrative, but its authen-
ticity is clear:

> Colonel Gadaffi ... recounts how he saved the Assistant Police
> Director of the Fezzan, who was practically trampled upon by the
> demonstrators; how he and others moved into one of the main

squares, and cabled Gamal Abdel Nasser denouncing Syria's sep-
aration and calling for Arab unity.

On October 29, 1961, in the early hours of the morning, he
was brought face to face with the Wali of Fezzan, the powerful
Sayf al Nasr. He was questioned by him about the demonstration
of October 5, and the demonstration planned for the Algerian
independence. Gadaffi was harassed by Sayf al Nasr, who questioned him in the most authoritarian way.

Part of Nasr's questioning was "Are you a commander of an
army?" "Are you the leader of a People?" "What is this defiance
of authority and threat to the regime that you think you are
making?" "You were all our slaves under our feet . . . you are the
only one asking questions . . . what do you know about freedom?
Arab unity?" Gadaffi remarked that Sayf al Nasr considered himself above the law and spoke to his people in the manner one
speaks to a dog . . .

Expelled from Sebha with his schooling incomplete, although he
was now two or three years older than his class group, Gadaffi
moved to Misurata, a town on the coast midway between Sirte and
Tripoli. According to Dr. Habib, his clash with the authorities in
Sebha

> made him more careful of his political activities. He stayed up
> late at night devouring all the books he could read. He had
> become more and more conscious of the political realities of
> Libya and the Arab nations. He stated that these books became
> an important part of his intellectual revolutionary formation, just
> as much as the poverty and backwardness of the Fezzan had
> formed his revolutionary conscience. . . .

At Misurata, Gadaffi was able to return to school studies in readiness for both university education and a military career. The university at Benghazi was opened in 1955, and in its first year had only
thirty-one students and by the time Gadaffi commenced an arts
and humanities course in 1963, also studying history, the numbers
of students enrolled had possibly reached around as high as fifteen
hundred, for it was up to 3,635 by 1969–70 and 5,221 by 1971–72.
He combined his university studies with attendance at the military
academy, which was housed nearby, and in each year at both insti-

tutions formed fresh cells of the Free Unionist Officers, one being civilian-oriented and the other military.

Another of his colleagues there was Omar el Meheishi, who took part in the revolution and became a member of the Revolutionary Command Council*. "We were all of us influenced to some extent by Ba'athist theories and those of George Habash," says el-Meheishi.

We were extremely keen in our support of the Cuban Revolution. That was before Castro turned to Marxism**. Our movement aimed at being exclusively Libyan and free from any other ties whatever. It was precisely because we wanted to attain our goal by our own methods alone that we decided to become soldiers ... when we entered the army and began recruiting our fighting force from among the officers, we had to change our methods completely. Ideology was not going to help us, for the officers were not ready intellectually to follow us in that field. So it was

---

*El Meheishi is a doubtful witness. Gadaffi never wholly trusted him, and soon after the revolution el Meheishi turned against him, leading the attempted coup in August 1975. When this failed, he fled the country and was given asylum in Egypt with other anti-Gadaffi plotters. Gadaffi's agents made many attempts to assassinate him and he, in turn, became a focus-point of the Libyans in exile.

**His references to Castro, Ba'athism, and Dr. Habash need to be set in a wider context. Castro converted to Marxism in 1961 whereas Gadaffi did not start studying at Benghazi until 1963. The Ba'athist theory that attracted them was the call for Arab unity under one Islamic government, but Ba'athism was mainly concentrated in Iraq and Syria. It failed to establish a broad following in Libya. A United Arab Republic was proclaimed by Egypt and Syria in 1958 and joined later that year by North Yemen. The union collapsed in 1961 when Syria withdrew, although Egypt continued to say it was part of the UAR until 1971. Other attempts to form a united Arab republic are detailed in the Chronology sections.

The reference to George Habash is also confusing. Dr. Habash formed the Arab Nationalist Movement in Beirut in the late 1950s, and then later the Popular Front for the Liberation of Palestine (PFLP). He advocated Marxism, and turned to terrorism in September 1970 with the hijackings at Dawson's Field in Jordan (see Chronology). There is a widely held belief, which the author shares, that nearly all, if not all, the terrorist acts attributed to Libya were, in fact, committed either by Habash's followers, or those of Abu Nidal, who led the other Palestinian group the Fatah Revolutionary Council (FRC). Gadaffi supported their political objective and provided them with funds, but there is no direct evidence linking him to any one specific terrorist act.

on nationalism that we had to depend, a sentiment deeply felt in the army, and on personal relations, on friendships.

Mohammad Khalil, who had known Gadaffi from childhood—at the schools in Sirte and Sebha and then at Misurata—was given the task of recruiting others to the group:

Reviewing the factors upon which we could count for ensuring the success of our Revolution, [Gadaffi] indicated that the army's support was essential, but that the army itself was, as yet, inaccessible to us. A military career was the preserve of certain families, and its officers, completely apolitical, thought of nothing but *la dolce vita* even when they were sent abroad for training, especially if they went to the U.S.A., where they would only too often engage in a whirlwind of amusements, if not dissipation.

As for the political organizations already in existence at that time, such as the Ba'ath and George Habash's group, Gadaffi said that he had seriously considered the expedience of making contact with them. But he had finally abandoned the idea, he added, convinced that such people spent most of their time in arguing, and that such a move would only waste our time, too.

We decided therefore to rely upon our own forces. We would start by enlarging the organization already set up at Sebha, recruiting new members among young people who believed in Arab unity, in the principle of liberty, and above all in the absolute necessity of radical change within the country. My own role was to take over the task in Misurata. The criteria for selection were: no weight should be given to social origins; the utmost caution should be used in approaching people older than ourselves; total independence should be maintained of any group or any support coming from outside. Thus, little by little, I succeeded in enlisting in our organization such people as traders, teachers, workers, and civil servants. . . . After graduating in 1963, we organized the first general meeting of the movement's leadership in which people from Sebha, Tripoli, and Misurata participated. During this meeting it was decided that three of us—Gadaffi was one, naturally—should enter the military academy so as to form a nucleus of free officers . . . who would undertake to win the army's support, without which nothing could be achieved.

By his early twenties, if we are to believe Gadaffi's own unpublished account acquired by Dr. Habib and those of his fellow conspirators given to Mirella Bianco with the help of official translators, Gadaffi was a totally committed revolutionary who had already spent seven years of his life studying politics, history, and religion, gathering around himself the nucleus of supporters who were to one day accompany him in his assault upon the Libyan monarchy. There seems little doubt that Gadaffi was naturally charismatic, possessing abilities as a speaker, organizer, and decision maker that set him apart from the others; qualities of leadership—and yet he also appears to have been modest, unassuming, and totally devoted in his perception of God.

He could have gone abroad on a scholarship for which he had qualified, but wanted to stay in Libya and continue the secret organization," wrote Dr. Habib.

In 1963 he joined the military college.... In 1964 he and his colleagues decided to reorganize the whole revolutionary movement. It was divided into a military section and a civilian section. The military section became the most important, and it was around this nucleus that the leaders of the revolution made their plans.

The army section established a Central Committee which was to direct all revolutionary activities.... The Central Committee met regularly for long and tiresome meetings, organized mainly on holidays and feast days, and usually outside the main cities and towns. Security was essential in setting up the meetings. Holidays were selected so that members of the Central Committee would not be noticed by their absence. The members had to travel hundreds of miles in the heat and in the cold, and always at their own expense, a financial burden for most of them who had to support their families on low salaries. They had to buy cars and endure many sacrifices, and for long periods they did not see their own families. In addition, rigorous demands were placed on members of the Central Committee. They were not to play cards, drink alcoholic beverages, or frequent nightclubs, they were never to abandon their prayers or their studies. Some of these rigorous demands also applied to other Free Officers but not to the same degree as to members of the Central Committee. They were also required to attend university courses in their free time. Colonel Gadaffi registered in the Faculty of Arts at Benghazi. Each officer was to specialize in a particular subject. No meeting of the Central Committee could be held if one member were missing. It was a difficult task, for all the members were under strict military supervision. In 1967, a severe penalty was imposed on a member of the Central Committee for having failed to attend a meeting.

Colonel Gadaffi, in his account *The Story of the Revolution,* says with genuine pride that the Free Officers in the Central Committee, and outside, made many financial contributions for the purchase of the cars to be used for the good of the revolutionary movement. At a meeting in Sidi Khalifa, it was agreed that the salaries of all Free Officers, including the members of the Central Committee, were to be placed at the disposal of the Central Committee without limitations or restrictions. In fact, salaries were used for air travel and assistance to families. . . .

The Free Officers were most concerned with Arab unity. Great hopes were raised when the new tripartite union between Egypt, Syria, and Iraq became a possibility. The Free Officers were soon disappointed when party differences destroyed the proposed union, even before it was born. The Free Officers were greatly influenced by Gamal Abdel Nasser, whom they considered as the elder brother of all Arab revolutionaries. They believed in the oneness of the objectives of the Arab revolution, and were opposed to its multiplication of views, such as the Algerian Independence Movement, the Ba'ath, the Arab Socialist Union, and the populism of the People's Republic of South Yemen. . . . Different political systems were discussed in special study groups; the Egyptian experiment, other socialist experiments, the French Revolution, Nazi Germany, Petroleum, the Cuban Revolt, and many other related topics.

There were no organizational links with civilians, largely for reasons of secrecy and security. However, contact with civilians was regular. Professors were consulted without, however, revealing the ultimate objectives of the Free Officers. The Free Officers were never separated from the people, for, as Colonel Gadaffi says, "We lived the people's feelings, problems, and aspirations; they were our parents, and we emerged from the desert and deepest depth of our people. . . ."

Although he insisted then, and even after the revolution, that he was part of a collective leadership, Gadaffi was already *primus inter pares,* emerging as a leader at Sebha and then establishing a natural authority within the university and the military academy between 1963–66. One of the few occasions that Gadaffi has discussed his personal role was in an interview with Egyptian television just six weeks after the revolution, recalling that one of their earliest meetings had been held on the beach at Talmisa in 1964.

"As these meetings became more and more frequent, we were faced with many difficulties," said Gadaffi.

We had to meet during vacations, and often late at night. We also had to seek out places far from the town, and sometimes had to travel hundreds of miles, and put up with long sessions in atrocious weather. We would often sleep out in the open, sheltered only by a tree or a rock. . . . So as not to draw attention to ourselves we would take care to be seen in this place or in that during the holiday periods, and while on the one hand the Committee exacted obedience from its members on such matters as abstention from cards, drink, and other pleasures, and also imposed certain obligations of prayer and self-education, of studying as hard as possible (many of us were taking courses at Benghazi University), we were careful on the other hand to let some of our members appear as card players, again in order to avoid attracting the attention of the authorities.

As for the meetings themselves, our rules were extremely strict: all committee members were obliged to be present, and the absence of only one of us meant that a meeting was invalid. Of all our rules, this one in particular was the most tiresome, for obviously we also had to comply with military obligations.

Another key member of the Central Committee was Suleiman Mahmoud, who went off to Texas for training while Gadaffi was in Britain. Mahmoud also insists that Gadaffi stood out from his peers by

his enthusiasm, his integrity and his piety . . . and there was much discussion about what was called his "hobby horse," the purity of the Arab language. You must understand that at that time—and this is still the case in the Arab world—there was a habit of interpolating French and English words in Arabic sentences. This infuriated Gadaffi, who never missed an opportunity of rebuking us on the matter. "The Arabic language is so rich," he would exclaim, "why should we ape the others? Why bastardize ourselves?" Really, you know, we were surprised at the strength of his feeling. All the same, little by little, we, too, began to think on similar lines, and we began to give more and more consideration to the subjects which Gadaffi kept raising: the future of the

Arabs, the work and deeds of Gamal Abdel Nasser, the necessity of ridding our country of the British presence, just as Nasser had freed Egypt and the Canal.

Gadaffi cited Nasser's example as the only hope of acquiring our own true independence.... Looking back now, I can see how necessary this preparation was, for, by imposing upon us this period of reflection and meditation, he guided our minds and led us quite naturally to the next phase, when he would enlist our services for the Revolution itself.... He painted a picture of Nasser as the supreme hope whom we should all rally around. We spent hours talking about him, analyzing his every action, his every decision, and since it was always Gadaffi who took the initiative in organizing our discussions, gradually his own name became known, and began to be on everyone's lips. He himself became an object of admiration and respect among the officers.

The Sublieutenant's Coup

By the time Gadaffi returned home from Britain, the fate of the King was sealed. Events could have turned out otherwise. Oil was now flowing in abundance through the desert pipelines. Plenty of work was available for those with skills. Forty-one oil companies were now drilling for new fields. And they were all bringing money into the country.

At last the Libyan government had the resources to ameliorate the poverty of the Bedouin and the seminomadic peasantry; but there was not the slightest indication that the government wished to do anything of the sort.

Instead of putting their oil money into farm machinery and irrigation to raise the quality of their own harvests, the government began neglecting the land, preferring to spend the money instead on imported food and other goods brought in from overseas. The number of people working in agriculture fell from sixty-three percent in 1960 to thirty-seven percent in 1967. Prices soared and the value of foreign imports rose from 31 million in 1953 to 645 million in 1968.

The King's supporters became rich quickly, their bribes from the oilmen paid into secret numbered bank accounts in Switzerland, where some bought houses and apartments while others acquired homes in Italy, France, and Spain in readiness for the moment when the Sanusi monarchy fell. There was little doubt that it would. Having banned all political parties early in his reign, and surrounded himself with a venal bourgeoisie, the King lost all contact with his people. He was also now a very old man, approaching eighty years of age, with no natural heirs, and little understanding of the yearnings of the younger Arabs. All his attempts to establish good relations with the Russians, the other Arab states, and the West had failed, for they all realized that he lacked commitment to any of them. There was no one to whom he would be able to turn in extremis.

American Presidents John F. Kennedy and Lyndon Johnson were both warned by the CIA that the situation in Libya was fundamentally unstable, and worsening. The gap between the poor and the rich was unusually wide, with abject poverty in the slums of Tripoli, without light or drinkable water, overcrowding, and a high incidence of infectious diseases—when they could see the oilmen and British and American servicemen based in Libya carousing around the bars and nightclubs. All those with access to Libya's new wealth—relatives of the King, government ministers, senior advisers—went abroad for medical treatment, or to avoid the worst of the Libyan summer, when the air turns intensely hot and humid in July and August. They built themselves vacation homes abroad, and mini-palaces at home, furnished with every imported modern convenience, driving across the vast open deserts on the roads the Italians built in huge Mercedes, Daimlers, and Rolls-Royces, having acquired a taste for what Gadaffi always describes as *la dolce vita*. This was an apt description, for wealthy young Libyans would fly across to Rome, Cairo, Malta, or Tunis, which were little more than an hour away by plane, for a weekend's shopping, drinking, gambling, and sex. The King himself was a modest man, simple in his tastes, but he failed to curb the behavior of those around him and, in the words of Dr. Habib,

> created no workable political system, nor anything like a political ideology. He did not even attempt to create a party system through which he could rule the country. In the words of Colonel Gadaffi, "the Revolution occurred because of national, popular, and human considerations." In his own unpublished account, Gadaffi suggests that "poverty, injustice, persecution of the people, and the lack of proper housing were instrumental in bringing about the Revolution: and "deplored the illiteracy of more than 90 percent of the population; lack of medical facilities, and the helplessness of more than 35,000 victims of tuberculosis," adding that "these people saw no doctor, no government officials, and

no responsible person. The money of the people was spent on royal palaces, medical treatment for the ruling classes outside Libya, while the Libyan people could not be treated abroad or elsewhere.... The people lacked hospitals, schools, highways, electricity, water, and arms to defend themselves.

There were many warnings that the Sanusi monarchy was coming to an end. A wise king would have heeded them.

In 1953, there were widespread demonstrations against the decision to allow the British and American military to continue occupying their bases.

In 1956, students took to the streets protesting against Libya's acquiescence in the Anglo-French invasion of Egyptian territory bordering the Suez Canal, and their complicity with Israel.

Between 1957 and 1964, Gadaffi himself was involved in some of the protests that took place constantly in different parts of Libya, protesting against Western "imperialism," demanding that the U.S. and Britain withdraw their troops, supporting independence for Algeria and Chad, opposing armaments deals with Britain, attacking Britain for its support for the deposed monarchy in Iran, abusing the West for its liaisons with the Shah of Iran, and attacking Syria for its failure to forge a comprehensive alliance with Egypt.

In January 1964 there were repeated demonstrations against the government, again demanding that Britain and the U.S. withdraw from their bases; this time, the government sent in troops to quell the rioting, and as many as twenty students may have been killed. Many more were arrested and held without trial.

After these years of public protest, Prime Minister Mahmud al Muntasir announced in August 1964 that the Western powers had agreed to leave the bases when their leases expired, only to find himself in opposition to the King, who was relying upon the British to rescue him if his regime collapsed.

That October, there were, as we have already seen, more riots when forces loyal to the King arrested antigovernment candidates during the preelection period; the following May (1965), another general election was held—to the accompaniment of widespread rioting and the bombing of five oil fields.

In June 1967, rioters took to the streets of Tripoli after rumors that the United States was deeply involved in the impending conflict between Israel and the combined forces of Egypt, Syria, and Jordan. These demonstrations continued for many days. To this day, the degree of U.S. backing for Israel remains uncertain—but that same month, on June 8, 1967, two Libyan army divisions crossed the border into Egypt, defying their own commanders, convinced that they were going to be part of an Arab army engaged in a war with Israel and America. They did not return home to Libya until after the revolution.

In October 1967, two Libyan airmen, Muftah al Sharif and Fethi al Tahar, flew a Libyan military plane to Egypt, hoping to join this Arab force, but were returned to Libya, put on trial, and sentenced to six years' imprisonment.

Gadaffi's movements during 1967 remain unclear. He was in Britain most of that year—and may not have returned to Libya until after the Six Day War, when the Israelis inflicted another humiliating defeat upon the Arabs. Israel won the war in the first two hours with a surprise attack upon Egyptian, Syrian, and Jordanian airfields, destroying their planes on the ground and leaving the runways virtually unusable. Left without air support, the Arabs were then easily beaten in the field, leaving Israel in possession of the Gaza Strip, the Sinai Peninsula, the Golan Heights, the West Bank of the River Jordan, and the Arab sector of Jerusalem.

The Libyan government expressed support for the Arab cause, but the army, navy, and air force were in no shape to take part in any war. Realizing that any threat to his throne might come from within the military, the King had curbed their expansion, making sure that far more money was spent on his own private army, the Cyrenaica Defense Force, who were better-paid, better-armed, and totally outnumbered the nation's official forces (even the police force was larger than the army, for the same reason).

Frustrated by what they saw as their government's lack of leadership, the oil workers—led by Dr. Sulaiman Maghribi, later to become Gadaffi's first prime minister—imposed an oil embargo, again in the belief that the U.S. was backing Israel. All supplies to the West were banned for a month, costing the Libyan government over 70 million a day in lost revenue.

Whether or not Gadaffi had any contact with Dr. Maghribi at that stage is not known; neither is it known whether Gadaffi took any part in the decision of the two army battalions to go to war without their senior officers' consent, although Sir Peter Wakefield, then British Consul General in Benghazi, told Lycett and Green that Gadaffi did join the battalions initially, but returned home rather than join them in exile. This claim is uncorroborated, and seems unlikely, since Gadaffi did not leave for Britain until the autumn of 1966 and would not have been back in Libya in time to participate.

However, there can be little doubt that the Six Day War triggered Gadaffi's coup. Belatedly, the government began trying to exercise authority, arresting activists in the oil fields (including Dr. Maghribi), imprisoning the two young airmen who flew to Egypt, and cracking down firmly on street demonstrations. But it was all too late. Libya was visibly falling apart at the seams.

"We all knew there was going to be a revolution," says John Wright, then working at the British Embassy in Tripoli, and now employed within the BBC External Affairs Department. "The King's overthrow was being openly discussed. It was the main topic at every dinner table. . . ." But none of the Western diplomats, oilmen, or intelligence officers operating within Libya had ever heard of Muammar Gadaffi—and there were at least three other groups also plotting to unseat the King.

The former prime minister, Abdul Hamid Bakkush, was involved with one group of senior officers; a second coup was being planned from within the higher ranks of the army, and it was widely believed that the King himself was supporting a third, led by the el Shalhi brothers—Aziz, the head of the army, and Omar, the Minister for Palace Affairs. The existence of this third group was widely known; it was reported both to the U.S. government in Washington and to Colonel Nasser in Egypt, and the el Shalhi plan was that the King would abdicate, allowing them to seize power and him to live out his final days in quiet retirement. But none of them knew what the Free Unionist Officers were planning. If anyone had mentioned Gadaffi's name, his intentions would not have been taken seriously for he was still only twenty-seven years old, with a rank no higher than sublieutenant*.

*   *   *

---

*In some accounts Gadaffi was described as a captain, but it has also been reported that Gadaffi was demoted from captain to sublieutenant in the months before the revolution for disciplinary reasons. He has sometimes joked about leading the revolution as a sublieutenant.

Until now, Gadaffi had put nothing in writing. The Free Unionist Officers planned all their meetings by word of mouth, driving to each other's homes or passing on messages by radio and telephone. Gadaffi was probably the only person who knew how the Free Unionist Officers were organized, for he had adopted the classic revolutionary pattern, grouping his followers together in separate cells, reflecting the years in which they joined the military academy, with each then operating independently of the others and himself the only link between them.

By early 1969 he felt confident enough in their organization to ask all cells to report back to him with information on where their respective army units would be based in mid-March, the weapons at their command, and their reserves of ammunition. A meeting was then called at the Armieh barracks in Tripoli. To allay any suspicions on the part of the authorities, this was timed to coincide with the officers' promotion examinations, which gave them all a good excuse to be there.

In his account of the revolution, summarized by Dr. Habib and partially reported by Mirella Bianco, Gadaffi recalled that,

We decided, after analyzing the situation, to launch the revolution the following month. . . . I therefore prepared a circular letter . . . and I sent it to Jalloud and the others, asking them to provide me with a complete picture of the movement's strength on that day and their estimate of the possibilities of maintaining control of the military forces. The information received, which included the number and the names of the striking force as well as the material and the arms available, made us reckon that there was a real possibility of us having the situation well in hand, and that there remained only to fix the day.

Meanwhile, I had put in for leave, which, since I had taken none since my enlistment, would amount to forty-five days. We made use of this for organizing some larger meetings, which included not only members of the Central Committee but many other officers of all ranks. Most of these meetings were held at Jalloud's house at Zawiya el Dahmani at Tripoli or in Mohammad el Mogharief's home in Banghazi. I had previously checked the strength of each group in the various army units, and I had met the officers of each battalion individually. We decided then that March 12th would be D Day. . . ."

No doubt this date was chosen partly for symbolic reasons. It was the King's eightieth birthday, and every year March 12 was a public holiday. The country would be at ease, with shops and offices closed, police stations and military bases running at minimum strength, and most families staying quietly at home. However, to their horror, the plotters discovered that the date had also been chosen to stage a gala concert starring the Egyptian singer Umm Qalthum, a legendary singer in the Arab world with a popularity rating on a par with that of Sophie Tucker, Frank Sinatra, or the Rolling Stones. Her concerts attracted vast open-air crowds, with performances usually starting around 10 P.M. and often continuing through the cool night until dawn. Rather than upset her audience, Gadaffi and the Central Committee decided to postpone the revolution for a fortnight.

"At the appointed hour, most of the men concerned would be at the concert, mingling with a multitude of spectators," wrote Gadaffi.

For this reason and also, be it said, out of a certain sense of propriety, we abandoned that project.

At the end of the meeting during which March 12 had been appointed as the date, I was returning from Tripoli to Benghazi in my Volkswagen with Lieutenants Abdel Hamid Shammas and Abdel Hamid Zayed. We stopped at Sirte to see my parents and continued our journey very late. That night was so dark that we lost ourselves in the desert, and we had to wait until dawn before carrying on. It was then that we heard over the radio of the tragic death of Abdel Mon'eim Riad (the Egyptian Chief of Staff, who was killed near Suez). We were grief-stricken.

Suddenly, a tire burst. The car, driven by Lieutenant Shammas, lurched violently, left the road, and rolled down a long slope. Fortunately, after a bounce or two, it came to a rest. This was a critical moment, for we had a large packet in the car containing pamphlets and, indeed, the famous circular letters. My first thought, of course, was to recover this packet, and the three of us, miraculously unscathed—for the car was a wreck—rushed to recover it from the debris.

A bizarre detail: we had brought water with us, in a wine bottle. The first people who came to help thought we were drunk and were pretty scathing in their comments.

A few days later Lieutenant Muftah Ali Gadaffi contacted Mohammad el Mogharief at home in Banghazi and told him I ought to go to Tripoli without delay, as things there seemed to be taking a suspicious turn. I took the first plane, and was received by Lieutenant Khairi Nuri, who told me that Colonel Shalhi had ordered all armored units to bring their complete forces from the barracks at Tarhuna and Homs, and to rendezvous at Bab al Aziziya; all contact with the officers of these units was forbidden. Moreover, it had been decided that all transport of the Tripoli units would be sent to Benghazi without their officers. But that was not all; apparently Major Ali Sha'aban and Major Suleiman el Fakki, as well as officers of the Deuxieme Bureau, were making lightning visits to these barracks at all hours of the day and night while Staff Colonel Aun Rahuma and Colonel Shalhi were patrolling the streets in private cars. Staff Colonel Hasuna Ashur was quite openly sleeping in the munitions stores with members of his staff.

From these anecdotes, it would appear that Col. Abdul Aziz el Shalhi, the Army Chief of Staff, who was planning a separate coup with his brother Omar el Shalhi, Minister of Palace Affairs, had been tipped off that other preparations were also afoot. Gadaffi continues:

Upon this we held a meeting at Khairi Nuri's house, where we were joined covertly by some of the Free Officers. We decided to launch the revolution on the following Sunday—that would be March 24. I spent the night at Khairi's, keeping well away from the barracks, for I was sure that I was being followed. In fact, military intelligence officers admitted later that an order for my arrest had been issued on March 15 but had not been acted upon.

The next day I returned to Benghazi, where Khuweldi was awaiting me. Then slap in the middle of our preparations came the news that King Idris was about to go unexpectedly to what was called his fortress, the town of Tobruk, where he felt himself protected by the soldiers at the British base. This departure made us revise everything, for our plan presupposed the presence of both King and Crown Prince in Tripoli; now that Idris was off to Tobruk, everything changed and we had yet again to reorganize our plans.

Well, we passed some very critical hours, for everything was ready: for a moment we even thought of going to attack the King's refuge. However, we finally abandoned this idea for fear of claiming too many victims among the Tripoli police. On March 24 the garrison at Misurata made something of a false start, beginning to put into operation our original plan. But, on full consideration, we felt certain that some informer in our ranks had communicated our movements to the military command. By good fortune, the authorities did not take the information very seriously: presumably because they did not imagine that an affair of this kind could really endanger the monarchist regime. It was said that they went so far as to doubt the truth of the stories which had reached them! Nevertheless, this didn't prevent the King from leaving Tripoli and repairing hastily to his palace in Tobruk, so as to gain the protection afforded by the British base. In general, many of us thought that these postponements would not turn out to be favorable to us, but would risk giving the enemy a chance of striking first, which would have meant an irremediable end to all these years of work and organization.

The King and the el Shalhi brothers may have been playing a waiting game. Gadaffi knew he had at least one informer among the Free Unionist Officers, but in which cell? How much did he know? And was he the only one? Were the el Shalhis waiting for Gadaffi to implicate himself, or perhaps for their informer to identify the extent of their treason? With the Free Unionist Officers grouped on a cellular basis, never knowing who else was involved in their conspiracy, Gadaffi knew there was a good chance that any "leak" could be contained. There were also logistical reasons for keeping calm. Britain was about to supply Libya with Chieftain tanks, fighter aircraft, a radar defense system, and a new generation of Thunderbolt and Rapier missiles. The separate deals involved in this program totaled over 400 million pounds, which was an enormous sum for a country with a population of little more than one million largely illiterate peasants, who posed no serious military threat to anyone—and the Free Unionist Officers were worried that the weapons were being acquired not to defend the country, but to enable the el Shalhi brothers either to stage their own coup*, or to defend the King against his own people. Both factions were now aware of each other, but the el Shalhi brothers had taken

---

*The Free Unionist Officers suspected that 40 million pounds in bribes was paid to the King's entourage to secure these contracts, and after the revolution claimed to have found documentary evidence to back up this suspicion. One of the new regime's first decisions was to cancel all the British contracts.

the precaution of letting the Russians and the Egyptians know in advance of their intentions, and may have been so confident of their ability to act that they underestimated the potential strength of a junior officers' coup, for Gadaffi's account continues:

And then, just as we were trying to light the first spark of the flames which would one day liberate our country, I received orders for my immediate transfer to the Fernaj barracks at Tripoli. There I was given a fine house complete with garden and grape vine, but no serious work came my way. I arrived late at morning parade: nobody took any notice. And what's more the officer commanding the battalion treated me with great courtesy. Eventually I was given the job of organizing some communication centers. Once I had made up my mind that none of this implied anything really serious, I decided, in agreement with my comrades, to pursue my activities from Tripoli, while they would do the same in Benghazi.

On August 13, 1969, Army Command decided to arrange a great military conference in which the whole High Command would take part, together with most of the officers from all units in the Benghazi region. This meant that the only officers remaining in barracks would be those on duty. The purpose of the conference was to give Colonel Shalhi ... an opportunity to explain the importance of air defense and the advantages of the work he had been doing, or rather that the British had been doing for him, in this field.

The conference was to be held in the Benghazi Military Academy's amphitheater and was to last from morning till evening. By this time we were completely ready to launch ourselves into this adventure which would strike the decisive blow against the monarchist regime: we would arrest the entire High Command assembled in the amphitheater, and bring out all the other officers, to whom we would communicate one by one the tasks they were to undertake. Some of us would have to avoid attending the conference and remain in barracks, so as to control things here and organize the various tasks. The execution of this plan having been agreed, the necessary instructions were sent out. However, owing to the lack of time, and because no meeting of the Central Committee had been held before the decision was taken, our instructions did not reach all the units. I myself had decided to remain at Gar Younis with Kharrubi and Mogharief, and I had ordered Mohammed Nejm to do the same in the military academy, to which he belonged. With the help of his comrades, he was to hold it from within, while I looked after the barracks at Gar Younis.

The attack was planned for the morning. Each officer was to take over his unit in the absence of its commander. Once the success of the coup and the seizure of the academy was assured, we would send messages to the Tripoli area so that our companions might begin to take over their respective units there too. We would have to keep everything under control till nightfall and only then announce the revolution; if it should prove impossible to keep our actions secret, everyone would act on his own judgment.

Everything was planned for this. But at the very moment when we were closing the meeting Abdel Moheim phoned us from Tripoli to say that so far he had not succeeded in calculating the actual chances of taking control of the Tripoli units nor the turn which events might subsequently take, above all in full daylight. He added that in his opinion the operation risked becoming a veritable suicide affair, not only at Tripoli but also for us in Benghazi.

To avoid the risk of compromising everything, we decided to await a more favorable occasion and once again to postpone the start of the revolution.

The revolution had now been thrice postponed. This put the Free Unionist Officers in a quandary. What if the King chose this moment to abdicate, cutting the ground from beneath their feet? Having failed to produce an heir, and with no apparent loyalty to any other members of his family, Idris might help the el Shalhi brothers take over the country, letting them make whatever changes might be necessary to contain the constant waves of unrest. There was more to this possibility than mere speculation.

After hiding away in his palace at Tobruk for months, the King left Libya in June with four hundred trunks of baggage. No one knew what was in them. Was this what kings needed when they went on holiday—or had Idris literally packed his bags? It was said at the time that the King was seeking a medical cure, but he spent the next three months at holiday resorts in Turkey and Greece, accompanied by Omar el Shalhi and other members of his court. Early in August, he summoned the Prime Minister and the President of the Upper House to Athens, where he told them that he was planning to abdicate. This was not the first time Idris had mentioned abdication. He made a similar announcement five years earlier, and then changed his mind. This time he said he meant it.

The King's decision was not known to the Free Unionist Officers, but they realized something was afoot when eighty junior officers were suddenly told that they would be going abroad on September 3 to attend overseas courses. Realizing that this probably meant that the el Shalhis were trying to get them all out of the country while they staged their own coup, Gadaffi moved fast, and set a new time and date for the revolution—2:30 A.M. on September 1.

Worried that they still had an informer in their ranks, Gadaffi kept his plans secret until the latest possible moment. Gadaffi said that he and Mohammad el Mogharief would lead the coup from Benghazi, first capturing the army barracks at Gar Younis and then seizing the radio station. This would enable them to establish radio contact with all other units. Those with longer distances to travel were told to set out between 1 and 1:30 A.M., so that they could all act together at 2:30 A.M. Also based with Gadaffi at Benghazi were el Kharrubi, two lieutenants Mohammad Aun and Ahmed Abu Lifa together with Mohammad el Sadiq and Abdel Fattah Unis. In Tripoli, operations were led by Omar el Meheishi, Abdel Moneim el Huni, Abu Bakr Yunis, and el Khuweldi Hamidi.

The most reliable account of what happened that night was provided by Gadaffi himself a year later. In a Libyan television program arranged to mark the first anniversary of the coup, he described how the drama unfolded, saying that the Central Committee had agreed to leave him to make whatever radio announcements were necessary, and "to take all necessary decisions on any unforeseen events which might occur after the proclamation of the revolution— foreign intervention, for example, or serious internal resistance in the country."

Until the moment of revolution, the Free Unionist Officers had no way of knowing what would happen next; whether the el Shalhi brothers would lead a countercoup, or the British and/or the American forces come to the King's defense. The U.S. force at Wheelus Field was nearly twice the size of the Libyan army, and with its superiority in weaponry and military skills would have had no difficulty rounding up the Free Unionist officers.

"Broadly speaking," claimed Gadaffi, "the operation went according to plan"—although he did admit being badly let down at

Benghazi. To maintain a semblance of order during the revolution, the Free Unionist Officers agreed that any arrests should be made by the police. In Benghazi, they had the support of the commanding officer of the military police; or thought they had. When the time came for him to make arrests, none were made. "He did damn all. He was a bastard," said Gadaffi.

Speaking of unforeseeable factors, he was one, all right, but thanks to Mustafa el Kharrubi, we were able to rectify things at once. At the time I had no knowledge of this defection, and, indeed, knew nothing about it until the next day, but Kharrubi, as soon as he realized that this particular gentleman was late in carrying out his work, had the presence of mind to take it over himself. The result was that we got by with fewer arrests than we had foreseen. People gave themselves up of their own accord.

I changed only one detail in the execution of my own part in the plan, just one. I took a different route. That was because this villain of an officer I mentioned had sent us, barely ten minutes before we went into action, false information, according to which the authorities had got wind of our uprising, had increased the number of men in the barracks, and had mined the roads leading to them. Believing this information, I asked Mohammad and Abdel Fattah to go and occupy the Berka barracks. I must confess that I was within an ace of believing that the operation had really been discovered, but in any case it was too late to turn back now, and I said to myself that we must face up to it, cost what it might.

With the help of two soldiers I crammed my jeep full of munitions and light machine guns, so convinced was I that we were going to meet resistance either en route or on arrival, and that all hell was going to break loose. Kharrubi took command of the group which was to occupy the Berka barracks and off he went. I jumped into my jeep and drove to the head of my column. I took the Jilyana road as planned, and then took a left fork. The vehicles following me, which were supposed to come with me to occupy the Radio Station . . . went straight on ahead, heading for Berka. I had stopped my jeep to await the rest of the column when I suddenly saw all the other vehicles tearing like demons toward the main road. It then dawned on me that the entire Gar Younis barracks were streaming along in the one direction and that the drivers in their enthusiasm were following one another without worrying much about where they were supposed to be going. Clearly, I had to turn round, go back and rejoin them. I had to reorganize my column virtually vehicle by vehicle, and by the time I'd done it we were practically at Berka!

To crown all, some of the vehicles turned right when, by now, the only thing we could do was to approach the radio station from Berka. The fact is that el Kharrubi, having occupied the Berka barracks, had decided to steer for the police school, where, among other things, a totally unforeseen resistance was being organized. He was to pick up some of his officers there. Anyway, when I turned left en route for the radio station, I found myself alone once more, in my jeep, bowling along the road to Benghazi. No column. No lights. Nothing.

At this, I said to myself, let's go to the radio station as arranged and see what's going on, and what a pleasant surprise I had. Large numbers of vehicles, full of soldiers, were emerging from the direction of the Port. They had entered Benghazi after driving all round and were just reaching the radio station from the far side.

At the radio station, Gadaffi decided to make an immediate broadcast, drafting it there and then, on the spur of the moment:

The previous evening at Gar Younis we had decided to prepare a series of communiques and announcements to read over the radio, but we didn't have the time. We were far too busy putting out instructions to everyone concerned. These orders, in envelopes sealed with red sealing wax, were to be distributed in the various barracks.

Mogharief and I went personally to the El Abyar barracks and met the officers there. We made contact, too, with the officers of the El Marj battalion, who were told of the whole plan of operation throughout Libya, as well as of the specific tasks entrusted to each one of them.

Altogether I had no time to think of anything else. So I grabbed a file of blank paper with the idea of drafting the communique when we had occupied the radio station. However, when the announcers arrived I had to check their identity myself. Meanwhile, to fill in the time, we broadcast military music, marches, and so on. Then, and only then, did I begin to write the text of the communique. Just as I was reading it on the air, I recollected that there were foreigners living in Libya and that they ought to be reassured of their safety, and that the armed forces ought, after all, to be responsible for their security. So I delivered impromptu the sections about them, and these passages were broadcast, too.

One of the most crucial roles in the Revolution was entrusted to Omar el Meheishi, but, for security reasons, he was not told what it was until the very last minute. The day before the coup, el Meheishi went to Gadaffi's office at the Gar Younis barracks in Benghazi "and found him quietly at work as if nothing was happening. Most unfortunately there were several people in his office, and I was forced to join them and drink a glass of milk until we were finally able to retire to his room."

Gadaffi confirmed that the coup was timed for 2:30 A.M. the following morning and gave el Meheishi an air ticket to Tripoli. It was then midday, and when el Meheishi arrived at Benghazi airport he found all seats on the plane were booked. "By sheer luck, I stumbled upon a company employee who knew me well and who, ignoring the rules, got me on to the aircraft," said el Meheishi in the same TV program, but this was not to be his last moment of panic. The plane was delayed. By the time el Meheishi reached Tripoli it was 9:30 A.M. He caught a taxi into the center of town to liaise with Abdel Moneim el Huni, but could not find him; tried to contact Jalloud, but found that he was out on night patrol. Then el Meheishi remembered that he had left his revolver and ammunition in the back of the taxi—and could not trace the driver. It was midnight before el Meheishi arrived at the Tarhuna barracks, where he was given his sealed instructions to go to the private house of the head of the army, Abdel Aziz el Shalhi, and arrest him!

Abu Bakr and I went off at once to the Shalhi house in a Ford armored car commanded by Abu Bakr. We infantrymen flung open the great gate so that the armored car could drive into the garden, but shots awakened everyone in the house. The sentry had given the alarm. It looked as though the operation was well and truly done for, since el Shalhi, being a career officer, understood what was happening and fled in his pajamas. We hadn't the least idea where he might hide. We learned later that he hid in the swimming pool, diving into the water just as he was. We searched the house room by room with no success, and were finally obliged to take the members of his family as hostages. We treated them with great respect, of course, but we had no choice. El Shalhi was arrested next morning about 10 A.M.

As revolutions go, Gadaffi's was unusually peaceful. Only one person died; a soldier loyal to the King who started to shoot when asked to lay down his arms. Elsewhere, there was hardly any resistance—which was just as well because the Free Unionist Officers had little more than a few light machine guns, one or two armored cars, their jeeps, and service issue revolvers. They were relying upon their cause rather than superiority in arms. In the television broadcast, Abdel Moneim el Huni described how he and Abdel Salam were assigned to take over the antiaircraft defenses:

The station had about six hundred men, and for them there were only 1,050 rounds of ammunition. By good luck, the El Rabha regiment was on night exercises just then, and thus we had a chance to alert a large number of reliable NCOs, members of the movement, and to tell them that the uprising would start at 2:30 A.M. As they were returning from their exercises toward 11:30 P.M. we succeeded in rounding them all up in a cinema where we distributed their ammunition.... After that we decided to embark on a tour of inspection in the town, to check on strategic points and make sure whether the guard had been reinforced, or if all was normal. It was already past midnight and there was nothing special to report. On the contrary, we found out that the police had been put on alert the previous night, but the order had been canceled.

On our way back to the barracks, we remembered that we had had nothing to eat since early evening. We were ravenous, and one cannot very well launch a revolution on an empty stomach— so we stopped off at a café which was still open. The proprietor— an Italian, of course—was kind enough to serve us some *brioches* and milk. Afterward we looked in at the Club, where we found twenty officers, twelve of them members of our movement, and eight who did not belong. Since we needed every man we could get that night, for it had not been possible to contact all our people, for various reasons, we decided to recruit these men on the spot. They jumped at the chance, to a man. We knew them well, of course—this goes without saying—and we knew we could trust them.

Our entire armament consisted of five service revolvers. I had two. Abdel Salam Jalloud had two, also, and Abdel Salam Boukhila had one. There was one more revolver lying about somewhere, I don't remember whose. We armed our new recruits with these six revolvers and arranged to meet them at 2 A.M. precisely. As for the officer on duty, who had not the slightest suspicion of all this, we went to get him out of bed, thinking we might be able to enroll him, too, but he had no wish to be involved. So we locked him up, warning him to keep quiet until morning.

Then we set about our work. The first thing was to awaken the men, and then there was a ludicrous incident. An air force sergeant who had only just returned from the air defense exercise was completely drunk. He joined with the other NCOs, all the same, in waking the men. We had not yet dared to tell them the real object of the operation, confining ourselves to giving the order to get up and get ready, in battle dress, helmets, and all the rest.

When the men and some of the air force officers were assembled, we began to explain the situation—and what did that drunkard do but refuse to budge unless he was told every detail. We tried everything we knew to convince him, but he kept on saying, "Oh no, you don't. I'm not a robot. Let's get everything straight. Where are you taking us?" shouting at the top of his voice. It was three o'clock in the morning, and in the silence of the night this made a devil of a row . . .

Eventually they managed to quiet him and around 4 A.M. on September 1 joined up with el Khuweldi and went to seize the Tripoli radio station, where they met some resistance from five or six soldiers on guard duty. There was an exchange of fire. Three soldiers were wounded, with one later dying from injuries. Later in the night, there was more gunfire when a police detachment tried to recapture the radio station, but this was repulsed without any loss of life.

At this point in the television program, Gadaffi intervened to say:

We felt, all of us, in those hours, that whatever happened we must do our duty, that the possibilities of success or of failure had been analyzed and weighed up before the coup, and that we had given our own side the maximum of advantages. So when the time actually came we gave no further thought to the danger. Whatever the chances, we had to go through with it. I can tell you now, though, that before the coup we calculated that we had about a sixty percent chance. But if we had given too much importance to this kind of arithmetic, we would never even have started.

Abu Bakr Younis, el Khuweldi, Omar Hariri, Mohammed Sha'aban, and others went to the Tarhuna barracks and seized armored vehicles, which gave their unit extra mobility.

Moreover, our group was reinforced by four civil defense officers who were to support us on Gadaffi's own orders. They had been brought to us by car, but they could not possibly be accommodated in the barracks, for that would have aroused suspicion. We dressed them in civilian clothes and sent them, each with a little bag, to a hotel, where they registered as students.

Later they met in a field, allocated groups of three or four officers jobs to do, and handed out the ammunition, forty-five rounds.

Obviously, we could hardly have opened the ammunition depots before the coup. They were controlled by officers of higher rank than ours, and if we had made any such attempt we should have had to arrest them. This was out of the question, for it would have entailed the risk of our being locked up for mutiny or something of the sort. Anyway, having arrested a certain number of officers, whom we had brought together in one room, we allotted among us our various jobs. My job, with el Hadi and el Rimah, was to wake the soldiers. When everyone was ready we burst through the depot doors and each soldier helped himself to arms and ammunition. Then I boarded the first armored vehicle which I came across and I literally stuffed it with arms and ammunition, especially with submachine guns. Gadaffi had strongly advised us not to stick together, to keep a fair distance one from the other, so as not to risk being caught, and to control the situation better. So I jumped into this armored car and stayed there, standing, to have a complete view of the operation. My machine was at the ready, and. . . .

"You know, your plan wasn't altogether a safe one," commented Gadaffi, as Abu Bakr Younis continued, "I had hardly got into my vehicle when a soldier came running and shouting that flames were coming from one of the tanks. I leapt down and rushed to the tank, which was full to bursting with arms and ammunition . . . "

"If that lot had exploded the whole barracks would have blown up," said Gadaffi, intervening again.

"Yes," said Younis, "and that wouldn't have done any good to the morale of the troops. So I slid inside the tank, where a soldier was trying to repair the damage, and I tore out the wire."

"You certainly risked your life," added Gadaffi, as Younis then went on to describe how he and el Khuweldi then moved off from Tarhuna to join el Meheishi and seize Aziz el Shalhi.

El Khuweldi had also been given another important task, arresting the Crown Prince, and in the television program he described how he teamed up with Jalloud and Abdel Moneim at the Jalo barracks before going out to the Crown Prince's palace to have a preliminary look at its layout: "We observed that the two gates were about a kilometer apart and that the palace, which was surrounded by a high wall, was guarded by a number of policemen . . ." They then left, agreeing to meet again at 2:30 A.M., and el Khuweldi called in to see his mother.

This part of the coup did not go quite as planned. When el Khuweldi went to arrest the officer in charge of the army depots, he found that he had gone to the cinema—and when he went to the cinema, he discovered that a number of other senior officers were there as well, which made it difficult to arrest him.

Then, while we were driving along the Bir Mirji road my car took a dangerous bend at too high a speed and the vehicle following me, with Lieutenant Musa Abdel Salam in it, crashed into it. Musa was injured, and so was the soldier traveling with him. We had to leave both cars and go on with Lieutenant Hairi, who commanded the armored cars. . . . We had just started off again when some police passed by, and seeing two vehicles by the roadside asked to see the officers' papers and the car documents, too . . . Musa asked them to take him back to the barracks for medical attention, and once arrived there he had them arrested . . . .

Meanwhile, we had reached the Crown Prince's palace. There, things began to go wrong. I had twenty-five men with me. As soon as we arrived, two of them hoisted me up on their shoulders so that I could take a look over the wall. Unfortunately I had my rifle with me. The sentry saw me and took to his heels then and there, disappearing into an olive grove. I dropped down and started to run after him, trying to catch him, but in vain. Then most of us entered the garden, leaving the vehicles outside and some soldiers on guard. We forced the locks and found ourselves inside the palace. It was pitch dark and there wasn't a sound. We thought it was empty, but the Prince was there all right, as we soon found out.... Meanwhile the armored forces under Omar Hariri, which had arrived after me, also broke into the palace. They made a quick search, found nothing either, and they were just going off, leaving one man behind them. But this man on his own initiative began searching again and ended up by routing out the Prince. He dashed downstairs calling out to Hariri that he had found what they were looking for. Omar turned back and captured the Prince.

Mohammad el Mogharief gave his description of Gadaffi's role that night, the seizure of the radio station at Benghazi:

Leaving Gar Younis with Kharrubi and the rest we set off for Berka, where we secured barracks and other strategic points, my personal task being that of keeping the main entrance to the barracks under control, to repel any eventual attack by the police or other opposing force. I had to ensure this control until such time as arms and ammunition had been distributed all round.

However, we also ran into trouble just before operations began ... about 1 A.M. we had seen a military police Land Rover drive up to the barracks. A policeman got out and walked straight toward me. "There has been an accident some kilometers from here," he said. "The injured man has been taken to hospital but his moped is still there. Would one of you come with me to bring it in? The poor devil risks having it stolen on top of everything else."

Of course, we didn't believe a word of that. We thought at once that the police had come to look round the barracks. However, I went to the Land Rover, saying I was ready to accompany him, and to my immense relief there really was a damaged moped by the roadside.... [After the policeman left] we drove into town and straight to the radio station. There was only one sentry on duty. We disarmed him. It was about 4 A.M. and our objective was achieved. We realized at this point that we knew none of the announcers nor their addresses, yet we must get hold of them. All routes into the town were blocked, but we ordered that those who worked at the radio station should be allowed through. They came in finally between 6 and 6:30 A.M. The technicians and the announcers on Radio Benghazi knew nothing of what had happened and they were in such a state that Muammar decided to take over the microphone himself. He first made contact with Tripoli, however, and when we heard that station broadcasting military music we were absolutely delighted. It was then that Muammar broadcast Communique Number One.

Part III

GADAFFI'S COUP ASTONISHES
THE WEST. BRITISH AND AMERICAN
INTELLIGENCE AGENCIES PREDICTED THE
KING'S FALL, BUT NO ONE EXPECTED
A TWENTY-SEVEN-YEAR-OLD LIEUTENANT
TO LEAD THE REVOLUTION.
COUPS WERE USUALLY LED BY COLONELS,
AND, SURE ENOUGH,
GADAFFI ROSE THROUGH THE RANKS
TO COLONEL IN A MATTER OF HOURS. . . .
THE WEST WAS REASSURED WHEN TOLD OF
HIS TRAINING IN BRITAIN,
THE NEW REGIME'S OPPOSITION TO
COMMUNISM AND ITS WILLINGNESS
TO KEEP SUPPLYING OIL.

ON HOLIDAY IN TURKEY,
KING IDRIS DECLINES AN OFFER
TO RETURN HOME AS A PRIVATE
BUT "HONORED CITIZEN,"
INSISTING THAT THE
COUP IS "A TRIFLING AFFAIR."
HE SAYS HE WILL SOON BE BACK,
WITH THE SUPPORT OF THE BRITISH.

THE YOUNG COLONEL
PROCEEDS TO OUTWIT THEM ALL,
FOILING PLOTS TO OUST HIM,
OVERSEEING THE OVERALL STRATEGY
OF THE REVOLUTION, WHILE HIS
NUMBER-TWO, MAJOR JALLOUD, A CLOSE

FRIEND SINCE SECONDARY SCHOOOL,
AND A MEMBER OF THE NEIGHBORING
EL MEGHARA TRIBE IN SIRTE,
TACKLES DAY-TO-DAY ADMINISTRATION,
INCLUDING RENEGOTIATING TERMS
WITH THE OIL COMPANIES.
GADAFFI BEGINS TO IDENTIFY
THE NEW REGIME WITH
RADICAL CAUSES IN AFRICA AND
THE MIDDLE EAST, SUPPORTING
THE PALESTINIANS EVEN WHEN THEY
RESORT TO TERRORISM.

REPEATEDLY HE CALLS UPON THE
ARAB STATES TO UNITE AGAINST
ISRAEL AND THE WEST,
WHILE ACQUIRING WEAPONS
WHEREVER HE CAN.
INITIALLY EGYPT, SYRIA, AND
SUDAN AGREE TO WORK TOGETHER WITH LIBYA
TO CREATE A UNITED ARAB REPUBLIC,
BUT, AS THE YEARS GO BY,
ALL HIS ATTEMPTS TO FORGE
AN ARAB FEDERAL STATE
COLLAPSE.

THE WEST STANDS BACK
—BUT THEN BECOMES ALARMED,
SEEING GADAFFI AS A THREAT TO
THEIR INTERESTS IN THE
REGION, ESPECIALLY WHEN HE
ENDORSES TERRORISM, AND BEGINS
TO ARTICULATE AN ECONOMIC
ALTERNATIVE TO CAPITALISM AND
COMMUNISM,
HIS "THIRD UNIVERSAL THEORY"
WHICH GADAFFI
DEFINES IN HIS OWN WORK,
THE GREEN BOOK.

September	3	With the Russian Fleet still engaged in maneuvers, the Free Officers take control of Tobruk.

September 4 — Egypt reveals the existence of secret clauses in the 1953 Anglo-Libyan Treaty whereby Britain agreed to airlift forces to Libya from Britain, West Germany, Malta, and Cyprus in the event of Egyptian intervention in a Libyan coup. Omar el Shalhi meets Michael Stewart, who says the treaty only applies if there is an *external* threat to Libya. Russia and Egypt recognize the new Libyan regime without knowing the identity of its leaders; they are swiftly followed by the United States, Britain, France, and Italy.

September 7 — The Crown Prince renounces all claims to the Libyan throne and supports the revolution.

September 8 — Mahmud Sulaiman el Maghribi becomes Prime Minister. The West is reassured to learn that Maghribi studied at the George Washington University in the U.S. and had been a lawyer for Exxon. He was jailed in 1967 for leading a Libyan oil workers' strike. Gadaffi is promoted from captain to colonel and identified as the leader of the revolution; this is the first day his name has been mentioned.

September 13 — Gadaffi appointed President of the Revolutionary Command Council, the body that is actually running the country.

September 29 — The Libyan Revolutionary Command Council announced that the agreements with Britain and the U.S. over military bases will not be renewed.

October 16 — In his first major speech, Gadaffi calls for Libyan neutrality, says that all foreign bases will be evacuated, urges the abolition of all political parties, and emphasizes that Arab Unity will be the main aim of Libyan policy.

October	26	The Revolutionary Command Council sets up a People's Court to try those accused of political offenses against the state.
October	29	Britain and the United States are asked to evacuate their bases within eight months. Barclays Bank's local branches are nationalized. Libya says it will cancel its 400-million pound defense contract with Britain.

1969

November	14	Libya takes fifty-one percent interest in all other foreign banks. Negotiations for new royalties begin with the oil companies. The new regime says there has been no increase in the royalties since oil was discovered ten years earlier. And they now learn that Libya's known oil reserves are estimated at thirty thousand million barrels.
December	7	A counterrevolutionary coup foiled. Thirty army officers arrested together with Minister of Defense Adar al Hawaz.
December	11	The Revolutionary Command Council announces a new constitution and declares that any further attempt to overthrow the new regime will be dealt with severely. Leading plotters will be executed. Islam is declared the religion of the state with freedom of religion accorded to all other faiths.
December	23	Agreements signed for evacuation of British bases by March 31, 1970, and U.S. bases by June 30.
December	26	Presidents Nasser of Egypt and Numeiry of Sudan visit Tripoli.

1970

January	9	New cabinet announced with Gadaffi as Prime Minister.
January	10	Former Prime Minister Maghribi arrested and accused of complicity in previous month's attempted coup.

January	21	France agrees to supply Libya with over a hundred Mirage jet fighters; previously Libya only had ten planes, all of them American. France agrees to train Libyan pilots.
January	27	Libya and Algeria agree to cooperate on oil policy.
February	25	Marshal Tito of Yugoslavia visits Tripoli and agrees on a policy statement with Gadaffi emphasizing each country's wish to be nonaligned.
March	15	Libya establishes Libyan National Oil Corporation. In its first year the company handles 0.33 percent of the country's oil production, rising to 61.53 percent by 1974.
March	31	Britain evacuates its bases.
March/June		All Italian settlers ordered out of the country. Many have been living there thirty years. Some leave with the bodies of their families, having exhumed them from local graveyards. Gadaffi is anxious to remove all trace of Italy's occupation.
May	22	Libya signs an oil agreement with Iraq and Algeria, establishing a common policy "confronting the exploiting companies."
May	25	Gadaffi advocates a pan-Arab oil policy, pooling all national resources against Israel.
June	11	The U.S. vacates Wheelus Field, leaving a fully equipped mini-town behind. The base occupied an area of twenty-three square miles, totally surrounded by walls.
		Libya forces the oil companies to reduce their output to 3.7 million barrels per day.
July		Former U.S. ambassador to Libya David Newsom tells the Senate Foreign Relations Committee that the former King was probably organizing a coup against his own Crown Prince just as Gadaffi seized power.

July	7	Libya nationalizes the oil distribution system jointly owned by Esso, Shell, ENO, and Petro-Libya. LINOCO becomes Libya's oil distributor.
July	21	The Revolutionary Command Council announces the confiscation of all Italian-owned property.
July	24	Another and much more serious plot is foiled. Two former prime ministers, Abdul Hamid Bakoush and Hussein Mazik, are said to be implicated. The eleven ringleaders are arrested. Their plan was to bring in a five-thousand-strong mercenary force through Chad, take power, and install Idris's nephew Prince Abdallah Abdel Sanusi on the throne. There is suspicion that the U.S. and France colluded with the Chad government.
August	27	Chad breaks off diplomatic relations, accusing Libya of supporting an attempted coup.
		Armand Hammer breaks ranks with the other oil companies. He agrees to pay an extra thirty cents per barrel, rising to forty cents in five years, with an extra eight percent local tax. Gadaffi and his negotiator Jalloud use this breakthrough to squeeze similar terms from the other companies. Iraq, Algeria, Kuwait, and Iran follow suit.
September	6	The Popular Front for the Liberation of Palestine hijacks three planes and has them flown to Dawson's Field near Amman, Jordan. They demand the release of their followers jailed in West Germany and Switzerland, and the release of Arab prisoners in Israel.
September	15	After a long, drawn-out drama at Dawson's Field, the PFLP frees the 375 hostages and then blows up the planes.
September	17	Apparently in retaliation, King Hussein orders his forces to attack Palestinian camps near Amman. Fighting continues for

		eleven days with over a thousand Arabs killed.
September	22	At a meeting in Cairo called to end Hussein's action against the Palestinians, Gadaffi says King Hussein should be hanged.
September	28	President Nasser dies after being taken ill at the summit in Cairo.
October	1	Libya begins training helicopter pilots for a Malta land force after Britain starts to reduce its military presence on the island.
October	3–6	Gadaffi attends the Arab summit in Cairo where he meets Russian Prime Minister Kosygin.
October	20	Algerian oppostion leader Belgasim Krim found strangled in his hotel room at the Frankfurt Intercontinental a few days after meeting Omar el Shalhi to discuss cooperating in a coup against Gadaffi.
November	5	Omar el Shalhi's latest coup aborted when his boat develops engine trouble at Bari. The plan was to carry mercenaries to Tripoli where they would release prisoners from the jails and stage a counterrevolution.
November	27	General Assad seizes power in Syria.

1971

January	24	Gadaffi says he will not be a candidate for the presidency under the new constitution.
January	26	Gadaffi says that he will stand after all in response to popular demand.
February	24	President Boumedienne of Algeria follows Gadaffi's example and announces that Algeria is taking a fifty-one percent share in the French oil companies and will be nationalizing the pipelines and the country's oil and gas deposits.
March	21–23	The Italians foil Omar el Shalhi's latest attempt to seize power in Libya. He had been plotting the coup with the founder of the British SAS, David Stirling, and a

		corps of mercenaries. Someone tipped off the CIA and the British MI5, who contacted the Italians. The plotters' boat was seized leaving Trieste.
April	17	Egypt, Syria, Sudan, and Libya announce formation of a United Arab Republic in effect as of September 1. The plan is to put their four armies under one command with the Republic governed by a sixty-member federal assembly. The scheme founders over Egypt's attitude to Israel.
June	7	Libya signs a friendship treaty with Niger, agreeing to cooperate on oil exploration in their frontier areas.
June	26	Russia awards Gadaffi the Order of Lenin "in recognition of his efforts for world peace."
July	10	Libya backs an attempted coup against King Hassan of Morocco. The royal palace is attacked with rockets and machine guns. The King escapes by hiding in a toilet. Libyan radio praises the coup before news comes through that the King is still alive. Ninety-two people are killed and 133 injured.
July	14	Morocco breaks off diplomatic relations with Libya.
July	19	Attempted coup against Numeiry in Sudan. Gadaffi cooperates with Sadat in putting down the coup.
July	22	Libya orders down a British plane carrying two of the Sudanese plotters. The men are returned to Khartoum and hanged.
August		Libya helps Pakistan in its war with India, sending several squadrons of fighter bombers.
August		Libya announces a 12-million dollar loan to Malta.
August	27	Chad suspects Libya of involvement in another plot against the government and again breaks off diplomatic relations.

September	11	Gadaffi offers to resign after a referendum has approved the new constitution and then disappears for a month.
September	18	Libya recognizes the opposition group in Chad, the Chad National Front.
October	7	On his return Gadaffi says that he submitted his resignation to the Revolutionary Command Council "to protest at the shortcomings of the administrative apparatus in carrying out social, economic, and industrial projects."
November	17	King Idris sentenced to death in absentia; his wife to five years' imprisonment; Omar el Shalhi to life imprisonment, and the Crown Prince to three years' imprisonment.
December	7	After Iran occupies three islands in the Gulf, Libya accuses Britain of complicity and withdraws all its deposits from British banks. Libya nationalizes the assets of British Petroleum.
December	14	Libya expelled from the sterling area.
December	19	In a speech at the Tripoli mosque, Gadaffi uses the phrase "cultural revolution" for the first time, saying that it has "certainly not come to us from China; it has been foreshadowed in Islam for centuries."
December	30	Maltese leader Dom Mintoff visits Tripoli.

1972

January	5	Gadaffi announces that in future the police will be a civil authority with all officers graduates of the Faculty of Law. "There will no longer be a police state in Libya," he says.
January	25	Libya formally terminates its treaty with Britain signed on July 29, 1953.
February	5	Libya formally terminates its treaty with the U.S. signed on September 9, 1954.
February	15	Gadaffi visits Mauritania, unaware that Morocco's General Oufkir has suggested shooting down his plane.

March	4	Libya signs a treaty with Russia for joint production of oil and refining.
April	13	After Iraq signs a fifteen-year friendship treaty with Russia, Libya recalls her ambassador to Iraq saying the treaty is "contrary to the charter of the Arab League."
April	22	Diplomatic relations restored with Chad.
May	30	The Revolutionary Command Council decrees that anyone belonging to a political party other than the Arab Socialist Union may be sentenced to death.
June	5	Libya asks Britain, Russia, and the U.S. to reduce their diplomatic missions.
June	11	The British and U.S. ambassadors walk out when Gadaffi makes a speech at a ceremony to mark the second anniversary of America's departure from Wheelus Field. Gadaffi offers to help the IRA against the British, the Black Power movement against the U.S., and the Palestinian resistance movement against Israel.
July		Treaty signed with Malta on joint development of culture, tourism and economy. Libya and Malta agree a common boundary for oil exploration in the Mediterranean.
July	16	Jalloud becomes Prime Minister, with Gadaffi administering the oath live on television as Chairman of the Revolutionary Command Council.
July	20	Russia asked to withdraw military advisers.
July	22	Gadaffi welcomes the expulsion of Russians from Egypt by Sadat.
July	23	On the twentieth anniversary of the Egyptian revolution, Gadaffi makes a speech urging that Libya and Egypt be brought together in "total union."
August	2	Sadat agrees to Gadaffi's proposal. They agree a timetable with September 1, 1973, as the date for amalgamating the two

		countries, setting up joint committees to coordinate foreign, social, and economic policy—but these plans later collapse.
August	16	Another attempt to assassinate King Hassan of Morocco. Three planes from his own air force attack his plane as he is flying over the Mediterranean. The King takes control, announces his own death over a radio microphone, and foils the plotters. Planes later attack his palace.
November	26	Gadaffi mediates in the war between North and South Yemen, inviting the heads of both governments to Tripoli, where they agree to a settlement.
December	16	Gadaffi calls for unity with Tunisia.
December	26	Gadaffi drives to Tunis to speak at an Arab Unity rally. President Bourguiba hears his speech on radio, immediately drives to the meeting before Gadaffi has finished, and tells the audience "Tunisia does not need to be told how to organize its affairs by the leader of a backward country."

1973

February	20	Libyan Foreign Minister Abu Zayed Durdeh accuses Russia of being responsible for student riots against Sadat.
February	21	Israel shoots down a Libyan Arab Airlines over Sinai, killing 108 people, including the former Foreign Minister Salah Masoud Bousair. It seems to have been a genuine error on Israel's part. The plane overshot the runway at Cairo in a violent sandstorm and was thereafter ten miles off course. It just happened to stray near an Israeli radar station. Gadaffi swears revenge.
February	22–23	Riots in Tripoli and Benghazi as the bodies are brought home. The Egyptian consulate in Benghazi attacked by protesters angry that Egypt did not retaliate against Israel.

March	6	Two American and one Belgian diplomat executed by Palestinian commandos at the Saudi Arabian embassy in Khartoum. Sudan accuses Libya of complicity.
March		The Irish navy intercepts the SS *Claudia* off the Irish coast carrying five tons of weapons for the IRA, accompanied by IRA leader Joe Cahill. The weapons have come from Libya.
April	15	On the anniversary of the birth of Mohammed, Gadaffi launches the Cultural Revolution with a speech at Zuwara. People's Committees set up to run schools, factories, the radio station, etc., etc.
April	17	Gadaffi said to have ordered the commander of an Egyptian submarine stationed in Libya (and subject to Libyan control) to sink the *Queen Elizabeth II* with two torpedoes. The *QEII* was carrying Jews to Israel to celebrate its independence. The commander duly left the submarine base at Tobruk and then sought confirmation of these instructions from Sadat, who stopped it.
May		Libyan forces occupy the sixty-mile-wide Aouzou Strip on the border with Chad. Libya claims the strip was ceded to Libya by France in colonial days (which it seems to have been). The area has rich deposits of oil, gas, and uranium ore. Gadaffi argues that the strip was part of Libya when its boundaries were agreed by the United Nations. A long war ensues.
May	14	Gadaffi talks for the first time about his Third Universal Theory, an economic and political philosophy that is neither capitalist nor communist, requiring mankind to return "to the Kingdom of God."
June —July	22 9	Gadaffi goes to Cairo with his new wife Satiya, a former nurse, and their young child. This is the first time he has been

seen with his family. They stay at the Tahra Palace.

July	11	Gadaffi again offers his resignation, which is refused by the Revolutionary Command Council. Crowds take to the streets urging him not to resign. At first, the furor is a mystery, but it transpires that the plans to amalgamate Libya with Egypt are not going well.
July	15	Russia supports Egypt as the dispute with Libya spills over into the international press.
July	18	A crowd of forty thousand Libyans begin marching across the desert toward Cairo, demanding unity with Egypt. After three days, Egypt blocks their way with buses parked across the roadway. After an appeal from Sadat, Gadaffi urges the crowd to return home.
July	23	Gadaffi says he is withdrawing his resignation, adding that "fusion with Egypt is inevitable, even at the price of a civil war."
August	5	Passengers on a TWA flight at Athens attacked by Palestinians. Three killed; fifty-five injured. The attackers say they belong to the National Arab Youth for the Liberation of Palestine.
August	12	Armand Hammer agrees to Libya's demand for a fifty-one percent stake in Occidental's operation in Libya.
August	16	Libya announces that it has taken a fifty-one percent stake in Oasis and that three other Companies—Continental, Amerada, and Marathon—have agreed to similar arrangements.
August	25	Gadaffi and Jalloud go to Cairo to confer with Sadat.
September	1	Libya takes a fifty-one percent share in Shell, Exxon, Texaco, Mobil, and Standard Oil of California.
September	8	Gadaffi addresses the Non-aligned Confer-

		ence in Algiers, arguing that all non-aligned nations should refuse to have foreign bases on their soil. He also urges them to break off diplomatic relations with Israel.
September	9	Cuba becomes the first of thirty nations to break with Israel.
September	10	Egypt and Libya announce that they are appointing resident ministers in each other's country.
September		The Italians arrest five Libyans in possession of SAM-7 antiaircraft missiles, having found two more missiles in a raid on a house in Ostia. It is claimed that they intended to shoot down an Israeli plane, although Libya denies this.
September	19	Libyan Mirage jets strafe an Italian corvette thirty-three miles off the Libyan coast. Libya apologizes to the Italian government for the incident.
September	24–28	Gadaffi visits Cairo, meets Nasser's widow, and visits Nasser's tomb on the third anniversary of his death. When Sadat fails to send a car for him to attend a meeting, Gadaffi interprets this as a snub and returns home.
September	24	On hearing that the U.S. is threatening a boycott of Libyan oil, Gadaffi tells *Newsweek:* "How can one boycott something that everyone needs?"
October	6	The fourth Arab/Israeli War begins with a surprise attack by Egyptian, Syrian, and Saudi Arabian troops on Yom Kippur, the Jewish Day of Atonement. The Arab troops occupy Israeli forward lines but are soon pushed back.
October	7	Gadaffi tells *Le Monde:* "This war is not mine . . . Assad and Sadat took their decision and implemented their plan without consulting me." Libya later announces that it supports the struggle but "disagrees

		with the strategic plan and the aim of the war."
October	15	Libya denies that its Mirage jets have taken part in the war, but is later reported to have sent two squadrons plus twenty-four self-propelled 155mm guns and one hundred armed personnel carriers. Libya is said to have contributed $500 million to the cost of the Arab invasion.
October	16	Gadaffi congratulates the West on keeping out of the war—and then three days later doubles the price of Libyan Crude to $8.925 per barrel.
October	22	Russian leader Brezhnev sends military observers to the Middle East.
October	27	President Nixon puts all U.S. forces on alert.
November		Gadaffi announces that Islamic Sharia law would become part of Libya's new penal code.
November	15	Gadaffi protests against Egypt's agreement to a Middle East ceasefire.
November	18	Gadaffi pooh-poohs Western theories that Russia stands to gain from the Middle East conflict. "Russia is just another super-power like all the others," he says.
November	23–25	Gadaffi visits Paris for a long meeting with President Pompidou and to take part in a seminar organized by *Le Monde*, at which he again articulates his Third Universal Theory. He is accompanied by the Grand Mufti of Tripoli, Sheikh Alzawi, and Sheikh Sobhi, Secretary General of the Society of the Muslim Call.
December	17	Terrorist attack on Pan Am airliner at Rome airport. Thirty-two people killed; eighteen wounded. Gadaffi is accused of organizing it to encourage Arabs to call off the peace negotiations with Israel that were due to open in Geneva next day.

1974

January	18	Egypt and Israel sign an initial peace treaty at the behest of Henry Kissinger. Libya outraged.
February	11	Libya nationalizes three more American oil companies.
February	13–19	Jalloud visits Paris. France agrees to supply more military equipment. He then spends five days in West Germany.
February —March	18 9	Gadaffi visits Egypt, Saudi Arabia, Pakistan, Somalia, Uganda, Chad, and Niger.
February	25	Jalloud received in private audience by Pope Paul VI.
February	27	Libya signs an oil prospecting agreement with Italian company ENI.
March		Sadat grants Egyptian citizenship to former King Idris.
March	11	Libya signs an agreement with Compagnie Française de Petroles for prospecting, refining, and delivering oil in Europe and Africa.
March	23	Gadaffi denounces the Pope and the work of Catholic missionaries in "trying to impose their domination on the people of Africa."
March	30	Shell nationalized.
April	8	Gadaffi gives up all his political and administrative functions, but remains head of state and Commander in Chief of the Armed Forces.
April	14	Jalloud tells the Lebanese newspaper *Al-Nahar*: "Comrade Muammar is by nature averse to restrictions of formal ceremony."
April	15	Army coup in Niger after drought devastates the countries south of the Sahara. Lt. Gen. Seyni Kountche takes power and develops good relationship with Gadaffi.
April	20	Rebels attack Cairo Military Academy in Heliopolis. Eleven people killed. Egypt blames Libyan influence—which Libya denies.

April	26	Libya signs an oil agreement with Spain.
April	28	Gadaffi tells the newspaper *Assafir* that when he offered to unite Libya with Egypt he offered Libya's oil resources to develop Egypt's agriculture and industry. "They simply want the money without unity. They even want to portray us as though we want to realize unity through bribery. That is how they understand unity."
May	11	President Numeiry of Sudan insists that Libya was behind the attack on the military academy at Heliopolis.
May	12	Jalloud goes to Cairo with a message from Gadaffi. Sadat rejects it.
May	14–21	Jalloud visits Moscow to invite the Russians to invest in Libyan oil production, railway construction, the building of a desalination plant, and a factory making bricks and prefabricated units as part of a $12-billion arms deal. Russia agrees to supply Libya with three thousand tanks, MIG fighters, and antiaircraft missiles.
May	24	Sadat deplores Libya's attitude to Egypt before, during, and after the war with Israel.
May	28	The Egyptian newspaper *Akhbar el Yom* says Libya has spent "enormous sums of money" in trying to assassinate leaders of Egypt and Sudan.
June	3	Libya announces that it will continue its oil embargo against the United States.
June	4	Sadat forbids Egyptian civil servants to visit Libya.
June	18	Libya and Tunisia agree to build a railway between Tripoli and Gabes.
July	26	A bomb explodes inside a nightclub in Alexandria. Egypt blames Libya.
August	6	Sadat accuses Gadaffi of sending hit-men to blow up his summer home at Marsa Matruh.
August	6	The Egyptian Government releases the

text of a letter from Sadat to Libya asking that Gadaffi be removed from power and confirming that Libyan Mirage jets were based on Egyptian airfields during the conflict with Israel and took part in the war.

August	7	The Libyan Revolutionary Command Council rejects Sadat's letter and sends it back.
August	17	Gadaffi goes to Alexandria to meet Sadat. They agree to cease attacking each other.
September	1	On the fifth anniversary of the Libyan revolution, Gadaffi attacks the other Arab states for not continuing the oil embargo against the U.S. The new criminal code is enacted in line with Islamic law, providing for flogging and imprisonment for adulterers and homosexuals.
November	13	The PLO officially recognized by 105 member states of the United Nations. Yasser Arafat says he wants to see a democratic secular state established in Palestine where Christians, Jews, and Muslims can coexist equally.
December		Following its arms deal in May, Libya agrees to a $1.5-billion deal with Russia for the delivery of submarines.

1975

January	3	Germany agrees to export long-range radio equipment to Libya and Syria.
January	6	Libya and Morocco resume diplomatic relations.
January	20	Gadaffi says in a newspaper interview that he expects the U.S. to target Libya in any future military intervention in the Middle East.
April		President Tombalbaye killed in a military coup in Chad. He is replaced by General Felix Malloum.

Here are two official post-cards that were purchased by the author in The Green Book Shop in Tripoli. The photo to the left shows a smiling, relaxed Gadaffi, wearing traditional robes. The carpet hanging in the background suggests that Gadaffi was addressing visitors in one of the traditional Bedouin tents which are left standing specifically for this purpose. The photo below shows Gadaffi out meeting the crowds, greeting them from an open-topped military vehicle, possibly an adapted Land Rover which are widely used in Libya.

Gadaffi praying with two of his six sons. As a practicing Muslim, it would be his duty as a father to teach his sons the prayers that have to be said five times each day (see page 101).

Gadaffi with his parents and other members of his family, photographed in one of their tents. Two of his sons can be seen in the background. Their clothing and the tentwall decorations are traditional (see page 106).

The main square in the center of Tripoli, with Gadaffi's portrait prominently displayed.

Gadaffi's personal bodyguard, apparently drawn from many countries, in fatigues and standing by on the anniversary of the U.S. bombing raid upon his home. The author was invited to this evening of music and speeches, where Gadaffi was expected to make an appearance. An audience of over a thousand waited several hours for him. Gadaffi did not turn up.

Inside the room in which Gadaffi's adopted daughter Hana was killed during the U.S. bombing raid upon his home. The crowd in the foreground is looking at her photographs on the wall; beneath the photographs, but obscured by the people standing there, were toys and children's books that Hana had played with, preserved in two glass cases.

The author meets a total stranger while walking around Gadaffi's home. He asked to have his photograph taken and said that all Libyans were anxious to improve relations with the West. It was a strange encounter, with other Libyans looking on.

The crowd outside Gadaffi's house waiting for their Leader to appear. Note the bearing of the man in the center, and the other to his left wearing traditional white robes and brown hat, and the Western face to the right. The author did not ask for their names; he was standing inches away from Gadaffi's bodyguard, who all had rifles at their feet.

Gadaffi's back door, devastated by bomb-blast, with an armchair and other furniture visible inside.

Gadaffi's home, showing the bomb damage; note the spaciousness of the building and the large first floor verandah. The Libyans walking past give some idea of its dimensions. The building has been left just as it was after the U.S. bombing raid in 1986.

Gadaffi's bed, now encased in glass. Note the control panel on the left-hand side of the bed, by which he presumably controlled his TV and radio. The author was astonished by the illuminated picture at the head of the bed, showing waves beating on rocks in bright color.

Inside Gadaffi's lounge, with the furniture left as it was the night of the bombing and polythene sheeting in the background covering the windows that were devastated by bomb-blast.

The debris from U.S. planes (or plane), shot down over Tripoli during the 1986 bombing raid. Initially, the U.S. denied that any of their planes had been lost. And then later, Tripoli claimed several and the U.S. admitted one loss. The wreckage of one plane was paraded through the streets of Tripoli at the annual September 1st parade to mark the anniversary of the Revolution.

The oil painting glimpsed in the previous photograph. This is how a Libyan artist has portrayed the U.S. raid upon Tripoli, showing the Libyan anti-aircraft rockets zipping across the sky.

Inside the Libyan National Museum in Tripoli, housed within the 14th century Tripoli Castle. These statues came from the Roman city of Sabratha.

Inside the Libyan National Museum—the remains of an early Islamic frieze.

Inside the Libyan National Museum—and inside a Bedouin tent. This tent, with lifesize figures within, demonstrates the simple character of the Bedouins' life, with their tents divided into separate rooms, a wife & child on the left with their cooking pots & utensils, the room divided by a carpet from the one where the husband is sitting. At night, these would become separate rooms for sleeping. Gadaffi's family had lived like this for centuries, and he lived in a tent like this with them until his mid-to-late teens.

Map 1

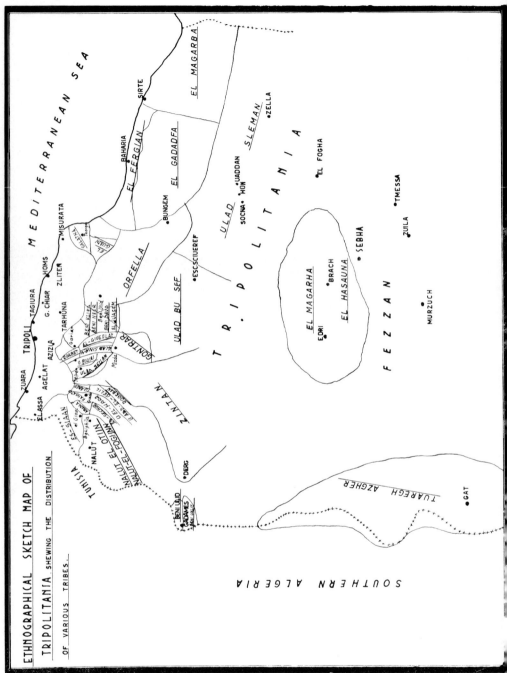

These two maps are from *TRIPOLITANIA: The Land and Its People* by Mohammed Murabet (Progress Press, Malta, 1951)

Map 1. The Ethnographical map gives some idea of the area occupied by Gadaffi's tribe (el Gadadfa) and Jalloud's (el Magarba). Between them they occupied practically the whole of the area under which oil was found.
Map 2. This map is interesting, too, it shows the caravan routes across the el Gadadfa's lands.

Map 2

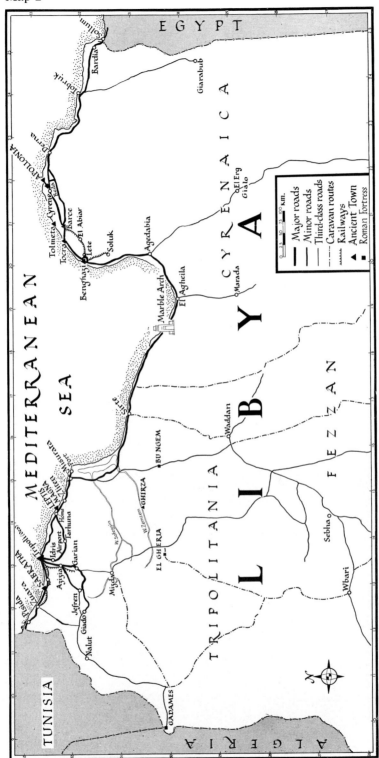

An elderly man begging on the streets of Tripoli. A crowd gathered and protested when the author took this photograph.

A one-man toolshop in the center of Tripoli. People are encouraged to start up in business on their own, and to work with members of their family or on a co-operative basis—but no-one is allowed to employ anyone else.

A street trader in Tripoli Market. Again, self-employment is acceptable—and the street trader could work with other members of his family, but under Gadaffi's laws he would not be permitted to employ anyone.

A crowd demonstrating outside the German Embassy in Tripoli. The demonstrators included a group from Malta, and Americans—from Chicago and Detroit— visiting Tripoli in defiance of the ban imposed by President Reagan. There were approximately thirty Americans in the demonstration. The demonstration itself was directed against the two British diplomats accommodated within the German Embassy, looking after British interests.

شركاء لاأجراء

الجماهيرية العربية الليبية الشعبية الاشتراكية
انتاج منشأة القرطاسية بمصنع المناديل الورقية
هاتف:٨٠٢٩٤٨/٣٥٦٢٤ طرابلس

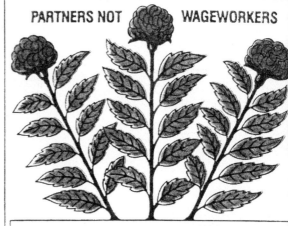

PARTNERS NOT   WAGEWORKERS

SOCIALIST POPULAR LIBYAN
ARAB JAMAHIRIA
PRODUCED BY THE TISSUES FACTORY OF
THE GENERAL STATIONERY ESTABLISHMENT
TEL. 35624 / 802948 TRIPOLI

This is the wrapping paper for a roll of official Government issue toilet paper, complete with pretty flowers, obligatory slogan, and the maker's imprint.

The Libyans are a very matter-of-fact people. They do not choose anything but functional names for their shops and factories. The supermarkets are called Supermarket No. 1 or Supermarket No. 2.

Likewise, the tissues are produced by The Tissues Factory and this is part of The General Stationery Establishment.

April	12	Sadat tells the Kuwaiti newspaper *Al-Siyasah* that Gadaffi is "one hundred percent mad," adding that Gadaffi is trying to make Egypt break its ties with the other Arab oil states.
April	16	The Libyan Revolutionary Command Council threatens to break off diplomatic relations with Egypt if Sadat does not stop his attacks upon Gadaffi. Libya expels 265 Egyptian workers. There are complaints that an Egyptian died after ill treatment by Libyan police.
April	30	Egypt accuses Libya of hiring assassins to murder leading Egyptian journalists Ihsan Abdel Qaddus and Ali and Mustafa Amin. The Libyans deny this and accuse the Egyptians of being engaged in a conspiracy with the U.S. against Libya.
June		The publication of Philip Agee's book *Inside the Company: CIA Diary* (Stonehill Publishing Co.) is taken as proof that the CIA is engaged in conspiracies against many governments that sympathize with Libya. Agee documents CIA plots to assassinate heads of state or destablize governments in Iran, Sudan, Syria, Guatemala, Ecuador, Guyana, Zaire, Ghana, Greece, Chile, Cuba, and Indonesia. Enormous harm is done to the standing of the U.S. in the Middle East.
July/August		Another plot to unseat or assassinate Gadaffi uncovered in Libya, this time led by one of his oldest friends, Omar el Meheishi, and Bashir Hawadi, both former members of the Revolutionary Command Council. Omar el Meheishi flees to Egypt. One hundred officers arrested.
September	1	Egypt and Israel sign a formal peace treaty. There is no comment from Gadaffi; this may be because Sadat warned Gadaffi of Omar el Meheishi's attempted coup.

September	Gadaffi announces a purge of the army and followers of el Meheishi. Another two hundred officers arrested.
September	Some time during this period (the date is not known), Gadaffi recruits two former CIA operatives, Frank Terpil and Edwin Wilson, who provide him with intelligence reports on the plots against him; equip him with computers, cryptographic equipment, and other electronic systems, and also begin recruiting former Green Berets who had served in Vietnam. The full scale of this exercise is never known, but Gadaffi soon has a corps of American merceneries.
December	Sheikh Ahmed Zaki Yamania, the Saudi Arabian oil minister and ten other Arab oil ministers are kidnapped at the OPEC meeting in Vienna and taken to Algiers where they are later released. Reports that this was organized by "Carlos the Jackal," a Venezuelan free-lance terrorist, with Gadaffi's backing—which Gadaffi denies to this day.
1976	
January	First meeting of Libya's General People's Congress, comprising three members/delegates from each of the 187 People's Assemblies.
January	President Pompidou approves the sale of one hundred Mirage jet fighters to Libya; this causes outrage in the United States, where there are public protests against Pompidou during his visit in February.
January	Student riots at Gar Younis University, Benghazi. Some reports say nine students died. This is denied by Gadaffi.
February	The Vatican sends representatives to a Muslim Christian Seminar in Tripoli after Gadaffi calls for dialogue among Christians, Muslims, and Jews.

February		Libya buys five Leopard tanks from West Germany.
March		Libya expels 6,387 Tunisian workers, claiming they have come into the country without work permits.
March	6	In Rome, Italian police seize three Libyans and accuse them of planning to hijack an airliner traveling from Rome to Cairo to kidnap Abdel Moneim al Hony, said to be a member of Omar el Meheishi's group.
March	8	Egyptian police capture seven Libyan commandos who are trying to seize Omar el Meheishi and take him back to Tripoli.
March	12	In an interview with the Egyptian newspaper *Al Ahram*, el Meheishi denies that he is still plotting against Gadaffi, whom he describes as a "dangerous psychopath."
March	20	The Egyptians capture another twenty Libyan commandos who are said to be trying to kidnap el Meheishi and al Hony.
March	21	The Tunisians arrest three members of Libyan intelligence and accuse them of trying to murder President Bourguiba. Tunis and Libya break off diplomatic relations.
April	7	Student riots in Tripoli.
April	28	Amnesty International claims that eight hundred students have been arrested.
July	1	Libya's senior diplomat Milhoud Seddik Ramadan ordered out of Egypt and accused of subversion.
July	2	Attempted coup in Sudan. Libya blamed.
July	6	Sudan breaks off diplomatic relations with Libya and cancels all air links, having complained to the United Nations and the Arab League that Libya and the USSR were behind the attempted coup.
November		Imelda Marcos visits Tripoli to persuade Gadaffi to cease funding Muslim rebels in the southern provinces of the Phillipines. The rebel leader Nur Misuari was living in Tripoli.

December	1	Libya acquires a ten percent share in the Italian car manufacturers Fiat for $415 million. This is later increased to around fifteen percent.
		A military court begins the trial of seventy-five officers accused of supporting el Meheishi's attempted coup.
	23	The Muslim rebels in the Phillipines agree to a ceasefire. Gadaffi invites both sides to peace talks in Tripoli. President Marcos agrees the southern provinces should have their own assembly and regional courts.
	25	The military court sentences twenty-five of the officers to death.

1977

January	4	President Marcos now says that his proposals will be put to a referendum. This is rejected by the rebels.
February	5	Marcos grants an amnesty to the rebels.
February	7	
—March	3	Negotiations between the rebels and the Phillipines government held in Tripoli. The proposals from President Marcos are rejected in the referendum. The rebels then break down into factions. Gadaffi loses interest.
March	2	Gadaffi proclaims that Libya is to be known in future as the Socialist People's Libyan Arab Jamahariya (the last word being the Arab word for Republic).
		Egyptian authorities arrest eight people accused of planning to disrupt the Afro-Asian Conference in Cairo. Seven of them are later executed.
April	2	Gadaffi authorizes the execution of twenty-two of the army officers convicted of being involved in the el Meheishi attempted coup.
April	7	The army officers are executed. Another

four civilians are also executed. This is the first time that Gadaffi has shown such severity, and there is widespread unrest.

April   10   Public demonstrations in Benghazi and Alexandria with Libyans and Egyptians accusing each other. The Egyptian government claims that the Libyan government planned the demonstrations to divert attention from the civil unrest over the executions.

May/July   Growing hostility between Egypt and Libya, with Egypt offering asylum to critics of the Gadaffi regime. There are many arrests in both countries.

Gadaffi puts his economic theories into practice. It is decreed that every house in Libya belongs to the family that lives in it. No one may own more than one property. All private renting prohibited.

July   Libya invades Chad with a force of four thousand troops. The Muslim tribes in the north back Libya. Egypt and Sudan both say they support the Chad government—and Gadaffi describes this as a declaration of war.

July   16–25   Libya at war with Egypt. This is sometimes referred to as the Four Day War, although fighting continued for nine. The war began with skirmishes in the Egyptian desert and developed into a major conflict with desert tank battles and jet fighters. Sadat ordered a ceasefire.

"This is going to be no ordinary revolution"

G adaffi's radio announcement gave the outside world its first news of the coup. His message was picked up by a BBC listening station in Cyprus and relayed to London and Washington. When the British and U.S. governments, the Foreign Office, and the State Department, contacted their embassies in Tripoli nobody there knew what had happened. Gadaffi was playing clever. The revolution was being waged anonymously ... in the name of the People.

Yes, the People. Always the People.

Whenever the Free Unionist Officers issued any announcement, it was stressed that they were acting on behalf of the People. When Gadaffi spoke at Sebha later that month, he invoked the name of the people seventy-seven times in one none-too-lengthy speech.

In that first radio statement, Gadaffi addressed himself directly to his audience—

In the name of God, the Compassionate, the Merciful, O Great People of Libya—in response to your own will, fulfilling your most heartfelt wishes, answering your incessant demands for change and regeneration and your longing to strive toward these ends; listening to your encitement to rebel, your armed forces have undertaken the overthrow of the reactionary, decadent, and

166

corrupt regime, the stench of which has sickened and horrified us all.

With a single blow your heroic army has toppled these idols and has destroyed their images. By a single stroke it has lightened the long dark night in which the Turkish domination was followed first by Italian rule, then by this reactionary and decadent regime, which was no more than a hotbed of extortion, faction, treachery, and treason.

From this day forward, Libya is a free self-governing republic. She will adopt the name of the Libyan Arab Republic and will, by the grace of God, begin her task. She will advance on the road to freedom, the path of unity and social justice, guaranteeing equality to all her citizens and throwing wide in front of them the gates of honest employment, where injustice and exploitation will be banished, where no one will count himself master or servant, and where all will be free, brothers within a society in which, with God's help, prosperity and equality will be seen to rule us all.

Give us your hands. Open up your hearts to us. Forget past misfortunes, and, as one people, prepare to face the enemies of Islam, the enemies of humanity, those who have burned our sanctuaries and mocked at our honor. Thus shall we rebuild our glory, we shall resurrect our heritage, we shall avenge our wounded dignity, and restore the rights which have been wrested from us.

You who have witnessed the sacred struggle of our hero, Omar el Mukhtar, for Libya, Arabism and Islam. . . . You who have fought at the side of Ahmed el Sherif for a true ideal; you, sons of the desert and of our ancient cities, of our green countryside, and of our lovely villages—onward! For we have work to do. And the hour is come.

And then addressing himself to the fears of the British and American governments with their large deployments of soldiers, airmen, and weaponry, and to the Italian settlers who represented such a large part of Libya's commercial establishment, Gadaffi continued:

On this occasion I have pleasure in assuring all our foreign friends that they need have no fears either for their property or for their safety. They are under the protection of our armed forces. And I would add, moreover, that our enterprise is in no sense directed against any state whatever, nor against the international agreements or recognized international law. This is purely an internal affair.

It was a speech of considerable cunning, all the more impressive for being made on the spur of the moment. Gadaffi found himself in the radio station without a script, faced by a microphone and announcers who were clearly terrified by the situation in which they found themselves, so distressed that they kept putting on the wrong music.

Diplomatically, the Free Unionist Officers showed similar adroitness, announcing their support for Colonel Nasser in Egypt and their wish to develop good relations with their Arab brothers in Syria, Sudan, and Iraq. This wrong-footed the nations of Western Europe and the United States, who had been anxious to improve relations with the Arabs since the Six Day War left the Suez Canal closed and its future thus under Egyptian control. The last thing the Western Allies wanted was a continuing vacuum in the Middle East, with Russia replacing them as dominant power in the region.

At five o'clock on the morning of the coup, Peter Wakefield, who had been up most of the night sending messages to the Foreign Office in London, walked back through the deserted streets of Benghazi to his home. Turning a corner, he met a group of Free Unionist Officers wearing army fatigues. They were as surprised to see him as he was to see them, and they invited him to accompany them to the radio station. There he was introduced to a "very dapper" young man wearing full army uniform. This was Gadaffi who, says Wakefield, "spoke with remarkable authority"—though he refused to say who the Free Unionist Officers were or identify himself as their leader. Gadaffi insisted that they were acting collectively on behalf of the People and that all decisions would be made by their Central Committee. Wakefield duly telegraphed this information back to London, although he did not know who he had been speaking to.

Initially Britain and the U.S. were reluctant to acknowledge the new regime, not knowing who they were, what they stood for, or whether they were in control of the country ... but Egypt swiftly announced its recognition, followed by Iraq, Syria, Sudan, and the USSR, and news began to filter out that the Free Unionist Officers were all young Libyans, mainly trained in Britain and the United States, committed to democracy and maintaining good relations with Western governments and the oil companies. They did not have to wait long for recognition after that.

King Idris was now on the Turkish coast, holidaying near Marmara with Queen Fatima. When told early on the morning of September 1 that the coup had been led by a group of unnamed and apparently junior army officers, he dismissed it as "a trifling affair" and predicted that he would soon return home in triumph.

The King's confidence was based on three false assumptions. He thought that after three generations of religious leadership by the Sanusi, he could rely upon the Bedouin tribesmen in the east of Libya, and he believed the Cyrenaica Defense Force would remain loyal, having always treated this mobile desert army as though it were his own private corps, paying them high wages, equipping them with helicopters, armored cars and light artillery. Lastly, the King thought he had an ace up his sleeve. Unknown to the Free Unionist Officers, secret clauses had been included in the Anglo-Libyan Friendship Treaty in 1953. This Treaty had been signed shortly after the downfall of the Egyptian monarchy, and Idris, foreseeing a possibility that one day Egypt might seek to annex Libya, sought a written undertaking that in the event of any *external* intervention in his country's affairs Britain would send in troops to defend him, airlifting them in from Malta, Cyprus, West Germany, and Britain. Now was the time for the King to invoke the treaty. Through the Libyan embassy in Ankara, the King asked that his Minister of Palace Affairs, Omar el Shalhi, be given immediate access to the British Foreign Secretary Michael Stewart. This was agreed and el Shalhi promptly departed for London . . . which was when the King's luck began to run out.

Before el Shalhi's plane touched down, members of the Cyrenaica Defense Force were willingly laying down their arms and committing themselves to the Free Unionist Officers. On September 3, the Free Officers took Tobruk. There was no resistance. The only reason they had not seized Tobruk barracks two days earlier was that with so much to do elsewhere, their resources were thinly stretched. When el Shalhi arrived at the Foreign Office in London, he was told that the King no longer had any known support within his country and that, anyway, the 1953 Anglo-Libyan Treaty provided for the British to intervene only if Libya was invaded by a foreign power; it did not require the British to defend the King against his own people.

Something else was worrying the British and U.S. governments. Two weeks before the revolution, Russia began a major naval exercise off Cyrenaica—and at the very moment that the coup was being staged Russia just happened to have ships deployed right along the coast, positioned between the Western bases in Libya and the British bases in Cyprus, blocking any potential movement by the Western powers. Was this just a coincidence? Or had the Russians been given prior warning of the Free Unionist Officers' coup? What would happen if Britain intervened on behalf of the King? Was Russia there at Egypt's invitation?

The probable explanation is that the senior officers' coup, the one that would have been led by the el Shalhi brothers, was all set for September 4—the day after they had hoped to neutralize the junior ranks by sending eighty junior officers out of the country, to begin overseas courses. (It should be remembered that the total strength of the army was about five thousand men, so the eighty junior officers represented a major part of the lower command structure.) By bringing his own plans forward to September 1, Gadaffi preempted them, more by good luck than good management, for he was not to know that the el Shalhis had already been in touch with the Russians and the Egyptians. Neither could intervene once a new de facto government had taken charge. Nor could the West.

But who were the Free Unionist Officers?

By September 5, the revolution was a fait accompli. That day the London *Daily Express* carried a sad interview with the deposed King, who agreed that he had wanted to abdicate five years earlier, and had met his Prime Minister and the presidents of both Houses of Parliament on August 4 to set his abdication in train.

"I cabled the two presidents saying ... that I would give them a formal declaration that I would stand down and leave my crown to Prince Hassan. They replied, 'Wait until your return' ... I agreed to do this, but said if they continued to refuse my abdication, then I would go away." Idris said that he had never really wanted to be King anyway, but accepted the throne "because of my feelings for Libya and for the Libyan people."

That same day the Crown Prince, Hassan al Rida, who was still in Libya, renounced all claim to the throne and gave his full support to the Free Unionist Officers, calling upon the Libyan people to forego any thought of resistance.

The radio stations in Tripoli and Benghazi were still playing martial and traditional music, with occasional statements from the Free Unionist Officers, asserting their belief in Islam, their confidence in Colonel Nasser as Leader of the Arab world, and their faith in three principles—liberty, unity, and socialism. These are words that have numerous meanings to different people, and in his subsequent speeches Gadaffi was careful to spell out precisely what these words intended:

By Liberty, we mean that individual and national liberty which shall eliminate poverty, colonialism, and the presence on our soil of foreign troops and foreign bases.

By Unity, we mean the unity of all the Arab peoples, be this in the form of a single great Arab government or of a federation of small governments. All will depend on circumstances.

By Socialism, we mean above all an Islamic socialism. We are a Muslim nation. We shall therefore respect, as bidden in the Koran, the principle of private property, even of hereditary property, but the nation's capital will be encouraged, in order to help the country's development.

To those who cared to listen with a sympathetic ear, this sounded more like the *liberté, egalité, fraternité* of the French Revolution than anything previously espoused in the Arab world, and Gadaffi was to say repeatedly over the coming months that, "This is going to be no ordinary revolution, with one dictatorial form of government taking over from another."

In Cairo, Colonel Nasser wondered what on earth to make of this anonymous group who had taken control in a neighboring oil-rich state, proclaiming faith in *him* and Arab brotherhood. Who were they? Where did they come from? What did they want? Why were they so pro-Egyptian? Would they survive?

On receiving a message from the Free Unionist Officers, via the Egyptian consulate in Benghazi, Nasser asked his close personal friend Muhammad Haykal, editor of the Egyptian daily newspaper *Al-Ahram*, to fly to Benghazi to meet the leaders of the new regime. A military plane was made available and Haykal left accompanied by an expert in military intelligence and a photographer. When he alighted at Bennina, Benghazi's airport, Mustafa el Kharrubi stepped forward to embrace him, crying with emotion.

"Where is Abdul Aziz el Shalhi?" asked Haykal, clearly believing that the el Shalhis had taken power.

"In prison," said el Kharrubi.

"Who are you?"

"I am one of the Free Unionist Officers," said el Kharrubi as they prepared to drive to the Egyptian consulate. "You will see our leader tonight. He is a sincere man. You can't imagine how pure he is."

At 2 A.M., an excited and unshaven Gadaffi walked into the building, looking even younger than his age. Haykal was astounded at the youth of them all, especially Gadaffi, who was still only twenty-seven years old, and listened with growing amazement as Gadaffi insisted that the revolution had been staged to unite the Arab world, and that they were willing to commit Libya's resources in the fight against Israel to avenge the Arab defeat in the Six Day War. Gadaffi told him how the Free Unionist Officers had formed their first unit at Sebha, and then others through each year at the Benghazi University and the military academy, developing both a military and a civilian wing.

"We have hundreds of miles of Mediterranean coastline," said Gadaffi. "We have the airfields. We have the money. We have everything. Tell President Nasser we made this revolution for him. He can take everything of ours and add it to the rest of the Arab world's resources to be used for battle.... We do not want to rule Libya. All we have done is our duty as Arab nationalists. Now it is for President Nasser to take over himself and guide Libya from the reactionary camp, where it was, to the progressive camp, where it should be."

Haykal advised caution, warning that moves to unite the Arab nations might have to wait until after the dispute with Israel had been resolved. While he talked the photographer took as many photographs as he could of Gadaffi and the Free Officers. That night, Haykal flew back to Cairo and went to see Nasser, who wanted the photographs developed immediately so that he might see for himself what Gadaffi looked like. He listened carefully while Haykal relayed Gadaffi's account of the Free Officers' history at Sebha, Misurata, and the military academy, how they had chosen to go into the army to prepare for a revolution, and were committed to Liberty, Unity, and Socialism, all with an Islamic emphasis, and wished to see the U.S. and Britain withdraw, and an end to Western imperialism.... It all sounded so familiar, like the student revolutionaries who had taken to the streets in Paris, London, Berlin, and some American cities, either demanding that the U.S. withdraw from Vietnam, an end to nuclear testing, or the end of colonialism.

"Are they really against us?" asked Nasser, a wary politician, doubting what he heard and rarely willing to take anything at face value.

"No, no, no," said Haykal, assuring him that the problem was far worse than that. "They are shockingly innocent," he said. "Scandalously pure."

And so indeed they were.

For Britain and America, as much as for the Egyptians, Mohammad Haykal's exclusive insight—revealed in the September 12 issue of *Al-Ahrem*—was equally daunting. No matter where one goes in the world, politicians are much the same. They talk the same language, employing the same gifts of evasion, half-truth, and compromise, saying one thing in private and another on camera, dissembling, and invariably leaving their options open . . . but, quite clearly, Gadaffi did not fit into that mold.

Initially he continued to insist that he was but one member of the Revolutionary Command Council, the new name given to his Central Committee. Its precise function was not disclosed; neither was its membership, but its members moved into the Bab Aziziya barracks in Tripoli and began ruling the country from there, living communally, each having a small private room, furnished like a monk's cell, with a bed, a desk, and little ornamentation apart from, in Gadaffi's case, a personal radio.

One of the Command Council's first decisions was to appoint Gadaffi a colonel, for they could hardly allow the country to be led by a sublieutenant; even revolutionaries are conscious of rank. Why a colonel? They did not say—but Nasser was a colonel, the colonels had seized power in Greece, and it was usually colonels who started Middle East coups. However, despite his sudden change in status— which was unexplained at the time—Gadaffi was careful not to create any impression that he was leading the country.

On September 8, having released Dr. Mahmud Sulaiman Maghribi from prison, the Revolutionary Command Council invited him to become Prime Minister, constructing his own cabinet or council of ministers. Maghribi had the right credentials to represent the Free Unionist Officers and also reassure the West. Born in Haifa to Libyan parents, he left Palestine as a refugee in 1948, was educated in Damascus, became a teacher and lawyer, eventually moving to the United States where he studied political science, economics, and law. Maghribi worked in the oil industry, advising Esso on petroleum law, and then returned to Libya, leading the oilfield workers in the oil embargo during the Six Day War. For that offense, he was jailed for five years and stripped of his citizenship by the King.

Maghribi's Cabinet was also comforting to the British and American governments, worried for the safety of their bases. Maghribi gave himself the finance, agriculture, and agricultural reform portfolios, inviting Salah Masoud Bousair to become Minister of Unity and Foreign Affairs. Bousair was strongly pro-Palestinian and opposed the British and U.S. treaties, but the West could live with that for he was a former Member of Parliament and committed democrat. The Minister of petroleum Anis Shiliemi was also recently released from jail, and the Minister of Education Mustapha ben Amer newly returned from exile, after running afoul of the King.

As they ran through the ministers' names, researching their backgrounds, Western intelligence officers could see that the new Cabinet was radical, but what did one expect after a revolution? On the other hand, its members seemed respectable, well-qualified, not overly militaristic, with only two ministers coming from an army background. Colonels Adam Hawaz and Musa Ahmed had supported the Free Unionist Officers' coup and were now being rewarded. To the West, this seemed a smooth transition of power and as Britain and the U.S. had already agreed to vacate their bases when the treaties expired, the demands of the new regime could be met without any loss of face.

The outside world still knew little of the revolution. Oil continued to flow. More and more countries were recognizing the new regime. Ministers were taking up their posts. There had been that one curious announcement that a Lieutenant Gadaffi was being promoted to colonel, but no signs of any resistance to the new regime or of forces rallying behind the Sanusi contenders, for Gadaffi had had another extraordinary stroke of luck.

The timing of his coup had been dictated solely by the turn of events in Libya, but it coincided not only with the presence of the Russian fleet in the Mediterranean—but also the absence of the world's press. Tripoli seldom attracted much attention in the European or American press, and those correspondents who might have been there had all been switched to Cairo, where President Nasser was holding an Arab summit. With the Suez Canal blocked and frequent skirmishes along its banks between the Israelis and Egyptians, the Arab leaders were gathered together, discussing whether or when to launch a fresh assault upon Israel.

One of the first Western journalists to arrive in Libya after the coup was John Cooley of the *Christian Science Monitor*, who entered via Tunis, where he spent a week trying to arrange a visa. The U.S. Embassy in Tripoli was barely functioning, unable to help with visas until it knew who was in charge of the new government, and so it was not until September 12 that Cooley was finally able to land in Tripoli, where he teamed up with Joe Morris, Middle East correspondent of the *Los Angeles Times*. Together they went to see the new Prime Minister, who assured them (as he had already told the oil companies) that life would continue as normal. They believed him.

Next day, Cooley went to the Foreign Ministry where Bousair was chatting to a group of dignitaries all dressed in white Arab robes (the *burnous*) with red caps (the *tarboosh*). An officer stood alone on a balcony just outside the door, dressed in khaki, wearing no insignia other than gold braid on his cap. It was Gadaffi. When they asked him who he was, Gadaffi replied in English, "Just one of the Revolutionary Command Council," adding, "None of us are giving interviews right now."

"Obviously, your group believes in collective leadership," said Morris.

"Just like the Algerians," replied Gadaffi. "You know the Algerians, the Algerian revolution? Like them, we are against the cult of personality."

Cooley told him that ten years earlier he had reported the campaign for Algeria's independence from the French, a conflict believed to have cost over a million lives. More might have died but for de Gaulle's decision to cut through the logjam and allow the Algerians to go their own way.

"Yes," said Gadaffi. "General de Gaulle was a great man, but did you meet Ben Bella and the Algerian leaders? We are like the Algerians. We are not after publicity. Maybe you will know our names later, but not now. . . . Now, if you will excuse me, we have some work to discuss here."

Unwittingly, Cooley and Morris had become the first Western

journalists to interview the new Libyan strongman, although it was
to be some time yet before they, or anyone else outside the Free
Unionist Officers' entourage, realized that this was Gadaffi's chosen
role, with his direction clearly defined.

Out in the Sirte Desert, still tending his flock, living in his goatskin tent, Mohammad Abdel Salam ben Hamed ben Mohammad
Gadaffi was also following these unfolding events with a sense of
disbelief. On the day of the revolution he was in Benghazi, "by
pure chance, of course, for I knew absolutely nothing of my son's
plans," he told Mirella Bianco.

> None of us knew anything about it, except one of his cousins,
> who was in the police and was a party to the plot.... We all
> knew that Muammar was passionately interested in politics—and
> what trouble this caused him when he was a student. We knew
> of his great admiration for Nasser and Ben Bella, but we knew
> no more....
> I went to Benghazi to see him and I was staying at the house
> of one of my nephews. We had our meal and waited; Muammar
> did not come. Next day it was just the same, and the day after,
> too. I began to be worried, for Muammar is a dutiful son and this
> was quite unlike him. Then one fine morning I heard shooting all
> around. So I went down the road with my nephew, and turned
> toward the sea. I could see no ship firing any guns. I looked up
> at the sky. There were no aircraft, no bombs. So the shooting
> was within the city. I turned happily to my nephew and said,
> "Muammar is behind all this, I'll be bound.

Within five months, Gadaffi was acknowledged as Libya's leader,
putting down an attempt by a group of more senior army officers
to take over the government, and becoming Prime Minister, but
initially, while it was still necessary to reassure the West that their
oil supplies were secure, he beavered away in the background,
based in the Bab Aziziya barracks with Jalloud and other members
of the revolutionary high command.

To an inexperienced eye, the new regime looked a shambles.
There was a government in situ—and this newly appointed colonel,
who was not a member of it, presiding over the Command Council,
touring the country as the spokesman for the revolution, giving
speeches, appearing on television and radio, explaining their aims,

setting the pace for social reform within Libya, and liaising with foreign powers without. His intellectual tone became clearer in a speech at Benghazi on September 16, commemorating the martyrdom of Omar el Mukhtar thirty-eight years earlier.

Gadaffi began with a warning that this was no conventional revolution, the mere replacement of one regime by another, and continued:

> The revolution does not claim that its leadership is the monopoly of the Revolutionary Command Council or its ministers. Government must revert to the people just as sovereignty must, and the final decisions. I hand over to the people the responsibility of governing. I hand over to the people responsibility for the philosophy of the revolution. They must make it part of themselves, with its foundations and its objectives; it is for the man in the street, the student, the peasant, the worker, the small official, and the merchant to work for the revolution. For should we announce that all is already achieved we should be liars; should we ask you to stay at home and promise you to realize our aims on our own, we should be deceiving you. On the contrary, what we do say to you is this: nothing can be achieved except by you, by your labor, your sweat, and your struggle.
>
> The revolution imposes very heavy responsibility upon you, the responsibility for its protection, its continuation, and its consolidation. These things can be achieved only by a day-to-day struggle, otherwise the revolution will remain a mere coup d'etat. What took place on September 1 was something quite different from a military coup; it was at once the logical consequence and the faithful reflection of the turning-point in history which our people are attaining at the present time.
>
> The revolution now demands that you assume responsibility for command and for reconstruction. To you the sacred task is given, the noble work of following and deepening and consolidating, for the revolution must not remain only a fortuitous event, a sort of collective festival.

Speaking on Egyptian Television a month later, Gadaffi referred more specifically to the situation in Libya under the monarchy, asserting that the causes of Revolution were "as much, social, political, and economic as historical"—

> The essential dynamic of the revolution must be sought in the underdevelopment of the Arab world, which has succeeded in

transforming the Arab himself into a backward individual, not even recognizing that he lives in the twentieth century. Libyan society before the revolution was rather similar to Egyptian society prior to July 1952. It was notoriously riddled with corruption, ruled by cliques of all sorts and by the ascendancy of foreign powers over every citizen. It was in the cruel grip of an intellectual and cultural imperialism which crushed our minds and dominated everything including even our own way of writing. One could not even have a visiting card printed unless it was done in bilingual form: Arabic and some foreign language. There is no need to underline the humiliation of all this, and its damage to our pride. And moreover the Libyan citizen did not even receive the minimum living wage necessary to any human being.

Seldom at a loss for words, but always avoiding the dull phraseology of Marxism, Gadaffi accompanied these frequent and often verbose speeches with a constant, driving, physical campaign against the forces, real and imaginary, that he thought might be threatening his revolution. Sometimes his targeting appeared fanatical, but he was, as el Kharrubi told Haykal, a man of total purity—committed to the Koran, eager to see its philosophy triumph over all other faiths.

First, he drove the few hundred remaining Jews out of Libya [others had left at the time of the Italian occupation with more departing for Israel with the foundation of the Jewish state]. He prohibited the sale of all alcoholic drinks, driving into Tripoli himself to close down Bowlerina's nightclub, marching out on to the dance floor with a revolver in his hand and ordering the dancing girls to leave ... maintaining that it was not he who was banning alcohol and *la dolce vita*, but the Koran. Symbolic gestures like these were important to Gadaffi in these early days, for he warned that the revolution was a continuing process that had to maintain its own dynamic. Each day, new targets were found.

Barclays became the first foreign bank to be nationalized, its assets and four local branches acquired by the newly created National Bank of Libya. ... The King's palace was thrown open to the people, and its contents dispersed ... the fancy Mercedes, Daimlers, and Rolls-Royce cars driven by the old regime were abandoned, their chauffeurs discarded. Gadaffi, Man of the People, drove around town alone in a battered Volkswagen, accessible to all. ... One day he drove up to the Tripoli hospital in disguise, saying he felt unwell; he was kept waiting for a long time and then told to come back tomorrow. At that, he revealed himself—and had the hospital staff removed from office. . . . He ordered that English language and Italian street signs and name plates be replaced by signs written only in Arabic . . . and workmen were to strip the ugly, grandiose Cathedral of the Sacred Heart, built by the Italians, removing all symbols of Christ and the Cross. Henceforth, its shell was to become the Gamal Abdel Nasser Mosque.

Most dramatically of all, the Italians were ordered to leave; every single one of them, all remaining thirty thousand to forty thousand men, women, and children. They left solemnly, emptying their family graves and departing with earth-stained coffins and the bones of their dead. More symbolically, perhaps, than even Gadaffi intended, Libya was breaking its chains with the past.

Misreading Gadaffi

By committing himself to neither East nor West, embracing neither conventional Marxism nor market theories, Gadaffi no doubt believed he could preserve Libya's neutrality. He overlooked one truth. World powers think only of their own interests; they have either friends or enemies—and precious little time to spare for nonaligned nations caught in between.

Gadaffi has never been of much importance to either bloc. Their governments do not care for his economic and social theories, disassociate themselves from his views on terrorism, and, insofar as they have any interest in Libya at all, think only of its strategic location, its oil and, in the long term, its gas and other mineral resources (which, ironically, will keep Libya to the fore as an economic force in the Middle East long after the Saudis, the Iraquis, Kuwaitis, and Iranians have exhausted their known oil reserves; Libya has enough natural gas deposits to keep production and exports going at their present levels for at least two and maybe three hundred years). This is said not in criticism, but merely as an acknowledgment of the pragmatism by which nations live. In world politics, little changes. Even revolutions usually mean no more than a new form of government. The fall of the Tsar, seventy years of Communism and its consequent demise barely affected the foreign policy pursued by Russia over the course of two centuries, defending its territorial interests. So it is with other nations in their relationship with Libya. At best, Gadaffi's regime has been a stimulant; at worst, a flea bite ... which is unfortunate, for there is a real possibility that the Libyan revolution was an event of wider significance, although not necessarily the same significance that Gadaffi ascribes to it.

Having taken power through personally directing the revolution, becoming Chairman of the Revolutionary Command Council, Gadaffi went on to assume the formal trappings of government when he succeeded Dr. Mahmud Sulaiman al Maghribi to become Libya's second postrevolutionary Prime Minister. This decision was forced upon him by events. The revolution was threatened. Other forces were emerging to challenge his authority, namely the two senior army officers appointed to the Maghribi Cabinet, Col. Adam Hawaz, Minister of Defense, and Col. Musa Ahmed, Minister of the Interior.

Early in December 1969, just three months after the King's removal, they were accused of "plotting against the state," allegedly with Maghribi himself—although he denied it and was soon released from house arrest. Habib suggests, "Either power went to their heads or they were military opportunists who thought they could imitate army officers in other parts of the world by plotting against their own colleagues. They failed to realize that the RCC was a united group who were in effective control. . . ."

Gadaffi has argued that the CIA were behind this first attempt to remove him, but there is little evidence to support him. Rather, it seems more likely that the senior officers in the army wanted to cooperate with the tribal chiefs and educated Libyans in establishing a more conventionally structured form of government. The freewheeling revolutionaries were beginning to scare them, driving around town in their battered Fiats and Volkswagens, carrying loaded revolvers, closing down bars, and stopping for prayer five times a day.

One has to remember, always, that the Libyan revolution was a piddling affair in itself, affecting just a few people but with thirty billion barrels of oil as its prize. The King's entourage probably numbered fewer than fifty people. His navy and air force each had a complement of fewer than two hundred men, partially because the King was reluctant to put powerful equipment in the hands of anyone who might turn against him. The strength of his army may have reached around five thousand but they were under the control of fifty-four British officers, with few Libyans yet trained for senior command—and, even though he may have underestimated them, the King was aware that the junior officers were listening more to the Voice of the Arabs than to him. True, the King had always been able to rely upon the Cyrenaica Defense Force in the past and maintained a police force twice the size of his army—but Gadaffi knew, as all revolutionary leaders learn from their textbooks (and especially from having studied the writings of Fidel Castro, Che Guevara, and Sun Yat Sen), that the lower ranks are trained to do as they are told, to obey whatever orders a senior officer gives them. Knock out the senior officers, and the infantry invariably lay down arms, raise their hands, and plead, "Please don't shoot!" So it was on the night of the Great September 1 Revolution, as they call it in Libya. There was chaos on the streets of Tripoli. Those with cars drove away from the gunfire as fast as their wheels would carry them. There were many road accidents, with far more people injured running away from the revolution than actually in it. Others took to their heels and ran out into the bush until the shooting stopped.

This is what happens in revolutions, although their leaders tend to say otherwise, always seeking to glamorize the actual events and to dress them up in the robes of a noble cause. Previous sections describe how *they* say the revolution unfolded and the political shape *it* acquired thereafter; but what of the illiterate peasantry who still numbered over ninety percent of the population? What of the wandering Bedouin tribesmen, still encamped in the Sirte Desert, and the impoverished thousands in the back streets of Tripoli, living off alms, and benefitting hardly at all from the oil boom?

These were the People for whom Gadaffi said the revolution was fought, and it needs to be said that he has never let them down. Whatever his other failings, Gadaffi has been a hugely successful social reformer, making hospital treatment, educational choices, and good housing available to all his people, and there is not the slightest evidence that he has ever sought to personally enrich himself, like so many of the African and Arab leaders who have plundered their countries these past two decades. The West is reluctant to acknowledge his achievements, but there are few countries anywhere in the world that have advanced as swiftly as Libya since 1969. Oil would have continued to flow if some other regime had emerged, but it was Gadaffi, aided particularly by Jalloud, who ensured that the benefits went to the People—with the result that none of the attempts to unseat him gained widespread support.

Immediately after the revolution was declared, Gadaffi doubled the minimum wage, *reduced* the wages of all ministers and senior officials (including his own), reduced all rents by between thirty and forty percent, and imposed price controls to prevent inflation. A massive housing program was started, with the help of West German contractors—and every Libyan family was told that a home would be available to them, as of right. This was not state benevolence in the sense that we have seen it in some socialist countries, but a determined drive to distribute the wealth of the state among the People. Gadaffi might proclaim a belief in socialism, but his government pursued a policy that was neither Marxist nor capitalist, but based on Islam. As soon as he was able to, Gadaffi introduced laws prohibiting private renting and anyone owning more than one house. For many years now, anyone traveling on Libyan Arab Airways has been able to read this slogan on his ticket— EVERY HOUSE IN LIBYA BELONGS TO THE FAMILY THAT LIVES IN IT.

Likewise, the Revolutionary Command Council speedily defined its other objectives, issuing a Constitutional Declaration on December 11, 1969 that continued the ban on political parties introduced by King Idris in 1952. "The RCC considered that Libyans had a great task in reconstructing their nation, and therefore had no time for partisanships and petty political intrigues and machinations," wrote Dr. Habib, adding ingenuously, "This view was expressed by George Washington when he warned his nation not to indulge in party politics.*"

The declaration began with a formal statement of aims:

In the name of the Arab people of Libya, who vow to recover their liberty, enjoy the resources of their land, and live in a society where every loyal citizen is entitled to well-being and prosperity;

Who are determined to break all the fetters which restricted their movement and progress, joining the ranks of their Arab brethren throughout the Arab Fatherland in their struggle to liberate every square inch of land desecrated by imperialism and removing the obstacles which impede Arab Unity from the Arabian Gulf to the Atlantic Ocean;

Who believe that peace can be based only upon justice, recog-

---

*A parallel like this may sound odd, but to the politically active Libyans their revolution is every bit as important *to them* as the French Revolution is to the French, or the American Revolution is to the citizens of the United States; they cannot understand why the rest of the world thinks otherwise, or seems to.

nize the significance of the ties binding them with all peoples of the world who struggle against imperialism and realize that the alliance between the reactionaries and imperialism is responsible both for the backwardness suffered by them in spite of their abundant natural wealth and the corruption prevailing in government bureaucracy, and

Who recognize their responsibilities for establishing a national, democratic, progressive and unionist government;

In the name of the popular will as shown by the Armed Forces on September 1, 1969, which overthrew the Monarchy and proclaimed the Libyan Arab Republic; in order to protect and consolidate the Revolution so that it may proceed to realize its targets of Liberty, Socialism, and Unity, we hereby proclaim this Constitution to be the basis for the system of government during the stage of completing the nationalist democratic revolution pending the preparation of a permanent Constitution that would reflect the accomplishments realized by the Revolution and define landmarks on the path lying ahead.

The first part of the constitutional declaration proclaimed that Libya would be a free Arab democratic republic—the Socialist People's Libyan Arab Jamahiriya—that would be part of the Arab Nation with the objective of overall Arab Unity. (The use of the word *Jamahiriya* puzzled the West, and still does. While researching this book I sought the views of a diplomat and, in passing, asked him what *Jamahiriya* meant. He said this was Gadaffi up to his usual silly nonsense, using words that the rest of the world does not understand—so I looked it up in a dictionary and found that *Jamahiriya* is no more than the Arab word for Republic.)

The second part of the declaration stated that Islam would be the state religion, which was not surprising for even then over ninety percent of the Libyan people were practicing Muslims. However, the declaration went on to recognize everyone's right to pursue his own private religious beliefs. It was also announced that Arabic would be Libya's official language, although in all parts of the country English and Italian are widely spoken.

The declaration goes on to recognize the family as the basis of society and all citizens as equal in law. Dr. Habib interprets the declaration as meaning,

Social justice is the objective of the state, it prohibits exploitation, and has as an objective the peaceful dissolution of class differences, and the attainment of a society of prosperity. In the application of socialism, the state shall be inspired by its Arab Islamic heritage, human values, and the circumstances of the Libyan society. . . . The Libyans did not wish to imitate others in establishing their social institutions, but wanted to look at their Arab and Islamic heritage. Thus, although public ownership was encouraged as the basis for the development and progress of society and for the realization of self-sufficiency in production, private nonexploitive ownership is safeguarded. Inheritance is recognized as a right governed by the Sharia (Muslim law). . . . The people are to work together and not fight each other as in some other social systems. All titles are abolished, extradition of political refugees prohibited, and the sanctity of the private house made inviolable against illegal entry or search. . . . Freedom of opinion is guaranteed within the limits of the people's interest and the principles of the revolution. . . . Education and medical care are guaranteed to all citizens. Education is compulsory to the end of the preparatory stage; it is free of charge at all levels, including the university level. Private schools are allowed to operate within Libyan regulations. . . .

If only as a declaration of intent, this went far beyond any assurances given to the People by the King. Already, they were acquiring a status in law that was soon to be enhanced by the provision of housing, schools, medical centers, and hospitals that gave each and every Libyan rights comparable to those enjoyed by the citizens of any European country. The declaration maintained that all Libyans should also participate in the daily life of their society, which they were to defend through voluntarily joining the armed forces. (National Service remains "voluntary"—but expected; all Libyans are brought up within their educational system to believe that it is "an honor" to defend one's country.)

Given that this was the attitude or tone that Gadaffi adopted for the revolution, providing benefits for everyone regardless of wealth or status, it is scarcely surprising that the People rallied behind him. The West has been slow to realize this, repeatedly pouring funds into one counterrevolutionary group after another, notably the National Front for the Salvation of Libya, which works closely with the CIA. The CIA also funded an anti-Gadaffi force based in Chad, [See Chronology, page 187] without understanding that his opponents had no natural following within the state. Gadaffi was shrewd enough to make this a Revolution *for* the People.

Gadaffi ordered the arrest of Prime Minister Maghribi, Defense Minister Colonel Adam el Hawaz, and Interior Minister Colonel Musa Ahmed together with thirty other army officers just four days before the Constitutional Declaration was formally proclaimed. After several days' interrogation, Maghribi was cleared of any collusion in what became known as "the army officers' plot." He returned to office as Prime Minister, briefly, but was then removed again on January 20 when Gadaffi himself became Prime Minister.

The fate of the conspirators was not announced, but it is probable that Gadaffi quietly allowed them (or most of them) to leave the country and go into exile. This was how opponents were treated in the revolution's early days. There were no mass executions of the kind one has seen more recently in Iran. Although Gadaffi permitted some executions after another attempted coup in 1977 (see Chronology) and earned widespread opprobrium between 1980 and 1984 in the West for hunting down his enemies abroad, he has been reluctant to authorize the death penalty. On the rare occasions that Gadaffi has done so, there have been reports of public disapproval and even demonstrations. The Libyans are an easygoing people with little appetite for revenge. Having lost by Gadaffi's estimates up to half their population during the Italian occupation, the Libyans have been in no mood for recrimination since gaining control of their own affairs. Gadaffi has respected that.

On the occasion of this first attempted coup, he created a military tribunal to judge the conspirators; introduced a law "to protect the Libyan Revolution" and went ahead with plans to introduce the new provisional Constitution, allowing himself just one sardonic comment on the attempted countercoup:

The one black spot, it must be said, is this rather náive, personal, and limited attempt which was organized by certain persons and which we deplore for their sake. We deplore it all the more since we ourselves had chosen these men for appointment to important posts, side by side with ourselves, in the service of the Revolution and of our people. These individuals, who, moreover, were not members of the Free Unionist Officers Movement, have taken advantage of their positions to organize an attempt at a coup d'état.

A much more serious attempt to overthrow the new regime came six months later when the Sanusi tried to maneuver themselves back into power, providing funds for Idris's nephew Prince Abdallah Abdel Sanusi to assemble a mercenary army of some five thousand men. The Prince was a charismatic figure, as black as an Ethiopian following an interracial marriage on his mother's side of the family. Naturally enough, he was known popularly as the Black Prince, and his intention was to assemble his private army in Chad, and then join forces with Gadaffi's longstanding opponent in Sebha, Sayf el Nasr, bringing mercenaries into Libya through the Fezzan, following the same route that the French had taken during the Second World War*. It was a logical military plan, for the Black Prince knew the southern Bedouin tribes owed little loyalty to the new regime and might well rally behind the Sanusi banner if convinced that he stood a real chance of winning.

However, somewhere along the line, the Black Prince's security collapsed. One of his supporters must have betrayed him—for when his first advance party of mercenaries landed in Sebha, Gadaffi's men were waiting to escort them off their plane and cart them off to prison. Gadaffi subsequently claimed—and remember, this was in July 1970—that the whole operation had been funded by the CIA, who he said had armed the Black Prince's men with a variety of weapons, including "poisoned daggers." Several of the mercenaries immediately confessed and a show trial was staged in Tripoli with twenty Libyans accused of conspiring against the state,

---

*Chad was part of France's North African empire, and it was the French who worked with the British to draw the boundary lines when the new Libyan state was formed. Their mapwork was clumsy, with the lines drawn across traditional grazing lands, between oases, and over mountains, leaving part of the Muslim population in Libya and part in northern Chad. The Chad Muslims were greatly outnumbered by the Christians in the south. This was to be a source of continual friction, with Gadaffi frequently engaging in wars with the Chad Muslims against the governments in the south (see Chronology). The fact that Chad also became his vulnerable underbelly was recognized by the CIA, who joined the French in sending money, men, and arms to the Christian south. In 1986, I discussed all this at length with two CIA operatives then working in Chad. At that time, so they told me, the CIA contingent in Chad was four-hundred-strong.

including two former Prime Ministers. Once again, there were no executions.

The Black Prince was also implicated in the third attempt to bring down Gadaffi, the bizarre misadventure catalogued by Patrick Seale and Maureen McConville in *The Hilton Assignment* (1973). This time the Black Prince formed a liaison with Omar el Shalhi, who had been living in Geneva since his own plans to seize power with his brother were thwarted.

Omar hatched an audacious plan to storm the main jail in Tripoli, where Abdel Aziz el Shalhi and other senior supporters of the King were all imprisoned together. The jail was code-named the Hilton, and the plan was to land a mercenary corps on the coast, storm the prison, release Abdel Aziz and over a hundred other senior army and police officers, equip them with weapons, and then mount a sudden attack that same night upon the Free Unionist Officers' base at the Bab Aziziyah barracks two miles away. Their exercise would be swift and bloody. No prisoners would be taken. Their aim was to assassinate Gadaffi and all members of his Revolutionary Command Council.

Realizing that they needed skilled military personnel for an exercise of this kind, the plotters sought the assistance of David Stirling, the British war hero who founded the Long Range Desert Group, forerunners of the Special Air Services (SAS). It was a shrewd move. Stirling knew North Africa well, kept in touch with his army comrades, and ran his own private security organization Watchguard, training and equipping private security guards for rich and powerful clients, whether Middle East oil sheikhs or African leaders, with reason to fear for their lives.

This sort of exercise appealed to Stirling. It was daringly simple and, if challenged, he could honestly reply that he was helping the former rulers of a friendly state remove their usurpers. As Seale and McConville say,

> The European mercenaries were wanted for just one night's work. . . . Of course, there were risks, but risks which could be calculated. This was not an open-ended mission whose success or failure depended on uncertain local politics. Instead, it was a short, sharp, in-and-out operation which could be appraised in strictly military terms. It was straightforward; it had the element of surprise; it could be carried out by a small hard-hitting force

of twenty to twenty-five men who, unless things went badly awry, need never take on Gadaffi's army. It had the further advantage that the logistical build-up could take place at the European end, with a minimum of Libyan involvement.

Stirling was left to organize the operation as he thought fit, setting up an office in Montpelier Street in Knightsbridge, London, almost opposite Harrod's, recruiting former SAS officers to lead his invasion team, and deciding upon the best means of transport to get them into Libya—and out again if the operation failed.

As Seale and McConville wrote:

They were looking for men between the ages of twenty-five and forty, tough, self-reliant, former soldiers who could handle all types of small arms and had been trained to kill, preferably men who had seen service in the commandos or the Parachute Regiment, tough enough to have survived it, and unimaginative enough still to be taking orders ... in practice, they were predominantly SAS ... trained to operate on the ground behind enemy lines, to destroy, to create confusion, and collect military intelligence.... This was a job that required hard men, not super fitness.

The men were recruited by word of mouth, which is how mercenaries find employment, and offered a down payment plus five thousand dollars per man when the mission was accomplished. They first met each other at the end of August. Stirling briefed them at Montpelier Street, not saying where they were going or which country they would be invading; only that the whole operation would take two weeks, allowing time for travel, to make their plans, equip themselves, and mount an attack.

As part of these preparations, two members of the team visited Tripoli posing as businessmen to find the best beach to make a landing, and to study the layout of the "Hilton" and its approach roads. They rented an apartment overlooking the prison and studied it carefully by telescope for three days ... but soon their plans began to change. As an ex-army officer and sound Establishment man, Stirling felt honor-bound to check that the British government was not opposed to any attempt to depose or assassinate Gadaffi. They may not have been, but the government was even more anxious not to be publicly identified with any exercise that would affect

Britain's standing with other Middle East governments. Stirling was warned off—and he promptly pulled out, closing down the office in Montpelier Street and paying off the men.

After three postponements, and with another team in charge, "Operation Hilton" was reset for March 1971. As their newly acquired boat *Conquistador III,* a fifteen-year old German coastal patrol boat, was about to cast off from her berth in Trieste "squads of well-armed Italian police and caribinieri poured aboard, arresting the captain and crew and questioning everybody"—and once again the mercenaries had to be paid off. In less than a year, Operation Hilton cost Omar el Shalhi over $1.5 million—and Gadaffi survived every attempt to remove him.

Neither the British nor the American governments would have been sorry to see Gadaffi fall, but ever since the Bay of Pigs they had been reluctant to risk ignominious failure; this project not only carried that risk, but if it went wrong the other Arab states might have felt compelled to publicly support Gadaffi, seeing him portrayed as a victim of Western aggression, or, even worse, Russia could have seized the opportunity to give extra support to the Arabs in their enduring conflict with Israel.

Gadaffi himself was careful not to alienate Western opinion. At the time of his assumption of power, Britain and the United States still had squadrons of fighter aircraft, tanks, armored vehicles, missiles, and a vast array of weaponry deployed in Libya: more than enough to remove him, had they wished. It made sense to avoid any provocation. All Gadaffi had to do was wait, remind them of their promise to go when the leases expired—and wait, while still agreeing to maintain Western oil supplies. It could even be said with apparent sincerity that his policy was evenhanded, for *all* foreign nationals were being ordered out with the express intent of creating a "Libya for the Libyans."

Likewise, the West could hardly object to his plans to use Libya's oil revenues to provide schools, hospitals, and health clinics, to develop home-grown industries, or to release more land for farming. These were laudable aims, and Gadaffi was careful to stress that his country would lean neither toward Russia or to the United States. His policies thus became even more popular with his Arab neighbors.

This position was explained in his discussions with Mirella Bianco, when Gadaffi argued that

> the interests and the strategy of the USSR are for all practical purposes incompatible, or ninety percent incompatible, with those of the Arab nations; and the same can be said about the USA. . . . In the last analysis the struggle between East and West is a matter of extending their respective zones of influence as widely as possible, and we are determined at any price not to fall under the influence of either of these two world powers.
>
> Look what happened during the First World War, when Sherif Hussein signed an agreement aligning himself with the Allies against Turkish imperialism. Once this imperialism was eliminated from his land, another took its place. The same situation was repeated during the Second World War: the only result of our alliances with the British and the Italians was that we found ourselves dominated by Great Britain. We do not want a repetition of this experience.

Gadaffi was no less trenchant in his approach to Russia, arguing that: "There is no reason for us to encourage the introduction of Communist doctrine here at home simply because the Russians sell us material. . . ."

Similarly, Gadaffi has not sought to conceal his reasons for supporting the IRA in Northern Ireland, the ANC in South Africa during the years of apartheid, or the independence movements he has funded in other parts of Africa, South America, and the Caribbean.

In the case of Ireland, he has consistently maintained that Libya's support for the IRA was in response to the IRA's campaign for independence from Britain:

> We are fomenting nothing whatever in Ireland. The troubles which broke out there are directed against England and answer the exact imperatives of an independence movement and a fight for freedom. Therefore, they raise with us essentially a question of principle, since we see ourselves as one of the supporters of world revolution. If we assist the Irish people it is simply because here we see a small people still under the yoke of Great Britain, and fighting to free themselves from it. And it must be remembered that the revolutionaries of the IRA are striking, and striking hard, at a power which has humiliated the Arabs for centuries. . . .

I would remind you that Great Britain persists in her criminal attitude toward the Arab world. . . . Great Britain is first and foremost responsible for the dispersion of the Palestinian people.

Aid to Ireland enables us to kill three birds with one stone. We still support liberation movements; we are showing the whole world that the Arab revolution is passing from the defensive to the attack; we pay Great Britain back in some way, even though minimally, for the harm she has done and continues to do in our countries. . . . The true Islam advocates the protection of all the weak, even if they are not Muslims. Whenever they ask for help they must be given help. Should we limit our protection to Muslims only, we would prove ourselves both fanatics and egoists. Islam is for the protection of everyone. . . .

Arguably the British and American governments, and the intelligence services upon which they rely, misread and also misrepresented Gadaffi from the start, never thinking that a twenty-seven-year-old sublieutenant, less than ten years removed from a Bedouin tent and generations of illiteracy, would master some of the skills of political leadership; perhaps, too, they overestimated his capacity to damage Western interests, believing his rhetoric, but never reading the small print, the minutiae of government that translates power into practice. Gadaffi outmaneuvered them all, and yet—if the quality of their intelligence work had been up to the standard that governments have a right to expect—the West would have known long ago that they were faced not by a fool or a terrorist but a wily political operator with a developed philosophy.

An Emerging Philosophy

In the early years of the revolution, Gadaffi dispensed with his army fatigues and adopted a more stylish, charismatic look. This was never quite as gross as those chosen by those two contemporary, self-appointed military heroes, Field Marshal Idi Amin of Uganda and Emperor Bokassa of the Central African Republic, who pillaged their countries and murdered their opponents, while parading in robes and uniforms trimmed in gold and adorned with medals and decorations.

No, Gadaffi was never that bad—but the fact that he was overdressed, wore highly decorative desert robes one day, tailored Italian jackets another, or took the salute at military parades in full dress army uniform and a breastful of strange and unexplained military decorations tended to give him an image that he did not deserve; it may also explain why the West felt free to make fun of him, rather than listen to what he said. Sometimes he appeared to have walked straight off the set of the Peter Ustinov play, *Romanoff and Juliet.*

It is always possible that his use of imagery was carefully planned, for when traveling abroad, visiting other heads of state, or attending the conferences of the Nonaligned Movement, he would not only travel with a strikingly attractive corps of female bodyguards, dressed to tempt and trained to kill, but also insist that his hosts provide space for his Bedouin tent and grazing for the two goats that both symbolized his origins and provided his daily milk.

These were eccentricities to the dark-suited politicians on the international circuit; dressing, thinking, and speaking with a due sense of propriety—but Gadaffi never pretended to be one of them. He was the man from the desert who had freed his nation from centuries of foreign rule. While Jalloud, his close friend since Sebha and Gadaffi's deputy to this day, was left to browbeat the Western oil companies, setting new prices for crude, upping the royalties and eventually taking the companies into Libyan ownership, Gadaffi continued to be the broad-strokes man, setting the tone, slowly defining a distinct philosophy, a genuine "middle way" between East and West*.

This philosophy is enshrined within *The Green Book* (see next chapter), a document that is meant to mean as much to any Libyan as the Declaration of Independence should to all U.S. citizens. It is Gadaffi's statement of personal philosophy and political belief translated into a program of action. *The Green Book* is part of every Libyan's life; it is studied at school, extracts are broadcast daily, and its slogans surround him as he travels to work or around the community where he lives.

With such an oversell, it is tempting to make fun of *The Green Book* much as cartoonists have Gadaffi's military caps and uniforms, but this would underestimate what Gadaffi is all about; he really has set out to achieve something more enduring than a military coup d'état, and not without some success.

Within days of the revolution, his Revolutionary Command Council began issuing decrees whose impact may have been minor in themselves but whose cumulative effect was to Islamicize the revolution and give it a character all its own. For example, the Libyans did not stop at replacing all their street signs; soon, every publication and every official document had to be printed in Arabic, without any translation—which still causes confusion to travelers who are given forms to fill in written in a language they do not under-

---

*Jalloud, from another Sirte tribe the el Meghara was widely held to have run rings around the Western oilmen, engaging in a subtle display of negotiating poker, unnerving the oilmen by rearranging meetings, holding them at unexpected hours, changing his position, convincing the oilmen in the process that concessions were their only way of making progress. His breakthrough came when Armand Hammer of Occidental Petroleum agreed to pay an extra fifty cents a barrel. After that, the other companies all caved in—and every other oil producer in the Middle East followed suit, securing similar terms.

stand before being allowed into the country. They are a form of entry pass, which has to be completed as one's boat or plane is approaching Libyan territory, and handed over with one's visa and passport.

Perhaps the oddest example of this policy to Western eyes is the sight of a familiar Pepsi Cola can, with the usual artwork in blue and pink, overprinted in Arabic. If anyone bothers to ask, they are told that the drink is KAWTHAR, i.e., the Libyans have a new name for it, the name of a river in heaven mentioned in the Koran. Does this matter? No, of course not—and if you ask for Pepsi Cola, you will still get it, but they have satisfied their own sense of honor by not using an American word. Gadaffi is shrewd enough to realize that these subtle, almost subliminal changes do matter; they are what people absorb each day, almost without noticing it—but it has been the structural changes that have been the real meat of his program.

Having banished the monarchy, removed all foreigners, reduced the influence of the tribal leaders, bumped up the oil revenues, nationalized the oil companies, and seen off the British and Americans and all their armaments, Gadaffi then began attacking the bureaucracy; a popular target in any modern state.

Here, too, his methodology was unorthodox, with the Revolutionary Command Council first ordaining that instead of political parties Libya should effectively become a one-party state, the Arab Socialist Union coming into being as "the popular political organization of the Libyan Arab Republic" (June 11, 1971). Gadaffi then went on to proclaim a "Cultural Revolution" (December 19, 1971), announcing that Libya would help revolutionaries all over the world, and especially those with campaigns directed against Britain and the United States (June 11, 1972), periodically throwing up his hands in protest at the failure of the Libyan people to follow his example, eventually giving up all formal executive and administrative functions (April 8, 1974) as a prelude to handing over power to the people through the formation of People's Committees and the General People's Congress, which came into being in January 1976.

Throughout this five-year period, while preoccupied with writing *The Green Book* and developing its theories, Gadaffi pointed the way his mind was going with a series of pronouncements, press interviews, and appearances on radio and television, that often seemed contradictory, but which, taken together, showed him firmly in control of the revolution, which was now adhering to the

Trotskyist principle that revolution should always be a continuing process—although Gadaffi would be the last to acknowledge any influence from that quarter.

"There are those who do not follow the Revolution," he said tetchily at Sebratha on October 7, 1971.

> If it were only a matter of one, or five, or ten, or twenty individuals, it would be of no consequence. They could be dismissed or sent into retirement. But it's the mentality of hundreds, even thousands of people, which is at issue. People who have many responsibilities and upon whom the Revolutionary Command Council should be able to depend for the carrying out of its decisions.... Nobody is doing anything, except for the sake of remuneration.... Nothing is performed, no mission accomplished, save in exchange for some reward. As a result, all production has edged toward bureaucracy. And bureaucracy has made inroads into hearts and minds. We cannot allow the people of Libya to be slaves to money or a crust of bread, to live in fear of poverty and illness.... There will have to be a real change of heart among Libyans. The revolution of September 1 was only a beginning.

Speaking at the Tripoli Mosque on December 19, Gadaffi returned once again to this argument:

> "The Cultural Revolution has certainly not come to us from China. It has been foreshadowed in Islam for centuries. We must embark upon a spiritual and cultural revolution, a revolution which ... will enable each of us to follow the path of righteousness. This is the true meaning of that verse in the Koran, which says, "Allah does not change a people's lot unless they change what is in their hearts...."

Similarly in interviews with visiting writers, especially those representing magazines published in other Arab countries, Gadaffi returned repeatedly to the themes of his revolution; or, rather, the course that he thought it should take.

Talking to Bassam Freiha, representing the Lebanese daily newspaper *Al-Anwar* (August 2, 1973), Gadaffi said:

We staged the revolution to give freedom to the masses.... Our revolution aimed, from the start, at smashing authority and handing it over to the People.... It is not necessary to have an army to stage a popular revolution or a cultural revolution.... The masses are taking over all the governorates, regions, and directorates to set up People's Committees. No one can crush the popular and mass movements ... when all the masses unite, as happened in the French Revolution, no one can impede or stop them. Hearing of the Fall of the Bastille, the masses marched on to take over the palaces of the princes and feudalists ... nobody could stand in their way or exterminate the revolution.

When he realized that by giving an interview to a foreign newspaper, he could be sure that that country's foreign minister would read his remarks, Gadaffi would seize the opportunity to emphasize Libya's neutrality, its cultural differences, its desire to stand apart from other nations' conflicts, and to avoid being embraced by either Russia or the United States.

After he had fallen out with President Sadat, who repeatedly described Gadaffi as "mad, totally insane," he found that Libya was not consulted when Egypt and Syria declared war on Israel in 1973*. Gadaffi made his position clear in an interview with Eric Rouleau for the French newspaper *Le Monde* (October 1973), knowing full well that whatever he said would be widely reported all over the world.

"This war is not mine," he said.

I have no advice to give. Assad and Sadat took their decision and implemented their plan without my approval and even without consulting ... though our three countries are members of a federal union whose constitution stipulates clearly that decisions on war or peace cannot be taken without a consensus by the three heads of state.... We have basic differences over the plan of war. I formulated a strategic plan for them in the past, but their

---

*Sadat, who could be vituperative, accused Gadaffi of interfering in Egypt's domestic politics, and, later, of attempting to foment a Revolution in Sudan; Gadaffi disputed this, but relations between them steadily deteriorated (see Chronology). Sadat was a pragmatic man and other Arab leaders took this to be a sign of moral weakness. They opposed his negotiations with Israel and the Camp David Agreement made during the Carter presidency. When Sadat was assassinated, hardly any Arab leaders attended his funeral.

respective Chiefs of Staff adopted another plan. I still insist that my plan is better than theirs, even if Egypt and Syria will gain victory over Israel. I can't take part in a war which I regard as a comedy ... [but I] automatically placed our oil and the funds of the Libyan State at their disposal. I don't believe they are in need of men and equipment because they have more than is necessary.

This was a brutal intervention on Gadaffi's part, for he would have known that Israel was the better fighting force; it was—and the Arabs were again overwhelmed by a numerically smaller army.

Gadaffi also took the *Le Monde* interview as an opportunity to rebuke King Hussein of Jordan, King Saud of Saudi Arabia, and the Emir of Kuwait, for being more interested in preserving their thrones than defending the Arab cause; he has seldom concealed his contempt for Hussein, whom he once said should be hanged (see Chronology), and has consistently argued that there is no place in the modern Islamic world for hereditary ruling families: "They are afraid of their peoples as well as the revolution raging at the gates of their palaces.... Their only concern was to mitigate the anger of their peoples. I deeply disagree with Presidents Sadat and Assad...."

The basic objective is not to restore the territories acquired by Israel in 1967 but to liberate Palestine, the whole of Palestine, from Zionist influence. I will not participate in any war unless its objective is the expulsion of the usurpers and the return of the Jews of Europe to the countries whence they came ... as for the Arab Jews, they are our cousins and brothers and will live in our midst as they did in the past.

A month later, with the Arab forces humiliated, sent home across the burning sands of Sinai in bare-stockinged feet, their boots confiscated, Gadaffi returned once again to the context of the Arab dispute with Israel in an interview with Asa'd al Muqaddam for the magazine *Al Usbua Al Arabi*. It was as uncompromising as ever, but showed him viewing the conflict in a broader context with an unspoken respect for Israel's military ability:

The ceasefire, peace, negotiations, withdrawal, the Security Council, America, Russia ... these are temporary solutions and sedatives, but the clash is inevitable as long as the contradictions exist. I mean that two forces or two entities are competing in the region which can accommodate only one entity.

In the Arab region are two nationalities, two entities, two religions, two civilizations, two nations, and two heterogenous histories, neither of which can absorb the other. . . . It is inevitable for the conflict to continue until one of two entities is finished off. Accordingly, the Arabs must be cautious and must not give themselves up to peace and relaxation. . . . Israel knows this fact, and never gives itself up to comfort. . . . It knows that the conflict is that of two entities and can never be ended except by the destruction of either of them. . . .

The conflict between Israel and us is natural and is one of the laws of nature. . . . I don't mean by conflict that we enter into battles in any way and we continue fighting in any manner. Pauses are likely to happen, but the conflict is continuous . . .*

What really bothers me is the fact that America and Russia regard themselves as policemen in the world able to stop the war whenever they please . . . each of them is working for its own interest and not out of sympathy for the Arabs or Israel. . . . Our problem, we the Arabs, is that our breath is short in envisaging the war and its duration.

The war should involve all positions and fields all the year round. Winter will succeed autumn, bringing with it some advantages to the war . . . one, two, three, and four years. . . . We penetrate into the depth of the enemy and the enemy penetrates our depth; we strike his cities and he strikes ours. Let the conflict take its full range and let other parts of the world explode, until we achieve victory.

(Anyone familiar with Gadaffi's speeches will recognize this final rhetoric. It is an unfortunate feature of his public persona that has led many CIA operatives into believing that he is threatening the United States, but, perhaps, it is just rhetoric, which is, after all, his forte.)

---

*Note the ambiguity in what Gadaffi says. It has already been mentioned that Libya quietly trades with Israel, exporting gas and oil and importing tinned foods, which are openly on sale in Libyan supermarkets. My own interpretation of these comments, and of other speeches that Gadaffi has made, is that he privately believes that Israel and the Arab states can coexist, but is not ready to break ranks and would probably prefer either to make no commitment, or to wait until a wider Middle East settlement.

Asked whether he wished to exterminate the Jews, Gadaffi continued:

We differentiate between two categories of Israelis: the Oriental Jews who used to live with the Arabs in peace and to whom no violence will be directed, and those who came after 1948 and who are still coming in great numbers from all directions as vagabonds and mercenaries. They are citizens of other countries and have no right to live in our homeland.... The Oriental Jews were already here, forming a community, a group, or a minority living in peace.... The 1947 partition was established on the basis that this area was sufficient for accommodating the Jews who happened to be there,* and that the other part was sufficient for accommodating the Arabs. We, the Arabs, did not bring anybody from abroad.

On occasions like these, meeting overseas journalists, Gadaffi has also tended to range over Libya's relationships with other countries, showing himself to be well-briefed, broad-thinking, outward-looking, and eager to forge new friendships, especially if by doing this Libya could replace Britain's interest in areas such as Malta. Libya now enjoys exceptional influence in Malta, both diplomatically and commercially**, even though Malta was a British Crown colony from 1814, became independent in 1964, and then a republic within the British Commonwealth in 1974.

The West should not be surprised by this; as long ago as December 1973, Gadaffi was saying this to the Lebanese magazine *Al-*

---

*Again, it should be conceded that Gadaffi is historically correct, although I happen to abhor his unwillingness to acknowledge the wider causes that led to the creation of the state of Israel. However, I discern in all his arguments an unspoken readiness to change ground when the time for a Middle East settlement draws near.

**Much of Libya's international trade now passes through Malta, which has its own banking system, deep sea port, and international airport. This tiny island even has a seat at the United Nations. In recent years, many international companies have set up offices in Malta so that they may deal with Libya without contravening President Reagan's decree. The Libyans have a substantial investment in Malta's banks, and there is constant traffic between Malta and Tripoli with staff of LAFICO (the Libyan Arab Foreign Investment Company) traveling in and out without arousing too many suspicions. There are two small hotels that cater almost exclusively to the Libyans.

Massa of his relationship with the then Maltese Prime Minister Dom Mintoff:

> I was discussing several issues with Mintoff, and the question of unity incidentally cropped up during the discussion. Mintoff was talking about the Arab language and how a great number of the Maltese spoke Arabic, as well as about the Arabic broadcast by Radio Malta. He pointed out that the Maltese were proud of their Phoenician origin and of Malta's role as a camp for the Muslims when they conquered southern Europe and made Malta a bridge for carrying out the conquest.... The conversation was merely an exchange of views, and it synchronized with the accelerated efforts for realizing unity with Egypt or Tunisia, with both of them or with any other Arab state.... Mintoff said during the conversation: "In the long run and if ever the Arab states are united, Malta's affinity with the Arabs is closer than its affinity with any other country."

Another opportunity to develop a relationship with a Middle East state at Britain's expense came in Oman, where the British helped Sultan Qaboos depose his father in 1970 and subsequently put down an insurgency in Dhofar. Once again, Gadaffi displayed his cunning, talking to both sides, sending a delegation to live with the rebels in Dhofar, allowing the rebels to open their own office in Tripoli, while still maintaining a continuing dialogue with Sultan Qaboos.

When the Popular Front for the Liberation of Dhofar first asked for assistance, Gadaffi was reluctant to intervene, thinking they might be Communist. Contrary to many opinions in the West, Gadaffi has always shied away from supporting Communist rebels, preferring always to fund what he describes as "independence movements," i.e., those seeking to take control of their own country after a period of what they perceive to be foreign occupation. Thus in Dhofar, he held back until he was quite sure what he was being asked to support. "A change took place in our point of view," he said in an interview with *Al-Dostoor* (April 1974),

> after a visit to Libya by a member of the movement's leadership who proved to us that the Dhofari people's major concern was to liberate the territory, spread social awareness, and to drive

out the British imperialism which dominates Oman economically, politically, and socially.

In order to have a clear picture about the situation we dispatched some Libyan military personnel to Dhofar, where they lived with the rebels, discovered how the majority of the miserable people live, and touched the determination of the people, who are entrenched with their weapons on the mountains, to struggle.

At that time, in particular, we had direct contact with Qaboos who visited Libya, and with whom I met in Algeria during the nonaligned summit and later at the Islamic summit in Lahore.... We did not conceal our contacts with the rebels, nor from them our contacts with the Sultan.... We told Qaboos about our contacts with the rebels and about the military men we dispatched, and how we were deeply concerned about the Dhofar armed people entrenched in the mountains.... [We told him that] we could not help him if he insisted on holding on to the British. To this, he replied, "How can I do without the British when I am in need of them? If I do that I'll lose my air force."

We said to him, "We can help you by training Omani Arab pilots to replace the British or we are ready to send Libyan pilots to replace them. If we could get rid of the British pilots and replace them with Omanis, we would have made a giant stride that would not run contrary to the Revolution's steps nor impede the achievement of its goals ...

Giving interviews like these, in the grounds surrounding the Bab Aziziyah barracks, where he would talk to visitors either in a symbolic Bedouin tent, by the tennis courts, or out in the open under a mimosa tree, Gadaffi would be at his most revealing, for within the society that he has created there is no one to whom he has to account for his actions. He may deliver a speech to the General People's Congress, or make a show of listening in the audience to what others say, but he is not answerable to a Parliament in the way that a British Prime Minister is. He does not have to secure Senate approval for his budget like a U.S. President, or produce a convincing manifesto to secure the votes of an electorate.

Even when there has been certain evidence that he has supported terrorism, or funded attempts to overthrow other Arab leaders, there has been no constitutional mechanism by which Gadaffi can be held to account. For the Libyan people, this is an obvious weakness in their system. Their leader acts in their name without them knowing what he does. There is another drawback, too. As he has never had to submit himself to the equivalent of a Parliamentary Question Time or the meetings of a Senate Committee, nor even the probings of an ill-tempered press conference, the West has no way of knowing which of the accusations made against him are true or false. Neither can the West be sure which terrorist movements Gadaffi has funded, or how much money they have had, for he is not required to secure approval through any Parliamentary process before allotting funds.

"No one can supervise the Colonel, who controls single-handed the budget of Libya," says his former friend and fellow revolutionary Omar el Meheishi, who was a member of the original Revolutionary Command Council and Libyan Minister of Economics until he sought to lead another countercoup in 1975.*

Gadaffi is a criminally inclined person with an unstable personality who operates on the assumption that he must use evil means internally and abroad to realize illusory and destructive dreams filling his mind. His reign is characterized by criminal insanity, for he has premeditated intentions toward the Libyan people and the Arab people in general which he believes he can only carry through by conspiracy and crime. He believes in crime and terrorism. He uses embassies and diplomatic privileges to help and is now dealing with professional criminals from all over the world. He is a deceiver.

Gadaffi tried to assassinate me eleven times in Tunisia and six times in Egypt. He even recruited the German mafia to kill me. After the OPEC raid when Carlos wanted to land the Austrian plane at Tunis Airport, he intended to bargain the life of one of the oil ministers for mine. But the Tunisians blacked out the airport so that the plane could not land there. It has been proved

---

*This quotation is taken from pp. 128–129 of *The Carlos Complex* by Christopher Dobson and Ronald Payne (1977). It should be noted that el Meheishi is an extremely hostile witness, having led an attempted Revolution that failed. He managed to flee the country and was given asylum by Egypt, which has consistently harbored Gadaffi's enemies. El Meheishi has been responsible for some of the wilder stories about Gadaffi, including the suggestion that Gadaffi fell off a camel as a child, injuring his brain. I find el Meheishi's argument suspect, but it is a point of view that should be included in a book like this—and its source carefully identified.

beyond a shadow of a doubt that Gadaffi participated in the attack on OPEC Ministers and that Carlos is in contact with him.*"

In nearly every other book about Gadaffi, there is a chapter titled "Terror, Inc.," detailing incidents like the OPEC kidnapping; reporting claims that Gadaffi sought to overthrow Colonel Numeiri in the Sudan, funded attempts to assassinate the late King Faisal of Saudi Arabia, President Sadat of Egypt, King Hassan of Morocco, and King Hussein of Jordan; that he gave 20 million pounds to the Black September Movement, who were responsible for the Munich Massacre; financed the murderous campaign of Carlos the Jackal; channeled arms and money to the IRA in Northern Ireland, and gave both arms and shelter to a wide variety of Arab commando groups engaged in hijacking and other acts of "terrorism" to bring pressure on the West in support of the Palestinians. These events are summarized in the Chronology, where one can see whether or not they fall into a pattern.

My own view is that Gadaffi's role in terrorism has been overestimated, although he has done neither himself nor his country any favors with his fiery rhetoric, fierce attacks upon the U.S. and Britain, arguing that he would lead the Arabs in a war against America (which is laughable), and openly supporting over sixty "independence movements" around the world. The totality of all this is almost impossible to summarize, but there is another side to it that has barely been explained.

Gadaffi is not alone in distrusting the West, and when he makes attacks like these (or funds those who might commit atrocities in his name) it is as well to remember that there are millions of Arabs and Africans who believe he is speaking *for* them; they have longed for their own independence; they have been subjugated by foreign powers and despotic kings; they do believe that the West has been far from even-handed in its relations with Israel and Palestine; they are aware that Britain shielded the apartheid regimes in South

---

*It should also be noted that Gadaffi has consistently denied any involvement in the kidnapping of the OPEC Oil Ministers shortly before Christmas 1975. Although the West has always refused to believe him, Gadaffi may well be telling the truth—for it was a Libyan economist Yousef Ismirli who was shot dead while trying to thwart the kidnap, and the Libyan Oil Minister Ezzedin Ali Mabruk was among the group of OPEC delegates seized in the Vienna kidnapping and held hostage.

Africa, and they look askance at much that has been done in the name of Christianity.

The other consistent theme of Gadaffi's leadership, enunciated first on the night of the revolution and proclaimed ever since, is his belief in Arab unity. Frequently he has offered to step down as leader so that Libya might unite with Egypt and Syria, or with Tunisia or Algeria, depending on the circumstances—arguing that there should be one Arab nation between the Atlantic Ocean and the Iranian Gulf.

Some years he has announced a form of union, said when it will happen (see Chronology)—only to see his proposals dissolve in acrimony, with the parties abusing each other.

However, there is a thread running through all this; he compares Arab unity with African struggles for independence, sees the West (or, rather "imperialism") as their common enemy, with Libya able to provide a form of leadership through its willingness to aid an unpopular cause, or assist an armed struggle when others might recoil (for many years, while Nelson Mandela was imprisoned on Robben Island, Gadaffi poured funds into the African National Congress, assisting their campaign against apartheid; the sums have never been disclosed, but almost certainly ran into many millions of dollars, for Gadaffi was one of the first people that Mandela visited on his release from jail).

"Our determination to drive out apartheid is a feeling of truth with ourselves," he said in that same interview with *Al-Dostoor*.

> Therefore, we visualize the situation in a practical manner and integrate words with deeds.... This is up to the Africans themselves if they are serious in liberating their countries and are willing to be trained and wage war against apartheid.... Libya is ready (to help them) at any time.... The call for liberation is a patriotic and national task. The liberation of Africa is inevitable, in order to safeguard the African resources against theft, exploitation, and looting and to restore dignity to the African national who has lost his language, characteristics, and dignity.

Asked whether he intended Libya to become a center for all revolutionaries, with himself their example, Gadaffi continued:

The Libyan Arab Republic . . . is the Mecca of the revolutionaries, [but] no one can consider another man his example unless this man's identity is sacrifice, and the happiness of man is his objective. . . . My aims are outlined in the liberation of every inch of the Arab territories to safeguard Arab nationalism, and every inch of Africa to safeguard Africa and her resources.

For me to explain why I have become an example is something I cannot do. However, anyone who follows the example of the policy of the Libyan Arab Republic can, for (when they believe in what they are doing) they are more capable of expressing their opinions.

In the next chapter, I shall explain how Gadaffi developed this emerging philosophy into written form in *The Green Book*, the personal credo that has since become the foundation of the Libyan state; but how does he see his relationship with other Arabs, especially the younger Arabs who will provide the next generation of leadership, and how does he reconcile his political beliefs with his faith in Islam? He touched upon both these subjects in his interview with *Al-Dostoor*, which showed him able to call upon unexpected depths of thought and intellect, when prompted.

Emphasizing that in Libya, the leaders of the revolution wanted open contact with the people Gadaffi touched upon "the style of rule which we adopted," clearly showing that all the imagery that I have mentioned, the Islamicization, and the use of symbols was consciously planned:

The style . . . could not be an upper sort of style, nor can we rule from behind the veil and live in sea shells. Rather, we should live with the people and directly react with them without intermediaries. We want to hear them and have them hear from us so that our judgment will be sound. . . . It would be good if I could meet with all the people, but we are trying to meet with youth as much as possible, and not necessarily with the Libyan youth, but Arab and world youth. . . . We even try to sit down together on the ground and get to know each other and hear the truth said simply by both sides. I feel that the Arab nation bears a message to the world, and the world nowadays needs such a message.

And then he opened out, quite unexpectedly, revealing himself in a way he rarely does, when the interviewer asked him a question about metaphysics and, whether or not, his theories were so based. "No agreement has been reached among metaphysicians on any one thing," he said,

and so [metaphysics] is an issue that enables one to advance his own ideas. Man studies the world around him to reach a result that leads him to believe in the existence of one power behind all phenomena. This is contrary to what another man may say, that the world we see is run according to certain laws and rules and seems to be a reasonable world.... The heavenly books rightly direct man and allow him to think, choose, study, and deduce freely, to conclude results; otherwise, what is man's role? The Koran and the heavenly books guide Man after informing him that God created the Universe, that it was justly created and is employed for the sake of Man. That is the logic of the start and the end.

Between the two, what does Man do? He has to labor to discover electricity, underground water, magnetism, the atom.... If God said: mix two atoms of hydrogen and one of oxygen to obtain water and directs us to produce things we need for life and development, Man will have no mission at all.... If Islam had been understood from the beginning, it would have been a real scientific, technological revolution. Unfortunately, Islam was understood in a very simple ordinary manner, so simple that when electricity was discovered it was thought to be antireligion. This is a misunderstanding of Islam. Islam says that all things are created in pairs. The verse in the Koran says,

'Praised be he who created pairs of things growing in ground and of themselves as well as things unknown to them'

This is in line with the negative and positive; the northern and southern that we know. Electricity, for example, consists of negative and positive poles.... However, the whole truth lies within the large framework of the Universe. Therefore, there is a certain aim to the Universe and this is what I mean by metaphysics and by what is behind Nature.... Behind all phenomena there is a power, and living things have a purpose to attain. This means that we ought to have a moral obligation.

The Green Book

All children in Libya spend two hours a week studying *The Green Book* as part of their school curriculum. Extracts from *The Green Book* are broadcast every day on television and radio; there are constant lectures and seminars relating to *The Green Book* in colleges and universities, and its slogans are to be seen wherever one goes—on the outer walls of public buildings, on roadside billboards, over the entrance to Tripoli Airport.

Only by going to Libya does one realize how Gadaffi's philosophy pervades every citizen's life. There is even a World Center for Researches and Studies of *The Green Book*, based in Tripoli with a general secretary and permanent staff, which organizes seminars in countries friendly to the Libyan regime. At these gatherings, papers will be presented by maybe thirty or forty lecturers with titles like "The Concept of Property in The Green Book," "The Humanitarian Economics of The Green Book: A Critical Analysis," "The Green Book and the Era of the Masses," "Power, Freedom and The Green Book," "Islam and Universality in the Political Work of Muammar Gadaffi," "The Methodology of The Green Book," "The Concept of the Party in The Green Book," "Women: Democracy and Power" or "Racism and Minorities." Always the titles are heavy and overpowering, without a trace of humor or lightness of touch; the Libyans have yet to realize that one witticism has more impact than a thousand theories.

After such gatherings have been held—in France, Eastern Europe, Columbia, or Venezuela—an account of their proceedings will then be published verbatim in massive volumes of up to eight hundred pages. These are difficult to obtain in the West, but at a bookshop in Malta—owned and run by the Libyans, there are hundreds of them, piled high like cartons of soap powder in a supermarket, always cover-printed in matching shades of green, and covered in dust. The shop assistant expressed astonishment when I wanted to buy some. In Tripoli, there is a bookshop in the airport concourse selling nothing but *The Green Book*, translated into every conceivable language, including some I had never heard of. There are eight salesmen sitting at desks waiting to sell *The Green Book*—but no customers.

Seminars are also arranged through another Libyan organization, the Mathaba, which invites delegates to conferences on *The Green Book* in Libya, produces magazines and newspapers describing the evolution of Libyan society, and assists groups in other countries with similar ideals. Occasionally the Mathaba has been described in the West, and by the CIA, as "a terrorist organization." This may be another Western error of judgment. Having been to Libya, met twenty or thirty people working for the Mathaba and discussed their work with the Libyan Foreign Office, my belief is that they are engaged in something far more pervasive . . . a highly articulate campaign to convince Libya's sympathizers that there is something deeply wrong with Western values.

Britain and America have found it convenient to treat Gadaffi as a lunatic on the questionable grounds that anyone who resorts to what we define as "terrorism" must be mad; there has been hardly any analysis of his life's work, which reveals him to be a far more subtle figure than he usually appears, with a guiding philosophy that is notably nonviolent—though it does challenge many fundamental principles of Western political life.

It was unfortunate for Gadaffi's standing that *The Green Book* followed so closely after Chairman Mao's *Little Red Book*. The Chinese Cultural Revolution was introduced three years before the Libyan revolution, and Gadaffi was undoubtedly influenced by it, partially modeling his career on Mao's in that he set the revolution's intellectual tone and then, like Mao, withdrew from daily participation in Libya's affairs, while remaining head of state, leader of the revolution, and leader of the armed forces.

Gadaffi always insists that *The Green Book* owes more to Islam and the Koran than any other source, and yet who can forget China's millions, marching in rhythmic unison, clasping their Red Book between forefinger and thumb, as they drove the middle classes out of every office, to work in rice fields or on the factory floor. So it was in Libya, to a degree, although *The Green Book* remains more persuasive. It may be naïve in some of its assumptions, but *The Green Book* is genuinely compassionate, and a surprising thesis for a man born of the desert.

The Green Book is concise, usually printed in a pocket-book format, 6½ inches by 4¾ inches, with only 110 pages of printed text, few bearing more than two hundred words, and many much less than that. It is divided into three sections—

Part One	The Solution of the Problem of Democracy—The Authority of the People
Part Two	The Solution of the Economic Problem—Socialism
Part Three	The Social Basis of the Third Universal Theory

These sections were published separately, the first late in 1975; the second early in 1977, and the third in September 1981. As with so many Libyan achievements, *The Green Book* only became known after its slogans began appearing on billboards. It was not formally launched in the way that books are published in the West.

Part One

The first part concentrates on the political structure of Libya, rejecting the usual concepts of parliamentary democracy. Gadaffi argues that all the world's political systems are the product of a struggle for power, either peaceful or armed, between social classes, sects, tribes, or political parties, and that they invariable end with one group exercising power over another "and the defeat of the people, i.e., the defeat of genuine democracy." He suggests that any electoral system that gives power to fifty-one percent of the people is "a false democracy, since forty-nine percent of the electorate is ruled by an instrument of governing they did not vote for, but had imposed upon them. This is dictatorship."

Gadaffi also rejects the concept of parliament, arguing that, "the mere existence of a parliament means the absence of the people" since its members are representing the people and are not the people themselves. Gadaffi goes on to argue that in Western democracies the electoral system separates those who govern from the people they represent—

immediately after winning their votes he himself usurps their sovereignty and acts instead of them. The prevailing traditional democracy endows the member of a parliament with a sacredness and immunity denied to other individual members of the people.

And so Gadaffi argues that people themselves can legitimately challenge such a system, taking power on the premise that there can be NO REPRESENTATION IN LIEU OF THE PEOPLE (one of the slogans that appears in public places in Libya).

Likewise, Gadaffi rejects the form of democracy in which different political parties campaign against each other for the electoral vote, arguing that—

if the parliament emerges from a party as a result of winning an election, it is a parliament of the party and not of the people. It represents the party and not the people, and the executive power assigned by the parliament is that of the winning party and not of the people.... Under such systems the people are victims, fooled and exploited by political bodies. The people stand silently in long queues to cast their votes in the ballot boxes in the same way as they throw other papers into the dustbin.... Thus it becomes clear that REPRESENTATION IS FRAUD [another slogan].

Gadaffi further develops the argument by suggesting that parliamentary democracy only came into being to counterbalance the power of "kings, sultans, and conquerors," and that once they had all been replaced, the leaders of the parliamentary democracies became too powerful themselves—

The most tyrannical dictatorships the world has known have existed under the show of parliaments.

Then he turns his attention to the political parties that operate within a democracy, arguing that they have become "the modern dictatorial instrument of governing"—

The party is not a democratic instrument at all because it is composed of people who have common interests, a common outlook, or a common culture; or who belong to the same locality or have the same belief. They form a party to achieve their ends, impose their outlook.... Democratically, none of these parties should govern the whole people because of the diversity of interests, ideas, temperaments, localities, and beliefs which constitute the people's identity.

And he goes on to ridicule the way parties operate, suggesting that they are driven by a constant need to denigrate their opponents, casting doubts on their rivals' plans even when these are known to be beneficial to society as a whole—

This is a battle which is inevitably waged at the expense of the higher and vital interests of the society.... The interests and programs of the society become victims of the parties' struggle for power. Such struggle is, therefore, politically, socially, and economically destructive to the society, despite the fact that it creates political activity.... It is a defeat for the people, a defeat for democracy.... The party game is a deceitful farce based on a sham form of democracy which has a selfish content based on maneuvers, tricks, and political games. All these emphasize that the party system is a dictatorial, yet modern instrument. The party system is an overt, not a covert, dictatorship. The world has not yet passed beyond it and it is rightly called "the dictatorship of the modern age."

Gadaffi proceeds to draw parallels between party systems and the tribal systems with which he was more familiar:

The society governed by one party is exactly like that which is governed by one tribe or sect.... Only blood-relationship distinguishes a tribe from a party and even at the foundation of a party there may be blood-relationship. There is no difference between party struggles and tribal or sectarian struggles for power ... both of them tread the same path and lead to the same end.

A parallel is also drawn with political systems based on social classes, arguing in each case that a minority view is always lost when decisions are taken by a majority, i.e., "If a class, party, tribe, or sect dominates a society, the whole system becomes a dictatorship." This all leads to his suggestion that a participatory democracy where people are involved in decision-making collectively rather than through choosing members of parliament, senators, or congressmen allows a wider variety of opinions to be heard before decisions are made—

> Under genuine democracy there is no excuse for one class to crush other classes for its own benefit, no excuse for one party to crush other parties for its own interests, no excuse for one tribe to crush other tribes for its own benefit and no excuse for one sect to crush other sects for its own interests.

There is, of course, some truth behind all this. In every Western society, there are groups of people who feel disenfranchised by the political system that operates within their community. Numerically, they are not loud enough to be heard. Arguably Ross Perot's followers believe this in the United States. Certainly in Britain there is a strong feeling that the electoral system is working unfairly because every recent government has been chosen by less than forty percent of the electorate. When Mrs. Thatcher was Prime Minister, her party won power with approximately thirty-four percent of the popular vote—at a time when she commanded the support of little more than half her own party (eventually she lost even that margin and was thrown out of office). These situations occur in a party system where a diversity of parties—a three-way split as happened in the U.S. presidential election in 1992 or the multiparty divisions that are a feature of Italian and German politics—enables the winning candidate to take office without securing the support of a majority of the electorate.

To that extent, Gadaffi's simplistic arguments may fall on fertile ground. Where they go wrong is in his solution—for *The Green Book* goes on to advocate the system of government that Libya now has. Basically the country is governed by 187 Basic Popular Congresses and 46 Municipal People's Congresses, which in turn appoint Popular Committees to implement policy. There are also a further twenty-two hundred Basic People's Committees operating at factory, office, shop, or workplace level. The Congresses have their own secretariats—and are represented at the General People's Congress, which meets annually in Tripoli, and sometimes more frequently, to decide overall policy. The system is not quite as simple as that, for the General People's Congress also appoints its own secretariat and a General People's Committee, whose members, in theory, run the government departments. But, there again, perhaps they don't—for Gadaffi also appoints a cabinet and departmental ministers.

What this means in practice is that Libya, a large country but with a population no greater than that of Chicago, is run by nearly twenty-six hundred committees, who are constantly talking, frequently countermanding each other's decisions—and never quite clear who is responsible for what. This creates a state of constant but thoroughly enjoyable muddle. When I was thrown off a Libyan ship in Valletta harbor, it was because the People's Committee on board—twelve men sitting around two tables, inspecting every passport and visa—decided not to accept the papers issued to me by the People's Committee in Malta at the request of the General People's Congress in Tripoli. They have every right to do this; the Committee at Tripoli Airport frequently refuses entry to people who have been invited into Libya by other People's Committees.

As might be predicted, *The Green Book* has a slogan to cover this situation—NO DEMOCRACY WITHOUT POPULAR CONGRESSES AND COMMITTEES EVERYWHERE—which can also be found posted on buildings and roadsides. Gadaffi asserts in *The Green Book* that by having these committees, while also abolishing all political parties and tribal systems (which he has), "the problem of democracy in the world is finally solved. . . . The people are the instrument of governing, and the problem of democracy in the world is completely solved." I am sure he is also aware that this diffusion of power means that no one can establish a power base in Libya to challenge his authority.

It would be wrong to suppose that because this Third Universal Theory would cause chaos if grafted on to any other Western society, it is necessarily wrong in itself. It may not be in Libya where, uniquely, Gadaffi was creating a new system for a people who had never known anything else, who had not previously enjoyed good health, education, *or* a democratic system—and now had all the time in the world, and as much money as they could ever need, while being told at the same time that it was they who would make all decisions. All I can say, having mixed among them, is that they are an undoubtedly happy people who believe that what they are doing is right for them.

This first section of *The Green Book* concludes that Gadaffi examining the role of law in any society, how society's conduct is supervised, and the responsibility of the press. Although he does not mention the Islamic penal code, the Sharia, in this context, Gadaffi argues—

Encyclopedias of manmade laws derived from manmade constitutions are full of material penalties against man, while traditional law seldom has these penalties. Traditional law imposes moral, not material penalties, that are appropriate to man. Religion embraces and absorbs tradition.... This law shows proper respect to man.

and it is a fact that Gadaffi frequently maintains the Sharia is the basis of Libya's system of justice; this previous paragraph could also be taken to mean that.

However, here again there is a subtlety in Gadaffi's approach to the problems of balancing religious belief against the social requirements of a modern state. Occasionally he will make a speech suggesting that the Sharia needs to be applied more strictly because of the levels of crime that may be prevailing at any one time. Everyone knows what he means; the Sharia provides that a thief may have his right hand amputated at the wrist, the left hand amputated in the event of subsequent thefts, that an adulterer may be stoned to death, a fornicator flogged, and the death penalty applied for a wide variety of crimes.

In some parts of the Islamic world, the Sharia is strictly applied. Anyone who brews home-made beer in Saudi Arabia can expect imprisonment and a severe flogging, up to three hundred lashes (although the sentences tend to be commuted when imposed on Western residents). Public beheadings are staged in the main square of Riyadh after Friday prayers—for murder, drug peddling, crimes of extreme violence, or economic crimes. According to Amnesty, one hundred five people were beheaded in Saudi Arabia in the 1992-93 year, of whom forty-eight were Saudis with the others from Pakistan, Nigeria, Yemen, Sudan, and the Philippines. Of this overall total, fifty-five were sentenced for murder, thirty-eight on drug charges (including one for repeatedly brewing alcohol), six for rape or sodomy, two for adultery, and one for apostasy. Three men in the northwestern town of Hakl, who raped and killed a Saudi woman and also murdered her children, were executed and their headless bodies then crucified. In another Gulf state in March 1993, two men were sentenced to have both an arm and a leg amputated after being convicted of piracy.

These punishments happen under Islamic law. Crime is viewed far more seriously than in the West. Muslims say that "a thief is lower than a dog"—and they mean it. Likewise, their punishments are meant to humiliate. The reason a thief has his right hand amputated is that the Koran ordains that this hand be used for feeding oneself, and the left for bodily cleansing—so a thief will be condemned forever to eat from the hand that also wipes his bottom.

In Libya, although Gadaffi insists that every aspect of the state's way of life is based on Islam, such punishments are unknown. I am not saying they never happen, only that not one of the British and American citizens whom I have interviewed after living there for long periods has ever heard of a woman being stoned, a man beheaded, or a hand amputated. At the same time, they tell me that Libya seems to be *almost* free of crime. As there is no alcohol publicly available, there are no alcohol-related crimes—no drunk driving, street mugging, or Saturday night violence. Theft seems to be relatively rare, since it is regarded as a "dirty" crime ("lower than a dog," etc.). A man who went to Tripoli as a visiting professor at the university told me, "If you left your coat on the pavement one night, it would still be there next morning, with the wallet inside, untouched. . . . They really are a very honest people."

Another visitor, an engineer from the north of England, told me that he saw a group of Libyans gathered around an Arab in Tripoli market, "smacking him around the head. When I asked them what had happened, they said he stole a packet of cigarettes and now they were punishing him . . . and went on to explain that, of course, he wasn't a Libyan, but came from the Sudan. They felt that they had to tell me that a Libyan would not steal a packet of cigarettes."

If this sounds astonishing, as it did to me when I first heard stories like these, the explanation may well lie in the way in which Gadaffi chooses to interpret the Koran. No one would dare be quoted as saying this, for all Libyans are forbidden to speak to foreigners, but apparently Gadaffi insists that the Koran is essentially a compassionate work of theology; he is said to argue that if a thief steals to provide food or shelter for his wife or children, then he cannot be punished—for it is society that would be at fault for allowing the situation to develop that forced him to steal.

Likewise, under Gadaffi, the Libyan courts avoid severe punishments wherever possible. Gadaffi has announced that he hopes to formally remove capital punishment from the statute book and close all prisons.

Answering his own question, "Who supervises the conduct of society?" Gadaffi suggests that in the kind of society that he is advocating, SOCIETY IS ITS OWN SUPERVISOR, which has become another of *The Green Book*'s slogans ... and he places full responsibility for this supervision on the People's Committees.

So do they also have a role in ensuring that crime is suppressed, i.e., in ensuring that the social forces within the state remain in balance? An outsider may never know for sure, for secrecy prevails at all levels of government; not least within the press.

The slogan that Gadaffi applies to the press is—DEMOCRACY MEANS POPULAR RULE NOT POPULAR EXPRESSION—which is capable of more than one meaning; his own is that—

The natural person has freedom to express himself even if, when he is mad, he behaves irrationally to express his madness. The corporate person also is free to express his corporate identity. In these cases, the first represents only himself, and the second represents no more than the group of natural persons comprising his corporate person.... The press is a means of expression of the society, and is not a means of expression of a natural or corporate person. Logically and democratically, the press, therefore, cannot be owned by either of these.

Any newspaper owned by an individual is his own and expresses only his point of view. Any claim that a newspaper represents public opinion is groundless because it actually expresses the viewpoints of a natural person. Democratically, a natural person should not be permitted to own any means of publication or information. However he has the natural right to express himself by any means, even if it is in an irrational manner to prove his madness.

Gadaffi continues this argument at considerable length, but what he is saying, in essence, is that in his ideal society anyone is free to express himself—but no one is allowed to *own* the means of expression, i.e., book publishers, newspapers, television stations, and radio stations must all be owned by the state because it is the state, i.e., the General People's Congress, that guarantees freedom of speech and thought. No doubt this thesis is well-intentioned. In every Western society, opinions are also broadcast freely—but the same opinions might not be allowed expression in Libya, where there are also laws prohibiting criticism of the revolution. The result is that, although Gadaffi probably means well (and may even believe in his heart that he is giving the People real freedom), in fact his society lacks the zest, vivacity, and general stimulus that comes when writers, artists, poets, and musicians compete for an audience, their ideas clashing in the punchbowl of popular opinion. Libya's two television channels produce a deadly diet of revolutionary fare—speeches often repeated night after night; dull discussions about factory production, imperialist aggression or *The Green Book*, and "entertainment programs" or plays, heavy on Message but lacking dramatic content. Likewise, Libya's books are miserably produced, with poor layout and substandard printing, and its newspapers are risible for their lack of news, their failure to express a variety of opinions, the banality of their criticism of the outside world, and the grossness of their cartoons, which invariable portray the United States as a bloated capitalist Uncle Sam, with the Union Flag stretched tight across a vast belly, a large top hot, and a cracking bullwhip.

Part Two

The second part of *The Green Book*, "The Solution of the Economic Problem—Socialism," is equally simplistic, but also well-intentioned. Gadaffi has looked at communism and capitalism, has some idea of their weaknesses (for no one has yet found a perfect system of society), and advocates in their place something that he calls "socialism" which is, in fact, very different from the kind of "socialism" previously practiced in the Eastern bloc.

Frequently, in public speeches, Gadaffi has argued that this is "Islamic socialism," and that its basic precepts—equality before the law, equality between races, and no one individual being permitted to exploit another—are soundly based in the teachings of the prophet Mohammed and predate Marxism by well over a thousand years. He would have been better understood had he not used the word "Socialism."

The crux of his argument is that tensions begin in society when individuals are allowed to profit through the exploitation of others, i.e., through the landlord making a profit from renting his property, the manufacturer employing labor below what Gadaffi would consider its true market price, or the shopkeeper employing labor to sell goods and thereby making a profit that, Gadaffi would say, has not been earned by the shopkeeper himself.

It is easy enough for a Western economist or politician to say that Gadaffi's theory is addled, for we all know that prices are reduced by minimizing the costs of production, distribution, and sale, and that there has to be a margin within which profit can be made to finance growth or expansion. Gadaffi makes no allowance for any of this, for he is primarily concerned by something else—the human relationship between workers and those who employ them.

In the first part of his thesis, he accepts that—

Important historical developments have taken place which contribute to solving the problem of work and wages, i.e., the relationship between the workers and the employers, between the producers and the owners. The developments include fixed working hours, wages for additional work, different types of leave, minimum wages, profit sharing, and participation in administration. In addition, arbitrary dismissal has been outlawed and social security has been guaranteed, along with the right to strike....

but then he goes on to say that the basic problem still remains unchanged, because "The wage-worker is like a slave to the master who hires him.... The ultimate solution is to abolish the wage-system, emancipate man from its bondage, and return to the natural law which defined relationships before the emergence of classes, forms of government, and manmade laws."

What he is saying, in effect, is that the relationships between men that were possible at the time Mohammed's writings were gathered together in the Koran could still be achieved if society were prepared to strip away much of its formal structure. This, too, is undoubtedly true. Society could dispense with all its factories, office blocks, transport systems, railways, highways, and communications systems, and its whole fabric of law and commercial interdependence, if we were prepared to live in goatskin tents and caves, as the Libyans were actually doing until just a few years ago.

This, I suspect, is the heart of the problem. Because Libya has so much land, oodles of money, and such a low population, Gadaffi is able to advocate and put into effect theories that would be lunacy anywhere else in the world; and because the Libyans have nothing else to compare their society with, he appears to them to be their savior in the process.

For Gadaffi has brought into being the solutions that he advocates in this second part of *The Green Book*. His basic premise is again put in slogan form—PARTNERS NOT WAGE-WORKERS—and this is the slogan that one sees most in Libya, for it embodies the system that he has created, which can hardly be called "socialism." Anyone can own a family business—as a farmer, market gardener, shopkeeper, sheet metal worker, electrician, engineer, or whatever—and other members of the family may work within that business, provided they share in it equally, sharing both profits and losses. They are not permitted to employ anyone else on a basis of paying a wage in return for labor. In the case of larger businesses, this means, in effect, they are all run as cooperatives—unless they form part of the state's own system of manufacture (in which case Gadaffi would argue that the same principles apply, since all citizens enjoy equal rights).

Gadaffi explains his theories with a historical parallel—

In the state of manual production the productive process involved raw materials, and man, the producer. Later, an instrument of production intervened between the two and man used it in the productive process. The animal may be considered as an example of the instrument as a power unit. It, then, developed and the machine replaced the animal. Raw materials increased in kind and quantity, from cheap, simple materials to valuable, complex ones. Likewise man developed from an ordinary worker into a technician and an engineer and a large number of workers began to be replaced by a few technicians. . . . The essential role of each factor has not changed. For example, the iron ore which is one of the factors of production, both past and present, was primitively manufactured by the ironsmith to produce a knife, an ax, or a spear. . . . The same iron ore is now manufactured in big furnaces, and from it engineers and technicians produce machines, engines, and all kinds of vehicles. The animal—the horse, the mule, or the camel, and the like—which was one of the factors of production has now been replaced by the vast factory and huge machines.

And then he goes on to argue that man will always be a part of this process, no matter what the scale of production, and addresses himself to the needs of the individual, which, he says, must always be considered separately from the productive process, because A PERSON IN NEED IS A SLAVE INDEED—

Man's freedom is lacking if somebody else controls what he needs. For need may result in man's enslavement of man. Need causes exploitation. Need is an intrinsic problem and conflict grows out of the domination of man's needs.

Gadaffi insists that this part of the problem can be solved if man's needs are met independently of his role within the productive process, i.e., if men own their own homes they cease to be slaves and become MASTERS IN THEIR OWN CASTLES—

The house is a basic need of both the individual and the family. Therefore it should not be owned by others. There is no freedom for a man who lives in another's house, whether he pays rent or not. All attempts made by various countries to solve the problem of housing are not solutions at all. The reason is that those attempts do not aim at the radical and ultimate solution of man, which is the necessity of his owning his own house.... In the socialist society no one, including the society itself, is allowed to have control over man's need.

No one has the right to build a house, additional to his own and that of his heirs, for the purpose of renting it, because the house represents another person's need, and building it for the purpose of rent is an attempt to have control over the need of that man and IN NEED FREEDOM IS LATENT

These concepts are difficult for us in the West to grasp, for we are conditioned to the idea that a certain part of our wages goes to meet our housing costs, with each generation passing through the hurdles of buying their first, second, or third homes, arranging home loan finance and paying taxes; Gadaffi is rejecting all of that, saying that first a citizen has a home, as of right—*and then*

income is an imperative need for man. Thus the income of any man in the society should not be a wage from any source or a

charity from anyone. For there are no wage-workers in the socialist society, only partners.

And he applies the same principle to car ownership; everyone is
entitled to a car—but only one car at a time—

The vehicle is a necessity both to the individual and the family.
Your vehicle should not be owned by others. In the socialist
society no man or any other authority can possess private vehicles for the purpose of hiring them out, for this is domination of
the needs of others.

This principle is also applied to the ownership of land, since, he
says, "Land is no one's property"—which, of course, it wasn't to
the Bedouin, whose ownership of wells might be defined by custom
and practice, but who were free to travel across the deserts when
the time came for the date harvest, or for their flocks to move on
to another pasture. Gadaffi argues that everyone has the right to
use land, "to benefit from it by working, farming, or pasturing. This
would take place throughout a man's life and the lives of his heirs,
and would be through his own effort without using others, with or
without wages, and only to the extent of satisfying his own needs."

What he is saying, and perhaps the West has been slow to understand this because of his use of the word *socialism*, is that the new
Libya might well benefit from the customs and traditions of its
past—

The purpose of the new socialist society is to create a society
which is happy because it is free. This can be achieved through
satisfying the material and spiritual needs of man, and that, in
turn, comes about through the liberation of these needs from
outside domination and control. . . .

Whoever possesses the house you dwell in, the vehicle you
ride, or the income you live on, takes hold of your freedom, or
part of your freedom, and freedom is indivisible. For man to be
happy, he must be free; and to be free, man must possess his
own needs. . . . The material needs of man that are basic, necessary, and personal, start with food, housing, clothing, and transport. . . . These must be within his private and sacred ownership.
They are not to be hired from any quarter.

Part Three

In its third section, "The Social Basis of the Third Universal Theory," *The Green Book* tackles a disparate range of issues that do not fit naturally into the earlier parts, but there is one important theme running through it; Gadaffi believes in the concept of nationalism, and he argues that a desire for a sense of identity is the common thread in all campaigns for independence—

These needs are in no way individualistic. They are collective needs, rights, demands, or objectives of a nation which is bound by a single nationalism. That is why these movements are called national movements.... The world is now passing through one of the regular cycles of the movement of history, namely, the national struggle in support of nationalism.... It is in the nature of the human group ... the nature of the nation. It is the nature of life itself. Other animals, apart from man, live in groups. Indeed, the group is the basis for the survival of all groups within the animal kingdom. So nationalism is the basis for the survival of nations.

Nations whose nationalism is destroyed are subject to ruin....

Gadaffi continues his argument with the suggestion that in most parts of the world the problems that exist within society are usually due to some form of suppressed nationalism. In this, he was remarkably prescient, for in all parts of Africa, Eastern Europe (and currently in the Balkans), South America, and the Middle East, recent years have witnessed a return to ancient forms of nationhood, with countries lost within wider boundaries proving that their sense of identity remains unbroken. Gadaffi was saying this fifteen years ago, before the breakup of the Soviet Union or the disintegration of Yugoslavia—

Man's life is damaged when he begins to disregard nationalism ... the social factor ... the gravity of the group ... the secret of its survival. There is no rival to the social factor in influencing the unity of one group except the religious factor.... Originally each nation had one religion. This was harmony. In fact, however, differences arose which became a genuine cause of conflict and instability in the life of the peoples throughout the ages. The sound rule is that every nation should have a religion.

Within such a binding concept of the role of religion, by which he means Islam in the case of Libya, Gadaffi believes that the family and the tribe are the basis of any nation—

To the individual man the family is of more importance than the state.... The family is his cradle, his origin, and his social umbrella. Mankind, as a matter of fact, is the individual and the family, not the state.... Societies in which the existence and unity of the family are threatened, in any circumstances, are similar to fields whose plants are in danger of being swept away or threatened by drought or fire, or of withering away.... The flourishing society is that in which the individual grows naturally within the family and the family itself flourishes in the society.... If human society reached the stage where man existed without a family, it would become a society of tramps, without roots, like artificial plants.

A tribe is a family which has grown as a result of procreation. It follows that a tribe is a big family. Equally a nation is a tribe which has grown through procreation. The nation, then, is a big tribe. So the world is a nation which has been ramified into various nations. The world, then, is a big nation. The relationship which binds the family is that which binds the tribe, the nation and the world.... The degree of warmth involved diminishes as the relationship moves from the smaller level to the larger one. This is a social fact only denied by those who are ignorant of it.... The social love, cohesiveness, unity, intimacy, and love are stronger at the family level than at the tribal level ... stronger at the tribal level than at that of the nation, and stronger at the level of the nation than at that of the world.

These arguments would be acceptable in most societies; where Gadaffi differs is that he specifically prefers a closely knit family structure within a small nation to anything larger; he does not say this in so many words, but there is an implicit criticism of "great nations," which he suggests will always disintegrate because the formal political and economic structures that they devise make their governments far removed from the People, i.e., the family that forms the basis of society. In this, as elsewhere, he is advocating a system of society, another aspect of his Third Universal Theory, that can be made to work in Libya's particular circumstances, but which would be impractical in more developed countries.

The last major section of *The Green Book* concerns the role of women within society, and here, too, Gadaffi is advocating ideas that verge away from the traditional concepts of Islam. He sees men and women as equal within the state, possessing equal rights in law and equal status. Once again, the way in which he develops this proposition may seem oversimplified to those who have lived through years of feminist debate, but his basic argument is revolutionary in the Arab world, where, in states such as Saudi Arabia, it is considered wrong for a woman to drive a car, or engage in any social activity outside the home. Here, rather than summarized, is Gadaffi's case, in his own words—

WOMAN

It is an undisputed fact that both men and women are human beings. It follows as a self-evident fact that woman and man are equal as human beings. Discrimination between man and woman is a flagrant act of oppression without any justification. For woman eats and drinks as man eats and drinks.... Woman loves and hates as man loves and hates.... Woman thinks, learns, and understands as man thinks, learns and understands.... Woman, like man, needs shelter, clothing, and vehicles.... Woman feels hunger and thirst as man feels hunger and thirst.... Woman lives and dies as man lives and dies.

But why are there man and woman? Indeed, human society is composed neither of man alone nor of woman alone. It is made up naturally of man and woman. Why were not only men created? Why were not only women created? After all, what is the difference between man and woman? Why was it necessary to create man and woman? There must be natural necessity for the existence of man and woman rather than man only or woman only. It follows that neither of them is exactly the other, and the fact that a natural difference exists between man and woman is proved by the created existence of man and woman. This means, as a matter of fact, that there is a role for each of them, matching the difference between them. Accordingly, there must be different prevailing conditions for each one to live and perform their naturally different roles. To comprehend this role, we must understand the differences in the nature of man and woman, namely the natural differences between them.

Woman is female and man is male. According to a gynecologist, woman menstruates or suffers feebleness every month, while man, being a male, does not menstruate and he is not subject to the monthly period which is a bleeding. A woman, being a female, is naturally subject to monthly bleeding. When a woman does not menstruate, she is pregnant. If she is pregnant she becomes, due to pregnancy, feeble for about a year, which means that all her natural activities are seriously reduced until she delivers her baby. When she delivers her baby or has had a miscarriage, she suffers puerperium, a feebleness attendant on delivery or miscarriage. As the man does not get pregnant, he is not liable to the feebleness which woman, being a female, suffers. Afterward woman breast-feeds the baby she bore. Breast-feeding continues for about two years. Breast-feeding means that a woman is so inseparable from her baby that her activity is seriously reduced. She becomes directly responsible for another person whom she helps to carry out its biological functions, without which it would die. The man, on the other hand, neither conceives nor breast-feeds.

All these innate characteristics form differences because of which man and woman cannot be equal. These, in themselves, are the realities that necessitate the distinction between male and female, i.e., man and woman; they assign to each of them a different role or function in life. This means that man cannot replace woman in carrying out these functions. It is worthy of consideration that these biological functions are a heavy burden, causing woman great effort and suffering. However, without these functions which woman performs, human life would come to an end. It follows that it is a natural function which is neither voluntary nor compulsory. It is an essential function, whose sole alternative is that human life would come to a complete standstill.

There is a deliberate intervention against conception which is the alternative to human life. In addition to that there is a partial deliberate intervention against conception, as well as against breast-feeding. All these are links in a chain of actions against natural life, culminating in murder, i.e., for a woman to kill herself in order not to conceive, deliver, and breast-feed, is within the realm of deliberate interventions against the nature of life embodied in conception, breast-feeding, maternity, and marriage, though they differ only in degree.

To dispense with the natural role of woman in maternity—i.e., nurseries replacing mothers—is a start in dispensing with the human society and transforming it into a biological society with an artificial way of life. To separate children from their mothers and to cram them into nurseries is a process by which they are transformed into something very close to chicks, for nurseries are similar to poultry farms in which chicks are crammed after they are hatched. Nothing else would be appropriate for man's nature, and would suit his dignity, except natural motherhood, (i.e., the child is raised by his mother . . .) *in a family where the true principles of motherhood, fatherhood, and brotherhood prevail,* rather than in a center like a poultry breeding farm. Poultry, like the rest of the members of the animal kingdom, needs motherhood as a natural phase. Therefore, breeding them on farms similar to nurseries is against their natural growth. Even their meat is closer to synthetic meat than natural meat. Meat from mechanized poultry farms is not tasty and may not be nourishing because the chicks are not naturally bred, i.e., they are not raised in the protective shade of natural motherhood. The meat of wild birds is more tasty and nourishing because they grow naturally and are naturally fed. As for children who have neither family nor shelter, society is their guardian, only for them should society establish nurseries and the like. It is better for those to be taken care of by society rather than by individuals who are not their parents.

If a test were carried out to discover the natural propensity of the child toward his mother and the nursery, the child would opt for his mother and not the nursery. Since the natural tendency of a child is toward his mother, she is the natural and proper person to give the child the protection of nursing. Sending a child to a nursery in place of his mother is coercion and oppression against its free natural propensity.

The natural growth for all living things is free sound growth. To substitute a nursery for a mother is coercive action against free sound growth. Children who are driven to a nursery are driven compulsorily or by exploitation and simple-mindedness. They are driven to nurseries purely by materialistic and not social considerations. If coercion and childish simple-mindedness were removed, they would certainly reject the nursery and cling to their mother. The only justification for such an unnatural and inhuman process is the fact that the woman is in a position unsuitable to her nature, i.e., she is compelled to perform duties which are unsocial and anti-motherhood.

The woman, whose nature has assigned to her a natural role different from that of man, must be in an appropriate position to perform her natural role.

Motherhood is the female's function, not the male's. Consequently, it is unnatural to separate children from their mother. Any attempt to take children away from their mother is coercion, oppression, and dictatorship. The mother who abandons her maternity contradicts her natural role in life. She must be provided with her rights and conditions which are appropriate, noncoercive, and unoppressive. Thus she can carry out her natural role under natural conditions. Anything else is a self-contradictory situation. If the woman is forced to abandon her natural role as regards conception and maternity, she falls victim to coercion and dictatorship. A woman who needs work that renders her unable to perform her natural function is not free and is compelled to do that by need, FOR IN NEED FREEDOM IS LATENT.

Among suitable and even essential conditions which enable the woman to perform her natural role, which differs from that of man, are those very conditions which are proper to a human being who is sick and burdened with pregnancy, i.e., bearing another human being in her womb, which renders her physically incapacitated. It is injust to place such a woman in this stage of maternity into circumstances of physical work incompatible with her condition. Such work is a punishment of woman for her betrayal of maternity and of mankind. It is also a tax she pays for entering the realm of men who are not, of course, of her sex.

The belief, including the woman's own belief, that the woman carries out physical labor of her own accord, is not, in fact, true. For she performs the physical work only because the harsh materialistic society has placed her, without her being directly aware, in coercive circumstances. She has no alternative but to submit to the conditions of that society while she thinks that she works of her own accord. However, the rule that "there is no difference between man and woman in every thing" deprives her of her freedom.

The phrase "in every thing" is a monstrous deception of woman. This idea will destroy the appropriate and necessary conditions which constitute the privilege which woman ought to enjoy apart from man in accordance with her nature on which a natural role in life is based.

To demand equality between man and woman in carrying heavy weights while the woman is pregnant is unjust and cruel. To demand equality between them in fasting and hardship, while she is breast-feeding, is unjust and cruel. To demand equality between them in any dirty work, which stains her beauty and detracts from her femininity, is unjust and cruel. Education that leads to work unsuitable for her nature is unjust and cruel as well.

There is no difference between man and woman in all that concerns humanity. None of them can marry the other against his or her will, or divorce without a just trial. Neither the woman nor the man can remarry without a previous agreement on divorce. The woman is the owner of the house because it is one of the suitable and necessary conditions for a woman who menstruates, conceives, and cares for her children. The woman is the owner of the maternity shelter, which is the house. Even in the animal world, which differs in many ways from that of man, and where maternity is also a duty according to nature, it is coercion to deprive the young of their mother or deprive the female of her shelter.

A woman is but a female. Being female means that she has a biological nature different from that of man. The female's biological nature differing, as it does, from that of the male, has imparted to a woman characteristics different from those of a man in form and essence. A woman's anatomy is different from that of a man just as the female in plants and animals are different from the male. This is a natural and incontrovertible fact. In the animal and plant kingdoms the male is naturally created strong and tough, while the female is created beautiful and gentle. These are natural and eternal characteristics innate in these living creatures, whether called human beings, animals, or plants.

In view of his different nature and in line with the laws of nature, the male has played the role of the strong and the tough without compulsion but simply because he is created that way. The female has played the role of the beautiful and the gentle, not because she wanted to, but because she is created so. The natural rule is just, partly because it is natural, and partly because it is the basic rule for freedom. For all living creatures are created free and any interference with that freedom is coercion. Noncommitment to these natural roles and a lack of concern toward their roles amount to an act of negligence and destruction of the values of life itself. Nature has thus been designed in harmony with the inevitability of life from what is being to what will become. The living creature is a being who inevitably lives until he is dead. Existence between the beginning and the end is based on natural law, without choice or compulsion. It is natural. It is natural freedom.

In the animal, plant, and human kingdoms there must be a

male and a female for life to occur from its beginning to its end. They do not only exist but they have to play, with absolute efficiency, the natural role for which they have been created. If their role is not efficiently performed there must be some defect in the course of life caused by certain circumstances. This is the case of societies nowadays almost everywhere in the world as a result of confusing the roles of man and woman, i.e., as a result of endeavors to transform a woman into a man. In harmony with their nature and its purpose they must be creative within their respective roles. For the opposite is retrogressive. It is a trend against nature, which is as destructive to the rule of freedom, as it is hostile to both life and survival. Men and women must perform, not abandon the role for which they are created. Abandoning the role or even a part of it only occurs as a result of coercive conditions, i.e., under abnormal conditions. The woman who rejects pregnancy, marriage, and femininity for reasons of health, abandons her natural role in life under these coercive conditions of health. The woman who rejects marriage, pregnancy, or motherhood, etc., because of work, abandons her natural role under the same coercive conditions. The woman who rejects marriage, pregnancy, or maternity, etc., without any concrete cause, abandons her natural role as a result of a coercive condition which is a moral deviation from the norm. Thus, abandoning the natural role of female and male in life can only occur under unnatural conditions which are contrary to nature and a threat to survival. Consequently, there must be a world revolution which puts an end to all materialistic conditions hindering woman from performing her natural role in life and driving her to carry out man's duties in order to be equal in rights. Such a revolution will inevitably take place, particularly in the industrial societies, as a response by the instinct of survival, even without any instigator of revolution such as *The Green Book*.

All societies nowadays look upon woman as no more than an article of merchandise. The East regards her as a commodity for buying and selling, while the West does not recognize her femininity.

Driving woman to do man's work is unjust aggression against the femininity with which she is naturally provided for a natural purpose essential to life. For man's work disguises the woman's beautiful features which are created for female roles. They are exactly like blossoms which are created to attract pollen and to produce seeds. If we did away with the blossoms, the role of plants in life would come to an end. It is the natural embellishment in butterflies and birds as well as the rest of the animal females which is created for that natural vital goal. If a woman carries out man's work, she will be transformed into a man abandoning her role and her beauty. A woman has full rights to live without being forced to change into a man and to give up her femininity.

The physical structure, which is naturally different between man and woman, leads to differences in the functions of their different organs which lead in turn to differences in the psyche, mood, nerves, and physical appearance. A woman is tender. A woman is pretty. A woman weeps easily. A woman is easily frightened. In general woman is gentle and man is tough by virtue of their inbred nature.

To ignore natural differences between man and woman and mix their roles is an absolutely uncivilized attitude, hostile to the laws of nature, destructive to human life, and a genuine cause for the wretchedness of human social life.

Modern industrial societies, which have made woman adapt to the same physical work as man at the expense of her femininity and her natural role in terms of beauty, maternity, and peace of mind—those societies are uncivilized. They are materialistic, uncivilized societies. It is as stupid as it is dangerous to civilization and humanity to copy them.

The question, then, is not whether the woman works or does not work. For it is a ridiculous materialistic presentation. Work should be provided by the society to all able members—men and women— who need work, but on condition that each individual should work in the field that suits him, and not be forced to carry out unsuitable work.

For the children to find themselves under adult working conditions is injustice and dictatorship. Equally it is injustice and dictatorship for woman to find herself under the working conditions of man.

Freedom means that every human being gets that education which qualifies him for work which is appropriate to him. Dictatorship means that a human being learns what is not suitable for him. That leads him to work which is not suitable to him. Work which is appropriate to man is not always appropriate to woman, and the knowledge that is proper for the child is not suitable for the adult.

There is no difference in human rights between man and woman, the child and the adult. But there is an absolute equality between them as regards their duties.

This section has been reproduced in full, because it illustrates both the best and the worst aspects of Gadaffi's theories, as expressed in *The Green Book*. There are occasional moments of cogency, but, on the whole, it is badly written, and his argument veers first this way and then that, sometimes barely holding together—and yet beneath it all is that quality new to the Arab concept: an acceptance that women should enjoy equal status with men, albeit their roles may be different.

And, to give him his due, it must be said that Gadaffi has been true to his argument. Women enjoy rights and career choices in Libya that are denied to them elsewhere in the Arab world. They do not have to wear *baraqi* (the veil) at all times, though no Libyan woman would dream of dressing immodestly. They are free to pursue careers, to study at university and abroad, to take up employment (there are women doctors and dentists), to train at their own military academy, to serve in the armed forces (even as members of Gadaffi's bodyguard), and there are opportunities open to them that Arabs in any other Middle Eastern state would find astonishing. Women play an active role in the People's Committees and the General People's Congress, and Gadaffi has even gone so far as to appoint a young, attractive, and extremely able member of his diplomatic corps, Ms. Hind A. Siala, as Ambassador to Malta, which is an important position, for Malta is within the Sterling Area, at least seven hundred Maltese citizens work in Libya (traveling to and fro by hydrofoil now that air flights are banned), and Libya uses its offices in Malta and its banks in its dealings with Europe.

Gadaffi made this commitment to giving women their due status in Libyan society even clearer in a speech delivered on September 1, 1981, to mark the anniversary of the revolution and the graduation of the first generation of women to pass through the women's military academy, after a three-year period of training. It was a remarkable speech, and, like so many of Gadaffi's more significant utterances, virtually unreported in the West—

We are proud that the first military academy for girls in the world is today graduating officers here in the Jamahiriya. This is something novel. . . . Ever since its inception, the Revolution has attacked all phenomena where women, especially European women, are bought and sold as a cheap commodity in reactionary, backward societies, including the bygone monarchical regime which had opened nightspots of pleasure where women were traded. European women who wrongly believe they have been liberated are in fact still being bought and sold, and are items of recreation in European armies. . . . We have resolved to totally liberate women in Libya, so that they may be masters of their own fate in a democratic milieu where they have equal opportunities with all other members of society.

And then he went on to draw a distinction between Libya's attitude to women and their standing in other Arab societies, clearly suggesting that the Gulf States should also be reformed in similar ways—

Inside the Arab nation, women have been dominated by forces of oppression, feudalism, and profit. We call for the outbreak of a revolution for the liberation of women in the Arab nation. . . . This is a bomb that will rock the entire Arab region and will drive the female prisoners of palaces and marketplaces to revolt against their jailers, exploiters, and oppressors. . . . Women now are not respected. What goes on at present does not agree with the true constitution of any Islamic society. Islam means freedom, equality, and a humane society. Current practices are no more than insults. Marriages, divorces, and other social activities being practiced are all contrary to the Koran, Islam, freedom, and humanitarianism. Unfortunately, Oriental societies espousing Islam have harmed our religion and are the most reactionary and infidel of societies. . . . We are determined to see this revolution destroy the citadels of reactionaries and their castles, and raid these high palaces where Arab women are being enslaved, destroying the palaces and liberating women, from the Ocean to the Gulf. . . . We would like to announce that Libyan military colleges and Libyan military schools are wide open not only for Libyan Arab girls but for all the girls of the Arab nation and Africa.

In this final section of the third part of *The Green Book*, Gadaffi also defends the rights of all minorities to be heard within his ideal society, and goes on to embrace concepts of multiracialism, which is also advanced thinking in the Arab context. Only fifty years ago, slavery was still being practiced in his own country (as we have discussed in earlier chapters). It continued to be practiced within the Maghreb until much more recently, and there are still Arab rulers and princes who employ negroes as though these practices remain unchanged. Gadaffi, who avoids any mention of Libya's past connection with the slave trade, puts the blame elsewhere—

> The latest age of slavery is the white race's enslavement of the black race. The black man will not forget this until he has achieved rehabilitation. This tragic and historic event, the resulting bitter feeling, and the search for satisfaction derived from rehabilitating a whole race, constitute a psychological motivation in the movement of the black race to vengeance and domination, which cannot be disregarded.

And he goes on to argue that THE BLACKS WILL PREVAIL IN THE WORLD.

The Green Book concludes with Gadaffi's views on "Melodies and Art" and "Sport, Horsemanship, and Shows", specifying in both sections how followers of his Third Universal Theory should approach the problem of how best to use their leisure time—

> Man is still backward because he is unable to speak one common language. Until he attains this human aspiration, which seems impossible, the expression of joy and sorrow, what is good and bad, beauty and ugliness, comfort and misery, mortality and eternity, love and hatred, the description of colors, sentiments, tastes, and moods—all will be according to the language each people speaks.

Gadaffi says it will not be enough for people to learn one language in one generation, for "a common taste" only comes when each generation can transmit its thoughts to the next in words that are understood; the words *melody* and *art* do not actually appear in the text, but what he appears to be saying is that traditional cultures keep people apart, and a common philosophy, a shared appreciation of values, of music, art, and literature, may be slow to evolve "because man does not speak with his brother one common language which is inherited and not learned."

In his attitude to other forms of leisure, Gadaffi argues that sport should be in the hands of the people—

> Public sport is for all the masses. It is a right of all the people for its health and recreational benefits.

And he argues strongly against spectator sports, saying that it is only "foolish people" who "crowd stadiums to view, applaud, and laugh . . . people who have failed to carry out the activity themselves." He upbraids them further for "practicing lethargy," urges them to take part in all sporting activities themselves as active participants, ending up with almost a tirade—

Those who are unable to perform the roles of heroism in life, who are ignorant of the events of history, who fall short of envisaging the future, and who are not serious enough in their lives, are the trivial persons who fill the seats of the theaters and cinemas to watch the events of life and learn their course. . . . Those who direct the course of life for themselves do not need to watch it working through actors on the stage or in the cinemas. Likewise, horsemen who hold the reins of their horses have no seat in the grandstands at the race course. . . . The sitting spectators are only those who are too helpless to perform this kind of activity because they are not horsemen.

Equally, the Bedouin peoples show no interest in theaters and shows because they are very serious and hard working. As they have created a serious life, they ridicule acting. Bedouin societies also do not watch performers, but perform games and take part in joyful ceremonies because they naturally recognize the need for these activities and practice them automatically.

Different types of boxing and wrestling are evidence that mankind has not got rid of all savage behavior. Inevitably they will come to an end when man ascends the ladder of civilization. Human sacrifices and pistol duels were familiar practices in different stages of human evolution. However, these savage practices came to an end years ago. Man now laughs at himself and regrets such acts. That will be the fate of boxing and wrestling after tens or hundreds of years. However, the more the people are civilized and sophisticated, the more they are able to ward off both the performance and the encouragement of these practices.

The Green Book is a strange hodgepodge of ideas and attitudes, jumbling constitutional theory with a mangled view of economics that owes nothing to Keynes or Galbraith, and yet invoking relatively advanced ideas on personal freedom, women's rights, and the ways in which each individual may play some part in a participatory democracy. Taken as a whole, its theories are impractical in all but the most primitive societies—and yet they have been made to work in Libya, where, uniquely, Gadaffi has no need to make economic growth or administrative efficiency his markers. Oil protects him from the harsher realities of the modern world.

Part IV

UNREST AT HOME,
OPPOSITION ABROAD
—AS GADAFFI'S REVOLUTION
DEVELOPS A PACE, AND HIS
PHILOSOPHY A SHAPE,
TENSIONS GROW BETWEEN LIBYA
AND ITS NEIGHBORS.

THE U.S. GOVERNMENT
BECOMES INCREASINGLY CONCERNED
WHEN THE JUSTICE DEPARTMENT
LEARNS OF GADAFFI'S ABILITY
TO BUY MILITARY HARDWARE
FROM EAST AND WEST,
AND EVEN CIA INTELLIGENCE
SKILLS THROUGH HIS RECRUITS
TERPIL AND WILSON.

CIA DIRECTOR STANSFIELD
TURNER PURGES THE CIA
ON DISCOVERING THAT MEMBERS OF HIS STAFF
HAVE BEEN COOPERATING WITH
TERPIL AND WILSON, ENABLING
GADAFFI TO BUY THE LATEST
TECHNOLOGY, INCLUDING NIGHT
SURVEILLANCE CAMERAS. THERE
ARE ALSO REPORTS THAT GADAFFI
HAS RECRUITED FORMER U.S. PILOTS
AND VIETNAM VETERANS.

INCREASINGLY GADAFFI IS PORTRAYED
AS A THREAT TO STABILITY IN
THE MIDDLE EAST, AND
HOSTILITIES DEVELOP BETWEEN
LIBYA AND NEIGHBORING STATES
CLOSELY ALLIED TO THE WEST.

SOON GADAFFI IS AT WAR ON TWO
FRONTS. HE INVADES CHAD WITH A FORCE
OF FOUR THOUSAND MEN (JULY 1977), SUPPORTED BY
THE MUSLIM TRIBES IN THE NORTH.
EGYPT AND SUDAN BACK THE
CHAD GOVERNMENT, BASED IN THE SOUTH.
THIS CONFLICT LASTS MANY YEARS,
WITH FRANCE AND THE U.S. ALSO
ASSISTING THE MAINLY CHRISTIAN SOUTH.

LATER THIS SAME MONTH,
EGYPT AND LIBYA BEGIN FIGHTING
IN THE WESTERN DESERT.
MINOR SKIRMISHES DEVELOP INTO A
MAJOR CONFLICT WITH DESERT TANK
BATTLES AND JETS STRAFING. THIS IS
SOMETIMES CALLED "THE FOUR DAY WAR"
ALTHOUGH FIGHTING CONTINUED
FOR NINE.

ACCORDING TO THE LIBYANS,
THEY LOST TWENTY-SEVEN MEN WITH NINE MISSING.
TWO OF THEIR PLANES WERE SHOT
DOWN AND NINE TANKS DAMAGED.
SADAT CALLS A CEASEFIRE, AFTER
EGYPT HAS REPORTEDLY SUFFERED
GREATER LOSSES.

THERE ARE SOME FEARS THAT THE
CONFLICT MAY BROADEN, WITH THE U.S.
AGREEING TO SEND ARMS TO CHAD, EGYPT, AND SUDAN,
AND RUSSIA OFFERING
LIBYA T-62 TANKS WITH LASER
RANGE FINDERS AND MEDIUM RANGE

MISSILES. SADAT'S
CEASEFIRE ENDS
THIS SPECULATION.

IN THE YEARS THAT FOLLOW,
GADAFFI WAVERS IN HIS ATTITUDE
TO THE WEST. HE COOPERATES
WITH THE CARTER ADMINISTRATION,
AND NOTORIOUSLY, RECRUITS BILLY
CARTER AS A SUPPORTER OF THE
LIBYAN REGIME, WHILE PURSUING
LIBYAN EXILES ABROAD.

GADAFFI COMES TO SYMBOLIZE PRESIDENT
CARTER'S WEAKNESS IN
CONFRONTING TERRORISM,
AND THUS AN
ISSUE IN THE 1980
U.S. PRESIDENTIAL CAMPAIGN,
LEADING,
ALMOST INEVITABLY, TO
A TRIAL OF WILL
WHEN RONALD REAGAN
WINS THAT ELECTION
... AND, EVENTUALLY,
TO THE U.S. TAKING
MILITARY ACTION
AGAINST GADAFFI.

1978

January		Said Hammami, London representative of the PLO, shot dead at his Mayfair office. Abu Nidal blamed.
January	26	Rioting breaks out in Tunis.
February		Another plot reported in Tripoli, this time led by Capt. Muhammad Idris Sharif and his brother-in-law Capt. Muhammad al Sayyid, head of Military Intelligence.
March		More reports of unrest in Tripoli. One of Gadaffi's aides Taher Sherif bin Amer dies in a helicopter crash with a visiting East German

leader Werner Lamberz. There is speculation that the plane was attacked in an attempt to assassinate Gadaffi.

May/June
The Italian government agrees to supply Libya with two hundred light aircraft, four corvettes, and military transport planes.

July   4
Former Libyan ambassador to Italy Gibril Shalouf visits Billy Carter, brother of the U.S. President at his gas station in Georgia and invites him to visit Libya. Billy says yes.

France sends bombers and Foreign Legion troops into Chad to shore up the government. After a peace conference in Tripoli, Malloum remains President and rebel leader Hissene Habre becomes Prime Minister. However, Habre still has his army—and Libya continues to occupy the Aouzou Strip.

August
Libya evacuates its three bases in northern Chad—at Bardi, Saya, and Zouar.

September   1
Gadaffi "liberates the wage earners from their slavery." Hundreds of firms are taken into cooperative ownership, run by People's Committees.

September   1
Imam Musa Sadr, a Shi-ite leader from southern Lebanon, disappears with two companions, Sheikh Mohammad Yacoub and Abbas Bedreddin. All three have been staying in Tripoli and are due to catch a flight to Rome. The Libyans insist they caught their plane; but they vanish. The incident later sours relations between Libya and Iran because the Imam was married to Khomeini's niece.

September
Libya donates four helicopters to Malta and supplies the training crews to develop an air-sea rescue service. By coincidence, there are floods in Malta the following month and many lives are saved. There were forty-seven Libyans working on the project.

September   5
Begin and Sadat agree to visit Camp David for discussions with President Carter "to

		seek a framework for peace in the Middle East."
September	25–27	Billy Carter and six friends from Georgia fly to Tripoli via Rome. After much heavy drinking, the party books into the Rome Hilton, where their room is "full of naked men and women and trashy prostitutes." The Libyans present Billy with a silver sword, a silver saddle, and four gold bracelets. Billy says he will try to do something to help the Libyans secure the release of eight Lockheed C130 aircraft which Libya has paid for, only to have them impounded by the U.S. government. The planes have been parked on an airfield in Atlanta for the past five years.
November	2	The U.S. State Department agrees to let Libya have two Boeing 727 aircraft. Two months later, Libya is allowed to take delivery of three Boeing 747s, having consented not to use them for military purposes. Libya also agrees to abide by the Hague Convention on hijacking.

1979

January	8	Billy Carter welcomes a party of Libyans at Atlanta airport. The party tour Georgia and visit the Carter family peanut warehouse. A Libyan-Arab-Georgian Friendship Society is formed. The President's mother, Lillian Carter, hosts a reception for the guests.
January/March		Renewed fighting in Chad with five different factions now fighting against the government. Libya supports the rebels.
February		Libya sends fifteen hundred troops to Uganda to help President Amin resist an invasion force from Tanzania. The troops are flown in by Boeing 727. This is enough to make the U.S. cancel its agreement for Libya to have Boeing 747s. Libya loses four hundred men when Tanzania captures Kampala at the end of March.

March	8–13	President Carter visits Cairo and Jerusalem, and announces on the last day that Sadat and Begin have accepted U.S. peace proposals.
March	26	Sadat and Begin sign the peace treaty on the White House lawn.
August	5	Billy Carter goes to Washington to meet Abdallah el Saudi, chairman of the Libyan Arab Foreign Bank, hoping to raise a loan.
August/September		Billy Carter and his wife Sibyl return to Libya with their son Buddy to help the Libyans mark the tenth anniversary of their revolution. Former CIA operative Frank Terpil acts as his interpreter. Billy is photographed with Yasser Arafat—but never meets Gadaffi.
November	4	Iranian militants seize the U.S. Embassy in Teheran with sixty-five U.S. diplomats taken hostage. The U.S. freezes Iranian assets.
November	19	Rosalynn Carter, wife of the President, asks Billy to contact his friends in Libya to see if they will intervene on the hostages' behalf. The National Security Adviser Zbigniew Brzezinski also phones Billy.
November	20	A statement is issued by the Libyan government: "In our view the hostages should be released...."
November	27	Billy Carter meets al Houderi at the Libyan Bureau in Washington and asks him to meet Brzezinski to discuss the hostage crisis—and they meet.
December	2	Rioters set fire to the U.S. Embassy in Tripoli.
December	6	Brzezinski takes al Houderi to meet President Carter at the White House. Carter says that if Libya helps free the hostages and gives assurances that U.S. diplomats would be protected in Libya, he will try to ensure an improvement in relations with Libya.
December	10	Gadaffi quoted as saying that he expects Libya's relationship with the U.S. to improve if Carter is reelected. "We have received assurances," he says. "We interpret them as

meaning a more neutral American posture in the conflict between the Arabs and Israel."

December 12   Al Houderi tells Brzezinski that Gadaffi has spoken personally to the Iranians to secure the release of the hostages.

1980

January   Libya attacks the Tunisian base at Gafsa, an area to which both countries lay claim and in which there are said to be oil reserves.

January   Rioters burn down the French Embassy in Tripoli. Thereafter, France increases its aid to the government forces in Chad.

February   Permanent Revolutionary Court established in Libya; Amnesty International later claims the court failed to meet international standards on fair trials.

February 6   Gadaffi reportedly authorized the "liquidation" of Libyans living overseas and hostile to the regime. There were twelve assassinations in the months that followed. At that time, thirty thousand Libyans were living abroad, mostly students on government grants.

March   Renewed fighting in Chad.

April   The Libyan Arab Foreign Bank lends Billy Carter $200,000. The loan is secured on his property. He uses the money to pay taxes and debts.

May 7   The U.S. State Department expels Libyans working at the People's Bureau in Washington. They are accused of harassing dissidents living in the U.S.

June 4   Jalloud justifies Libyan's pursuit of its nationals living abroad in an interview with an Italian newspaper: "Many people who fled abroad took with them goods belonging to the Libyan people. . . . Now they are putting their illicit gains at the disposal of the opposition led by Sadat, world imperialism, and by Israel."

		Britain expels three members of the Libyan People's Bureau staff in London after the shooting of two opponents of the Gadaffi regime.
June	27	An Italian DC-9 airliner is shot down off the northern coast of Sicily. A radar station at Marsala had been notified that it was a Soviet-made Tupolev on its way from Tripoli to Warsaw. Eighty-seven people are killed. A Libyan plane flying near the liner veered off and landed at Malta. At the time it was widely believed that Gadaffi was traveling on the DC-9 and that the U.S. tried to shoot him down with a missile.... This was denied by the U.S. Ten years later the remains of the DC-9 and fragments of a missile were found in the sea.
July	15	Billy Carter admits receiving the $200,000, creating uproar in the U.S. press just weeks before the presidential election. He says he received the other gifts and wrote to the U.S. government on behalf of the Libyans, but denies being a Libyan agent.
August		Reports of an attempted army mutiny at Tobruk, led by Major Idris Shehabi. There are also reports that Gadaffi has been killed, and then later that he survived another attempted coup with the help of East German forces. None of this is confirmed.
August	26	Dom Mintoff puts his planes and helicopters on alert in Malta.
August	27	Malta expels forty-seven Libyan military personnel.
August	30	Malta accuses Libya of endangering peace in the Mediterranean; the reasons for the dispute are a mystery—but a few days later war breaks out between Iran and Iraq. Libya backs Iran.
September	3	The day before he is due to stand trial in New York for exporting firearms to Libya, Frank Terpil vanishes. Later he is seen in

Beirut. A year later a reporter from *Newsweek* finds Edwin Wilson in Tripoli, running an import agency with a staff of American veterans from the Vietnam War.

September 4 The U.N. Security Council considers an urgent request from Malta. The mystery is still unexplained. The Libyan delegate to the U.N. insists that Malta and Libya are friends. The U.N. takes no action.

September 15 Italy formally recognizes Malta's neutrality. Malta agrees to allow no foreign bases on the island; neither the U.S. nor Russia can use its docks. Italy guarantees Malta's neutral status.

October Gadaffi provides testing facilities near Sebha for the West German company OTRAG. The firm tests weather, telecommunications, and educational satellites—and is later reported to have been testing medium-range ballistic missiles as well. This causes protests in the West. The tests are canceled after fifteen months.

October Col. Muhammad Yusuf al Mugarielhi, former Libyan Ambassador to India, leaves for Cairo and announces that he is joining the Libyan opposition. He accuses Gadaffi of "dictatorship, tyranny, and corruption."

October The U.S. Senate votes 47–44 against a proposed ban on Libyan crude and agrees to study other measures to confront Gadaffi.

October 30 Gambia breaks off diplomatic relations after allegations that Libya has been encouraging Muslim extremists.

October/November Gadaffi again invades Chad, this time with four thousand men. They occupy the city of N'Djamena. President Carter orders a U.S. satellite to be moved to cover Libyan troop movements. Tunisia asks for guarantees of support from the U.S. and France.

November Senegal breaks off diplomatic relations because of Libya's invasion of Chad.

November		Republican candidate Ronald Reagan defeats President Carter in the U.S. presidential elections. The U.S. hostages are still held captive in Iran, and Carter's failure to secure their release or confront the Arabs has been a prime issue.
November	20	All Sanusi *zawiyas* abolished with their employees offered other jobs within the state.
December		Gadaffi claims he moved Libyan forces into Chad to protect the Tuaregs who traditionally wandered across southern Libya and what are now Chad, Mali, and Niger.
December		Muslim rebels seize the city of Kano in northern Niger. They claim to have Gadaffi's support. This is neither confirmed nor denied.

1981

January		Gadaffi withdraws his forces from Chad after two of the rebel leaders, Habre and Oueddi, agree to join forces. They discuss uniting Libya with Chad.
January/February		Widely reported that the incoming U.S. President Ronald Reagan has such a low attention span that complex issues are best put to him in visual form. The CIA does just this, showing him a fifteen-minute film arguing that action needs to be taken against Gadaffi because he has shown himself to be anti-Israel, anti-Sadat, and anti-Hussein, anxious to unite the Arab and Muslim states in one federation, and keen to seize Chad because of its uranium deposits. Secretary of State Alexander Haig authorized to take action against Gadaffi.
February		Two Libyan businessmen attacked at Rome airport. Two Libyans arrested and later jailed.
February	11	A Libyan pilot lands a MIG-23 at Souda Bay in Crete and asks for asylum. The U.S. military take the plane apart and return it to Libya in pieces.

February		Haig reports that there were 760 international terrorist acts in 1980 in which 642 people died and another 1,078 were injured. He says that the U.S. will never again negotiate with terrorists as the Carter administration did in trying to secure the release of the hostages in Iran. Later disclosed by *Newsweek* that the U.S. began planning Sixth Fleet maneuvers for August, with target practice against pilotless planes near the Libyan coast, "because we wanted to tweak Gadaffi's nose."

March — Reported in the Swedish newspaper *Espressen* that Libya has purchased five large amphibious landing craft each fitted with 40mm Bofors rapid-fire cannon. Each carrier said to be large enough to transport eleven tanks and 240 troops. There are said to be ninety-six Libyans currently in Sweden training to operate radar, electronic communications, and computers.

March 15 — Libya denies asylum to hijackers of a Pakistan Airways plane. Gadaffi says he is against hijacking and the taking of prisoners.

March/May — Gadaffi angers the new Reagan administration by offering $100 million in aid to the Sandinista regime in Nicaragua. Russia offers wheat. Cuba sends military advisers. Rebel leaders in Salvador and Guatemala also told they will receive Libyan aid if they seize power.

May — The State Department closes down the Libyan People's Bureau in Washington and gives its staff five days to leave the U.S.

May — Reports of another attempt on Gadaffi's life as he is returning from a visit to Moscow. A decoy plane shot down; he survives.

May — Dr. Mohammad al Magharief, Libyan Auditor General from 1972 until 1977, publicly defects and becomes the focal point for U.S. attempts to overthrow Gadaffi.

July	15	France lifts the ban on arms sales imposed when Libya invaded Chad. Libya buys thirty-four Mirage fighter bombers, helicopters, submarines, and ten gunboats. In return, Libya allows the French company ELF-Aquitaine to prospect for oil.
August	19	Claims on Libyan TV that the U.S. is planning to murder Gadaffi as the Sixth Fleet begins its maneuvers off the Libyan coast. The fleet enters waters that are claimed by Libya. When the Libyan air force sends up two SU22 fighter bombers, these are shot down by U.S. Sidewinder missiles.
August	21–23	Gadaffi visits Ethiopia. Addressing 500,000 people at a rally, he calls on all the Mediterranean countries to deny military bases to the U.S. He signs defense treaties with Ethiopia and South Yemen.
August	25	Gadaffi visits Syria.
September	1	Gadaffi threatens to attack U.S. bases in the Mediterranean if U.S. ships and planes again enter the Gulf of Sirte.
September	1	Welcoming recruits from Libya's first military academy for women, Gadaffi calls for the "liberation of women within the Arab nation." He argues that the Arab states have failed to allow women to marry and divorce as provided in the Koran.
September		In London, the International Institute for Strategic Studies reports that Russia has deployed twelve surface-to-air missiles in Libya. These are said to be in bunkers outside Tobruk within range of Greece, Turkey, Egypt, and Cyprus, positioned to counter any U.S. strike against Libya.
October	6	President Anwar Sadat assassinated in Egypt.
October	7	The National Front for the Salvation of Libya set up under the leadership of Dr. Mohammad al Magharief. Later reported that the CIA is funding the Front with the support of

the White House and the Egyptian government. Dr. al Magharief says their aim is "to
rid the world of the scourge of Gadaffi's
regime."

October 11 Sadat's state funeral marked by rejoicing in
Libya and Syria. Western governments turn
out in force for the funeral, which is attended
by three U.S. presidents—but most Arab
leaders stay away. Of the twenty-four Arab
League states, President Numeiry of Sudan
is the only leader to attend. The others send
no representatives. This is because the Palestinians believe that Sadat sold them out at
Camp David.

November Gadaffi agrees to withdraw from Chad to
make way for an African peacekeeping force.
This fails to materialize because the African
states do not have the money to pay for it.

December The U.S. administration claims Gadaffi has
sent a team of Libyan hit-men to Washington
to assassinate the U.S. President. Armed
guards positioned on the roof of the White
House. Roadblocks set up to monitor traffic
movements in Washington. President Reagan
says: "We have the evidence and Gadaffi
knows it." When the names and photographs
of the "Libyan hit-men" are published, it tran-
spires that they are respectable *Lebanese*
businessmen.

December 10 On the pretext that Gadaffi is engaged in
hostile acts against the U.S., all American citizens are ordered to leave Libya. Senator
Howard Baker says: "The Libyans have been
behaving in a belligerent way." Libya reacts
by offering political asylum to any Americans
who wish to stay in the country. Libya says
it will not obstruct any Americans who wish
to return home and begins recruiting Cana-
dian, Iranian, and European workers to replace those that leave. It is estimated that
between fifteen hundred and two thousand

Americans ignore their government's instructions.

1982

February
Another attempted coup against Gadaffi. The leader said to be Rashid Abd al Hamid al Urfia. Twenty-one arrests. All are held without trial until March 1988 and then released under a general amnesty.

February
Gadaffi says on West German radio: "We have no wish to send our troops beyond Chad."

February/April
The Libyans open their own school in London, having purchased the former Kingsley School in Glebe Place, Chelsea, from the Inner London Education Authority.

May
An Argentinian mission arrives in Tripoli to buy SAM-7 antiaircraft missiles, air-to-air missiles, and infrared night-vision scopes for sniper rifles to use against the British in the Falkland Islands. Gadaffi authorizes deliveries to Buenos Aires. (This remains secret for five years until publication of *The Land That Lost Its Heroes* by Jimmy Burns (Bloomsbury Press). There was then speculation that the CIA secretly tipped off Mrs. Thatcher and that this explained her support for President Reagan's decision to bomb Tripoli).)

June
Civil war breaks out again in Chad. Habre seizes N'Djamena and Goukouni Oueddi asks Gadaffi for help.

November
Scottish engineer Robert Maxwell jailed for twelve years in Libya for bribery and espionage. The Libyans invite his wife to visit him, which she does over Christmas.

1983

January
Worried by his image abroad, Gadaffi invites a party of British and American journalists to Tripoli.

February
British Health Minister Kenneth Clarke vis-

	its Libya for five days. He visits hospitals and assures the Libyans that Britain is anxious to improve relations. There were then eight thousand Libyan students in Britain.
March	Reported in the British press and the BBC TV *Money Program* that Libya is funding a printing company that produces left-wing newspapers in Britain at specially reduced prices.
July	The Revolutionary Court sentences three people to death for being members of the pro-Iraqui Ba'ath Party. Amnesty International later reports that two of them, Muhammad Hilal and Mustafa al Nawari, were executed.
August	France intervenes in Chad to prevent Oueddi's rebel force and the Libyans from advancing farther south. After several months of fighting, the area south of the 16th Parallel is declared an exclusive zone.
September 3	The National Front for the Salvation of Libya holds its first demonstration outside the People's Bureau in London. The People's Committees respond by bussing in two thousand Libyan students from different parts of Britain to join a counterdemonstration. Similar demos are held for months (see April 17, 1984).
October 23	The People's Bureau in London writes to every M.P. saying that compensation should be paid to Libya for damage done by the wartime Allies, who left the Western deserts mined. Since then 1,956 Libyans have been killed by exploding mines with a further 1,777 injured. The Libyans claim there are still five people a year being killed on average, with ten in 1975.
November 2	Gadaffi writes to the Secretary General of the U.N. denouncing the U.S. invasion of Grenada and describing President Reagan as "the new Hitler of the world." He says that

the U.S. "has become a threat to the freedom of all the smaller nations and to world peace."

1984

January	21	Amar al Tagazi, head of the People's Bureau in Rome, shot dead in front of their premises.
February	18	Libya accuses Britain of providing sanctuary for "enemies of the Revolution."
February	18–20	In Tripoli, Gadaffi says the campaign against "stray dogs" (i.e., his enemies) will be increased.
March	10	Semtex bombs planted outside two London shops selling anti-Gadaffi newspapers, the Omar Khayyam restaurant in Regent Street, and the Auberge nightclub in Mayfair.
March	11	Three bombs planted outside a flat in Manchester occupied by a Syrian family believed to have connections with Libya.
April	15	Two leaders of anti-Gadaffi demonstrations publicly hanged at Tripoli University.
April	17	A large crowd of anti-Gadaffi demonstrators gathers outside the People's Bureau in London. Shots are fired at them from within the building in a ten-second burst of machine-gun fire, accidentally killing a young police-woman Yvonne Fletcher. Police then hold the Bureau under siege.
April	22	Home Secretary Leon Brittan says that even if the murderer were identified he would be covered by diplomatic immunity and could not be brought to trial. The Libyans are ordered to close the Bureau and remove all personnel with the exception of two, who are allowed to operate from within the Saudi Arabian embassy, handling consular matters.
April	30	Thirty expelled Libyans leave London.
May	1	Foreign Secretary Geoffrey Howe tells the House of Commons there is "no firm evidence" linking the People's Bureau to other recent bombing incidents.

May	8	Major disturbances in Libya after another attempted coup. There is an open battle near the Aziziya barracks in Tripoli where Gadaffi lived. It was reported long afterward that ninety Libyan soldiers were killed, and that afterward there were five thousand arrests. In February 1987, the *Washington Post* revealed that the CIA and the French Securité Exterieure were closely involved in the attempted coup. Members of the National Front for the Salvation of Libya were said to have been left dead on the streets of Tripoli as a warning to others. There were also reports of public hangings, but none of this has ever been confirmed in any detail.
June		At least eight people executed after being tried by the Revolutionary Courts. They were members of the Muslim Brotherhood, an Islamic fundamentalist sect.
August	29	Gadaffi opens the first section of Libya's Great Manmade River, the largest single civil engineering project ever undertaken anywhere in the world. This is a 350-mile double-pipeline carrying water from the underground lakes beneath the Sahara to supply Libya's coastal towns. At that time, the cost was said to be $14 billion.
September		France and Libya agree to withdraw from Chad.
September	28	During the British miners' strike, union executive Roger Windsor goes to Libya and meets Gadaffi. Libya contributes to their funds and says it supports the miners' cause.
November		Two Britons hired to assassinate former Libyan Prime Minister Abdul Hamid Bakoush seized by police in Egypt. They participate in an elaborate deception, with Bakoush pretending to be dead. When photographs of his "body" are published, the Libyan government falls into the trap—by saying the execution "has been carried out by a revolutionary

force, thereby implementing the decision of the basic People's Congress."

December   Terry Waite visits Gadaffi to discuss the release of British hostages.

1985

January   Mohammad Naas, head of the Libyan Arab Foreign Investment Company in Rome, says LAFCICO now has funds invested in ninety-four companies around the world, primarily in shipping, agriculture, mining, and manufacturing.

February   3   Terry Waite secures the release of four Britons held in Libya—Alan Russell, Robin Plummer, Malcolm Anderson, and Michael Berdinner. Four days later they leave for London.

February   The General People's Congress in Tripoli votes out a proposal from Gadaffi that all women should be conscripted into the Army.

April   General Numeiry deposed as President of Sudan. Libya had been backing an opposition group, the Sudanese People's Liberation Army.

June   James Abra, age fifty-seven, who worked for Plessey Radar, arrested at Tripoli Airport on his way back to London. The blueprints for Libya's radar system were in his briefcase. Accused of spying, he says he worked on the system when it was installed.

September   19   After receiving information from a Libyan dissident, police at Heathrow Airport, London, arrest Jordanian Dr. Rasmi Abdul Hafez Awad as he arrives from Geneva to collect and store six hand grenades.

November   After acting with total secrecy, Col. Oliver North stands on the brink of triumph. . . . He has agreed to ship U.S. spare parts for Phantom jets, helicopters, and Hawk missiles to the Iranians. The missiles are coming from Israeli stocks. The cargo will be taken to Iran on board a plane provided by Southern Air Transport, one of the CIA private airlines. "All the hostages are coming out," says North. But they don't. The deal collapses when the Iranians discover that the missiles are duds.

December 27 Palestinian terrorists attack Rome and Vienna airports. Twenty killed, including five Americans. One hundred eleven injured. The CIA blames Libya, and this is widely reported in the U.S. press. The Italian and Austrian governments link the attacks to Syria, revealing that this is where the terrorists were trained. Israeli Defense Minister Rabin agrees. The Austrian Minister of the Interior says: "There is not the slightest evidence to implicate Libya." However, for reasons that have never been explained, President Reagan and the CIA continue to accuse Libya.

1986
January 1 President Reagan signs an executive order requiring all U.S. citizens to leave Libya by February 1. Gadaffi again offers political asylum to any Americans who wish to stay in Libya.

January 1 Gadaffi says the Palestinian cause is "the holiest there is," but denies any involvement in the attacks on Rome and Vienna airports. He again says that he is against terrorism.

January 5 Gadaffi puts Libya's forces on a state of alert in case the U.S. launches a surprise attack. The Arab League says the Arab states will support Libya.

January 6 President Reagan presides over a meeting of the National Security Council, which decides to provoke Gadaffi by sending Navy ships and Air Force planes into the Gulf of Sirte. A Libyan response would then be used to justify bombing raids. Col. Oliver North suggests using Tomahawk missiles.

January	7	President Reagan says the U.S. has "irrefutable evidence" of Libya's role in the Rome and Vienna airport bombings. He announces the imposition of economic sanctions including a ban on all imports and exports. (The details for January 6, 7, and 17 were published in the Washington Post on February 22, 1987. The *Post* made the point that the President may not have realized that he was being boxed in by his staff, i.e., by Colonel North.)
January	17	President Reagan signs a secret executive order authorizing further contact with the Iranians and shipment of arms, waiving all regulations. The personnel implementing the order are CIA Director William Casey, National Security Adviser Admiral Poindexter, and his deputy, Colonel North. Casey is instructed not to tell Congress because of "security risks." The decision is not made known to Secretary of State George Shultz or White House Chief of Staff James Baker.
January/February		The U.S. National Reconnaissance Office orders the SIGNET intelligence satellite moved from the skies above Poland to monitor Libyan communications.
February	15	French planes attack Libyan radar installations at Quadi Doum in northern Chad.
mid-March		The U.S. transfers a third aircraft carrier to the Mediterranean, bringing the Sixth Fleet to a strength of three aircraft carriers and thirty other ships.
		In a British BBC TV program on the U.S. buildup in the Mediterranean, Senator William Proxmire says "the great powers must defend their right to sail in open seas." Reagan describes Libya as "an outlaw state," and Vice President George Bush calls Gadaffi "mad and unpredictable."
March	25–26	The U.S. provokes Gadaffi. All three aircraft carriers and the support ships are sent into

the Gulf of Sirte. Fifty Libyans are killed when the Americans sink four Libyan boats. U.S. aircraft also attack radar stations on the Libyan coast. Gadaffi appears on TV that night claiming that Libya repulsed a U.S. attack. It is also claimed that the U.S. refused to rescue survivors when the boats were sunk, although sixteen were later rescued by a Spanish oil tanker.

April	5	A terrorist bomb wrecks the La Belle Epoque discothèque in Berlin, killing an off-duty American and a Turk.
April	6	The CIA contacts President Reagan at the Western White House in California, claiming to have intercepted Libyan messages before and after the Berlin bombing.
April	12	Manfred Ganschow, chief of the Antiterrorist Police in Berlin, says that he "rejects the assumption that suspicion is concentrated on Libyan culprits."
April	12	James Abra, the Briton arrested at Tripoli airport the previous June, is sentenced to life imprisonment for espionage.
April	14	American F 111 bombers attack Tripoli and Benghazi. The Tripoli raid lasts eleven minutes. Nearly one hundred people are killed, including Gadaffi's sixteen-month-old adopted daughter Hana. Two of his children injured. Months later it is confirmed that the bombers targeted Gadaffi's home, hoping to kill him in his bed. It also emerges that the raid was carefully timed to coincide with the ABC TV early evening news. The bombers were allowed to use British bases by Prime Minister Margaret Thatcher, who took the decision without consulting her Cabinet. West Germany, France, Italy, and Spain all refused to cooperate, saying there was no proof that Libya had been involved in the terrorist attacks in Rome, Vienna, and Berlin.
April	14	President Reagan said he authorized the

bombing because of the raid on the Berlin discothèque: "Today we have done what we had to do. If necessary we shall do it again."

April 15   President Reagan tells the American Business Conference: "This arch terrorist has sent $400 million and an arsenal of weapons and advisers into Nicaragua to bring his war home to the United States. He has bragged that he is helping the Nicaraguans because they fight America on its own ground."

Many months later, after the arms-for-Iranian-hostages scandal had broken, it also emerged that planning for the hostages deal *and* for the raid on Tripoli had been handled by Col. Oliver North, since CIA Director William Casey was undergoing radiation treatment for prostate cancer.

In Britain, Mrs. Thatcher is widely attacked. Former Prime Minister Edward Heath said he would not have allowed the U.S. to use British bases as the raids were contrary to Article 51 of the United Nations Charter. Former Foreign Secretary David Owen said the U.S. "should have worked within the United Nations. No one can justify America breaking international law." Another former Foreign Secretary Dennis Healey said the raids would lead to more terrorism "with a further loss of British and American influence in the Middle East."

April 17   A bomb is seized as it is being smuggled aboard an El Al plane at London's Heathrow Airport. The plane was bound for Israel. The police later establish that a Syrian named Nezar Hindawi had tricked a girlfriend into carrying the bomb, which was timed to detonate in midair. Hindawi sentenced to forty-five years imprisonment. Hindawi's brother is later convicted in Germany of planting the bomb in the Berlin discothèque.

May 11   Terry Waite says on British TV: "It is not

impossible to talk to Gadaffi. I was able to go there and find a solution to our hostages' problem without any loss of face on either side."

May	28	Colonel North and Robert Macfarlane go to Teheran to negotiate the release of hostages, but the deal falls through.
June		Jalloud says Libya will resume supplying funds and arms to the IRA because of Britain's support for the U.S. raids on Libya. He says Libya has not been supplying the IRA for the past eleven years.
June	28	The U.S. Sixth Fleet begins fresh maneuvers in the Mediterranean. Gadaffi moves the headquarters of the Libyan air force and navy out of Tripoli in case Libya is attacked again.

Ali Treiki, Libyan Ambassador to the U.N., says that Libya is being used as a scapegoat.

August	12–13	Gen. Richard Lawson, Deputy Commander of the U.S. European Command, visits Chad and offers support in their conflict with Libya.
August	14	Admiral Poindexter submits a three-page memo to President Reagan advocating a campaign of deliberate disinformation against Gadaffi. This is discussed at a White House meeting presided over by Reagan. At one point, Reagan comments on Gadaffi's clothes and says: "Why not invite Gadaffi to San Francisco, he likes to dress up so much." Secretary of State George Shultz says: "Why don't we give him AIDS?"
August		Libya acquires two secondhand Airbus A310 jets from British Caledonian to use on domestic flights between Tripoli and Benghazi. British and French contractors agree to update the planes. This is criticized in the United States.
August	25	The Poindexter disinformation campaign commences. Most leading U.S. newspapers

carry false stories linking Libya to terrorism, talking of unrest in Libya and looming conflict with the U.S.

August   28   The U.S. stages Operation Sea Wind off Libya, involving aircraft carriers and jets, with practice bomb runs. Planes are sent within areas covered by Libyan radar. At the same time, the U.S. transfers eighteen F 111 bombers to the same bases in Britain that were used for the April raids. The U.S. government denies that any of this is provocative.

August   29   Britain's new ambassador in Washington, Sir Anthony Acland, tells the U.S. government Britain will require "hard evidence" before agreeing to another airstrike on Libya.

Gadaffi opens the second stage of the Great Manmade River at Braygah, accompanied by South Korean Construction Minister Lee Kyu-Hyo. Much of the building work was done by Korean contractors.

Part V

THE WAR OF WORDS CONTINUES
BETWEEN LIBYA AND THE
REAGAN GOVERNMENT, WITH
GADAFFI UNAWARE THAT THE
UNDERLYING FALSITY OF
REAGAN'S POLICY IS ABOUT
TO BE EXPOSED.

AS USUAL, THE LIBYANS STAGE
A MILITARY PARADE ON
SEPTEMBER 1, 1986,
TO MARK THE ANNIVERSARY OF
THEIR REVOLUTION, AND ALSO,
NO DOUBT, TO CONVINCE THE
WEST THAT GADAFFI IS
STILL IN CHARGE.

RUSSIAN VICE PRESIDENT
PYOTR DEMICHEV ATTENDS THE
PARADE, WATCHING EIGHTEEN THOUSAND LIBYANS
MARCH THROUGH TRIPOLI WITH
THEIR RUSSIAN TANKS AND MISSILES.
TRUCULENT AS EVER, GADAFFI
BRANDS PRESIDENT REAGAN AND
MRS. THATCHER AS "WAR CRIMINALS
WHO SHOULD BE BROUGHT TO TRIAL,"
AND DISPLAYS THE WRECKAGE OF
AN AMERICAN JET SHOT DOWN
DURING THE APRIL BOMBING RAID.

ON SEPTEMBER 5, PALESTINIAN
HIJACKERS SEIZE PAN AM FLIGHT 073
AT KARACHI AIRPORT. TWENTY-ONE PEOPLE ARE
KILLED. PAKISTANI COMMANDOS
STORM THE PLANE AND KILL
THE HIJACKERS.
ONCE AGAIN, THE CIA ACCUSES
LIBYA OF BEING INVOLVED—AND
GADAFFI PROMPTLY DENIES IT.

THIS SAME MONTH, COL. OLIVER
NORTH RETURNS TO IRAN, CARRYING
A COPY OF THE HOLY BIBLE AS A
GIFT FROM PRESIDENT REAGAN. AT
FIRST, THE U.S. GOVERNMENT DENIES
NEGOTIATING WITH THE IRANIAN
REGIME.... BUT THEN THE IRANIANS
DISPLAY THE BIBLE, PERSONALLY
INSCRIBED BY THE U.S. PRESIDENT.
UNFORTUNATELY FOR THE U.S.,
THIS IS WIDELY INTERPRETED AS
AN OFFENSIVE GESTURE. NO MUSLIM
WOULD EVER WRITE INSIDE A COPY OF
THE KORAN—AND THEY CANNOT
UNDERSTAND WHY THE PRESIDENT OF THE
UNITED STATES OF AMERICA
SHOULD WISH TO DEFACE
A HOLY BOOK.

THIS INCIDENT LEADS TO
IRANGATE, AND THE PUBLIC
EXPOSURE OF COLONEL NORTH AND ADM.
WILLIAM POINDEXTER, AND,
DURING THIS SAME PERIOD,
THE WASHINGTON POST AND
THE WALL STREET JOURNAL
REVEAL DETAILS OF POINDEXTER'S
AUGUST 14 MEMO TO THE PRESIDENT,
URGING A STRATEGY THAT
"COMBINES REAL AND ILLUSORY
EVENTS—THROUGH A DISINFORMATION

PROGRAM—WITH THE BASIC GOAL
OF MAKING GADAFFI THINK THAT
THERE IS A HIGH DEGREE OF INTERNAL
OPPOSITION TO HIM WITHIN LIBYA,
THAT HIS KEY TRUSTED AIDES ARE
DISLOYAL, THAT THE U.S. IS
ABOUT TO MOVE AGAINST HIM
MILITARILY."

EVENTUALLY IT BECOMES KNOWN THAT
COLONEL NORTH HAD BEEN USING TERRY
WAITE AS A COVER FOR HIS DEALS
WITH IRAN . . . AND SEYMOUR HERSH
REVEALS IN THE NEW YORK TIMES THAT
THE CIA HAS SPENT FIVE YEARS TRYING
TO ASSASSINATE GADAFFI.

GADAFFI BEGINS TO LIBERALIZE
THE LIBYAN REGIME, BUT STILL THE
CIA CONTINUES TO ACCUSE HIM OF
INVOLVEMENT IN TERRORISM,
BEFORE AND AFTER
THE BOMBING OF PAN AM FLIGHT 103
OVER LOCHERBIE. THE CIA ALSO
CONTINUES FUNDING HIS ENEMIES,
WHILE ATTEMPTS ARE MADE TO
PROSECUTE TWO LIBYANS ACCUSED
OF PLANTING THE LOCHERBIE
BOMB.

THESE EVENTS LEAD TO LIBYA'S
ISOLATION, AND THE IMPOSITION OF
SANCTIONS BY THE UNITED NATIONS . . .
AND ALSO TO A GROWING FEELING
THAT THE WEST HAS BEEN NEITHER
HONEST NOR EVENHANDED IN ITS
DEALINGS WITH GADAFFI.

October   2   The *Washington Post* and the *Wall Street Journal* disclose the contents of Poindexter's August 14 memo to the President.

October	8	U.S. State Department spokesman Bernard Kalb resigns: "I am dissenting from the reported disinformation." President Reagan insists: "No one on our side has been lying to anyone."
October	9	Kalb appears on CBS TV and says that he had never been aware of the government plan to deceive the media and had never knowingly given out "deceptive false information."

In Rome, three Libyans held in jail for attacks on other Libyans are exchanged for four Italians serving life sentences in Libya. |
October	30	Chad rebel leader Goukouni Oueddi announces in Tripoli that he is changing sides and will now support the government. The CIA reports that he has been shot dead by the Libyans. There are reports of a gun battle. However, Gadaffi is later filmed visiting Oueddi in the hospital and saying that those responsible will be punished.
November	19	Colonel North and Admiral Poindexter leave the White House after a fortnight of press and TV stories about their proposed arms-for-hostages deal with the Iranians. At first the deal is denied—but the Iranians produce the President's Bible! It transpires that North had been using Terry Waite as a cover for his deals with Iran.
December	11–12	Heavy fighting in northern Chad. Forty-five Libyans killed. Habre accuses the Libyans of using napalm and poison gas. The Libyans send in six thousand more troops.
December	12	The White House admits the President did not inform his Defense Secretary Caspar Weinberger or Secretary of State George Shultz of the arms-for-hostages deal.
December	21	Chad government claims that four hundred Libyans have been killed during a Libyan attack on towns in the Tibesti mountains.
December	31	On the eve of his latest mission to secure release of Western hostages, Terry Waite re-

fuses to confirm or deny that he has had six separate meetings with Colonel North.

1987

January	2	Libya attacks southern Chad, dropping five bombs on Arada, seventy-five miles south of the 16th Parallel. Chad government claims that 784 Libyans have been killed and a hundred tanks seized.
January	7	French planes again attack Libya's radar station at Quadi Doum in northern Chad. Libya retaliates with attacks on Chad villages.
January	12	Waite returns to Beirut—and is kidnapped. Nothing more is heard of him until August 1991 when released hostage John McCarthy says Waite was kept in solitary confinement for four years and then moved to join hostages McCarthy, Terry Anderson, and Tom Sutherland. The kidnapping comes in the wake of disclosures that hostage releases attributed to Waite had been accompanied by North's negotiations. The Arabs are now suspicious of Waite.
January	12	Gadaffi reported to have called for a *jihad* against Habre in Chad, accusing him of deserting his Muslim brothers and accepting aid from France and America. "He has gone to the ranks of the Christians, the Crusaders, the ranks of the enemies of Islam," says Gadaffi, arguing that Britain, France, and the U.S. have a historical hatred of Muslims.
February		The U.S. strengthens the Sixth Fleet in the Mediterranean, increasing it to thirty-five ships with the aircraft carriers *Nimitz* and *John F. Kennedy*. Nine people reported executed for murder and sabotage in Libya. Six civilians hanged in a public hall in Benghazi. Three soldiers shot. The executions were shown on TV.
February		Seymour Hersh reveals in the *New York Times* that the previous April's raid on Trip-

oli had been the culmination of a five-year campaign by the CIA to assassinate Gadaffi; he identifies the role of North and Poindexter, having interviewed seventy officials of the U.S. administration.

March — Asked about the recent executions, Gadaffi tells the *Observer*, a British newspaper: "They were secret terrorist groups like the Red Brigades and the Baader Meinhof groups, just like that. They were Libyan people. They killed people here, secretly. And they were guilty of intentional murder, premeditated murder."

March — Gadaffi warns France to take its "dirty hands" off Chad, where he predicts a "long and bitter struggle" until France withdraws its forces.

March 22 Libya suffers a major setback in Chad. Government forces overrun the Libyan base at Quadi Doum. Chad claims that thirty-six hundred Libyans have been killed and another seven hundred taken prisoner. Two thousand are said to have died of thirst in the desert.

April 29 British M.P. Ron Brown persuades Gadaffi to release the engineer Robert Maxwell, who was jailed for twelve years in 1982 for bribery and espionage.

May — Gadaffi invites Yasser Arafat and George Habash to Tripoli, saying that he has been so touched by the plight of the Palestinian refugees in Beirut camps that he wants the different factions in the PLO to unite. They agree, and at a subsequent conference in Algiers five different Palestinian groups unite under Arafat.

May/June Australia orders the Libyans to close their People's Bureau, accusing the Libyans of fomenting trouble in New Caledonia and East Timor, and supporting Aborigine protests in Australia.

June		Revealed in the *Washington Post* that the U.S. government colluded with Egypt and Sudan in 1983 in an attempt to bring down Gadaffi.
June	28	Reported that Gadaffi has called for the development of an Arab nuclear bomb, arguing that this is the only way the smaller nations can protect themselves against the nuclear powers.
August	7–8	Chad takes back the Aouzou Strip, claiming to have captured 437 Libyans. Libya had occupied the Strip since 1973. Libya retaliates by bombing government positions in the Tibesti mountains.
August	28–29	Libya sends in three thousand men, including paratroops, to reclaim the Aouzou Strip, capturing the key Aouzou oasis.
September	5	Chad claims to have destroyed twenty-six Libyan planes in an attack on the Maar tan as Sarra base in southern Libya. This is denied by Libya, who claim to have repulsed two attacks on the base. America sends $30 million in supplies to Chad.
September	7	French troops shoot down a Libyan bomber, a supersonic Tupolev 22 built in Russia, with an American-made Hawk antiaircraft missile. Libya sent two Tupolevs to bomb N'Djamena; the other escaped.
		Ceasefire announced between Libya and Chad, amid fears on both sides that the war might escalate. Libya estimated to have lost four thousand men, two hundred tanks, and forty-five aircraft since January. Chad losses not stated.
		Gadaffi switches support from Iran to Iraq in their war, after pressure from Egypt. Libya had previously been supplying Iran with surface-to-air missiles.
October	30	France seizes the *Eksund* inside its territorial waters. The boat had taken shelter during a gale, and is found to be carrying 150 tons of weapons worth £3.5 million, loaded in Tripoli and being taken to the IRA.

1988

March   9   Gadaffi announces the abolition of all courts set up by the People's Committees, and releases 400 political prisoners and another 130 foreigners held in Libyan jails. He acknowledges that Libya's penal system has not been working properly, saying some people have been wrongly imprisoned, and some wrongly executed. Many of those released were serving long sentences. Some were under sentence of death. Gadaffi says that in the future, "detention should take place only at the request of a public prosecutor." Gadaffi personally tears up the lists of those banned from traveling abroad; says he hopes to abolish the death penalty, and that "every citizen should be free to choose his education, job, and place of residence."

March   In an interview with a Kuwaiti newspaper, Gadaffi compares Libya with the French Revolution: "They said France was a terrorist state and all the kingdoms of Europe raged against it ... but with the passage of time those kingdoms became republics and monarchism disappeared."

April   Car bomb attack on the U.S. Club in Naples. Five killed. Seventeen injured. The Italian police name two members of the Japanese Red Army as suspects. The CIA blames Libya.

June   Gadaffi commutes all death sentences. Amnesty International later reported that this included six political prisoners who had been under sentence for many years, including one since 1970.

July   11   Gunmen open fire on the Greek cruise ship *City of Porus*. One gunman is killed. Later claimed that his gun came from a shipment sold to Libya in 1976.

    The U.S.S. *Vincennes* shoots down an Iranian airbus over the Persian Gulf; 290 people are killed. This provokes anti-American demonstrations throughout the Arab world. Suggestions afterward that this incident provoked the Iranians to seek revenge, with Iran giving money to the Popular Front for the Liberation of Palestine. It has been argued that this led to the bombing of Pan Am Flight 103 over Locherbie (see December 21, 1988).

August	31	Gadaffi announces plans to cut military service requirement from two years to one. No military parade is staged this year to mark the anniversary of the revolution. "Be rich," Gadaffi tells an audience. "Everyone is invited to become bourgois on condition that he does not do so by stealing the effort of another or by plunder."
August	31	Gadaffi takes the diplomatic corps on a cruise to the Tunisian port of Zarsis, where they pick up the Tunisian leader Ben Ali, and jointly inaugurate the offshore Bouri oil field, the largest so far discovered in the Mediterranean.
September	12	West Germany resumes diplomatic relations with Libya.
October		IRA reported to have acquired SAM-7 and Stinger missiles from Libya, thus stepping up their conflict with Britain.
		West German police arrest seventeen members of the Popular Front for the Liberation of Palestine and accuse them of planning to bomb an Iberian Airlines plane. This was known as Operation Autumn Leaves. Later it was argued this may have been Iran's first attempt to avenge the shooting down of their airbus (see July and December 21, 1988).
December		Gadaffi arranges the release of two French girls seized by the Abu Nidal group as the girls sailed through the Mediterranean with their mother fourteen months earlier.
December		In a major shift in policy, Yasser Arafat says

the PLO has renounced terrorism and accepts United Nations resolutions 242 and 388. They state Israel has a right to exist behind secure borders. Mrs. Thatcher comments: "This is a very considerable step forward, and we most certainly wish to encourage it."

December 21 — A bomb explodes on board Pan Am Flight 103 over Locherbie, Scotland, killing 259 people on board and 11 on the ground. Many months later it is revealed that a CIA unit was traveling back to the U.S. on the plane.

December — In a farewell interview with David Brinkley on ABC TV, President Reagan says he is considering a bombing raid on a Libyan chemical plant at Rabta. This shocks Britain and NATO, who had been given no warning of the President's intentions.

1989

January 4 — American planes shoot down two Libyan MIG fighters over the Mediterranean.

January 7 — After several days' controversy over the Rabta chemical works, Gadaffi walks into the Tripoli hotel where the Western press are staying, and says: "I didn't know you were here. I have just come for a cup of coffee." He accuses the U.S. of stirring up the Rabta issue to preempt a conference in Paris where 130 nations are considering chemical weapons. "We are against the use of chemical weapons," says Gadaffi, adding, "America must understand that her policy of surrounding us and using force against us will fail."

January 8 — Western journalists taken to Rabta. They are not allowed off the buses. Some claim to have seen missiles and radar installations. They are told to leave Libya within twenty-four hours. The German magazine *Der Stern* later reveals that thirty German, Swiss, and

Austrian companies have been working on the Rabta site.

January/April   Repeated clashes in Tripoli and Benghazi. Libya says these began when soccer fans protested that a World Cup qualifying match had been conceded to Algeria. Police reportedly fired into the crowd, killing a student. Twenty-four students arrested. Two years later, Amnesty stated that 392 people were detained and held without trial after clashes between Muslim fundamentalists and supporters of the Gadaffi regime. The truth of these stories is not known.

April   1   Chad military leader Idriss Deby flees N'Djamena with four hundred followers and sets up base near the Sudan border.

Russia agrees to supply Libya with fifteen long-range Sukhoi 24D supersonic jet bombers.

August   31   Libya and Chad sign an agreement in Algiers ending their war. Libya says its claim to the Aouzou Strip will be referred to the World Court.

September   1   At celebrations to mark the twentieth anniversary of the revolution, attended by eighteen heads of state, Gadaffi attacks U.S. imperialism.

September   19   A French UTA 772 plane explodes over the Sahara a few minutes after taking off from N'Djamena, killing 170 people. One theory is that it was shot down by a missile in the belief that Dr. Mohammed al Magharief, leader of the National Front for the Salvation of Libya, was on board. He was in N'Djamena at the time.

September   Gadaffi says he has stopped funding sixty liberation movements in different countries.

September   Gadaffi attends the Nonaligned Conference in Belgrade, where he again demands war reparations from Italy. He also urges that the power of veto be taken away from the five permanent members of the U.N. Security Council. The conference is attended by sixty-five heads of state and twelve prime ministers.

Libya joins the Interparliamentary Union. This is agreed by 105 votes to 9 with 12 abstentions. Those voting against include the U.S., Britain, Portugal, West Germany, New Zealand, and Israel. The leader of the Libyan delegation says the IRA will no longer receive support or assistance from Libya.

October   3   The liner *Granata*, which normally carries pilgrims to Mecca, is seized by 846 Libyans who set sail for Naples to protest Italy's failure to pay further war reparations. The ship is draped in black. Another 200 Libyans arrive in Rome by air to visit the graves of Libyans who died in exile. To coincide with these protests, Libya cuts all telecommunications with the outside world and declares a day of mourning. The protests are aimed at Italy's behavior during its colonial wars between 1911 and 1943.

1990
March   The U.S. government claims the chemical plant at Rabta is being used to make mustard gas. This is denied by the Libyans, who say the U.S. is trying to undermine Libya's attempts to create an economic union with Algeria, Tunisia, Morocco, and Mauretania. When asked if President Bush is planning military action, his spokesman Marvin Fitzwater says: "We aren't willing to speculate and nothing is ruled out."

March   14   A fire at the chemical plant in Rabta. Two people said to have died. This is followed by protests outside the Germany embassy [the main contractors were German]. A thousand Libyans gather with posters saying GERMANS OUT OF LIBYA. All journalists banned from

Libya after the fire. There is speculation that the fire has been faked.

| April | 10 | Three more French hostages released after Gadaffi's intervention, including the mother of the two girls released in December 1988. The French Foreign Minister praises Gadaffi. |

April 10 Three more French hostages released after Gadaffi's intervention, including the mother of the two girls released in December 1988. The French Foreign Minister praises Gadaffi.

October Gadaffi meets the Egyptian president Hosni Mubarek at the Egyptian coastal report of Mersa Metruh. Gadaffi says he has dropped all Libyan claims to the western desert. It is his first visit to Egypt since his disputes with Sadat. Gadaffi says: "I do not feel as a guest in this place. I am among my family and my brothers. . . . This soil is Arab soil. It is Libyan and Egyptian people and soil."

November 10 A new rebellion in Chad led by Idriss Deby and the Patriotic Salvation Movement. The U.S. accuses Libya of attempting to destablize the government headed by President Habre.

The U.S. declares support for Habre—but before it can act, Habre's government collapses and his troops begin throwing away their weapons and uniforms.

November 20 Chad rebels ambush government forces at Guered.

November 27 Chad rebels take the regional capital Abeche. French troops in the area refuse to take sides.

December 2 President Habre is deposed by Deby, who releases three planeloads of Libyan prisoners. After they have been flown home, Gadaffi sends Deby a limousine as a gift.

As the dust settles in Chad, it emerges that 650 troops commanded by the National Front for the Salvation of Libya have been based in Chad with the support of the CIA. Deby expels them. U.S. planes are sent in to Chad to help the Libyan rebels escape. The new Chad government takes journalists to the rebel bases, showing large stocks of U.S.

arms, including Stinger missiles, and long-range desert vehicles. It seems likely that another CIA attempt to invade Libya has been foiled.

Senegal grants asylum to former President Habre.

December 14   Press reports begin to appear linking the bombing of Pan Am Flight 103 with Libya.

1991

January   At the trial of the *Eksund* gun-runners in Paris, it is disclosed that four other shipments of arms were sent to Libya before the *Eksund* was seized in October 1987.

May/June   British Conservative M.P. Teddy Taylor visits Libya, meeting Gadaffi and Foreign Minister Ibraham Mohammad al Bushara. Taylor is given a letter aplogizing for the death of policewoman Yvonne Fletcher in 1984 together with a check for £250,000 as a donation to police charities. On his return, Taylor says: "I got the impression there has been a change in attitude, a complete sea change." Of Gadaffi, he says: "I found him a rather deep person. He was very well informed on world affairs. He was not the erratic and unstable person we are led to believe he is."

Amnesty International publishes its report claiming that there are still 467 political prisoners held in jail in Libya, "including prisoners of conscience reported to be held for reasons or under conditions which are contrary to international human rights standards."

June 9   Gadaffi offers to supply Britain with full details of Libya's arms shipments to the IRA. Libya's Ambassador the U.N., Dr. Ali Treiki, says: "We have broken all our links with the IRA." Libya subsequently supplies Britain with the names of twenty IRA members and says it sent ten tons of Semtex and hundreds of rifles and pistols.

August	27	Gadaffi opens the next section of the Great Manmade River, which he says will soon be pumping five million cubic meters of water a day through two aqueducts, each six hundred miles long.
October		A party of British Labour M.P.s visit Libya, including Tam Dalyell, Bernie Grant, Ronnie Campbell, Harry Cohen, and Jimmy Hood.
October	30	France issues warrants for the arrest of four Libyans whom it says were responsible for shooting down their plane over the Sahara in September 1989. They are accused of "conspiracy to commit murder" and include Gadaffi's brother-in-law Abdallah Sanusi.
November	14	Warrants are issued in Britain and the U.S. for the arrest of Abdel Basset Ali-Muhammad al Megrahi and al Amin Khalifa Fhimah, who are implicated in the bombing of Pan Am Flight 103 over Locherbie. That same day, the National Front for the Salvation of Libya issues a detailed briefing document on the bombing, naming the two Libyans.
November	16	Libya "categorically denies" any involvement in the Locherbie bombing, and says the matter should be referred to an international arbitration panel or to the International Court of Human Justice.
November	18	Terry Waite released.
November	27	Britain and the U.S. issue a joint declaration demanding the surrender of the two Libyans, disclosure of information about the bombing of Pan Am Flight 103, and compensation.
November	28	Gadaffi visits Egypt for discussions with Mubarek.
December	5	The twenty-one members of the Arab League express unanimous support for Libya, asking that Britain and the U.S. take no economic or military action against Libya.
1992		
January	2–3	Renewed fighting in Chad when former Pres-

		ident Habre returns with approximately four thousand men to capture two towns on Lake Chad.
January	10	Libya complains to the International Air Transport Association that aircraft from the U.S. Sixth Fleet have entered its airspace.
January	10	Gadaffi urges the General Assembly of the United Nations to meet to consider ways of eliminating terrorism.
January	14	Russia completes the withdrawal of all its forces from the Mediterranean.
January	21	The U.N. Security Council adopts Resolution 731 urging the Libyan government to comply with requests from the British and U.S. governments regarding the two wanted Libyans.
January	26	In an interview with the British newspaper the *Observer*, Gadaffi insists Libya has no chemical weapons. He also complains that, "The United Nations is dominated by the U.S.A. and Britain, who talk just like imperialists. The Security Council is now just part of the NATO alliance."
February	10	Press reports that the two Libyans have been executed to stop them from revealing Gadaffi's involvement in the Pan Am bombing.
February	11	Libyan judge Ahmed al Zawi denies that the men have been executed. They are said to be under house arrest and are duly shown on TV attending his court.
February	18	Unconfirmed reports that Gadaffi offered a Russian admiral $1 billion to leave behind a submarine with nuclear missiles when the Russians withdrew from the Mediterranean.
March	1	A key witness in any trial of the two Libyans is said to have defected to the West. Libyan intelligence officer Abdu Maged Jiacha was working at Luqa airport in Malta with the two Libyans.
March	3	Libya applies to the International Court of Justice in the Hague for an order against Britain and the U.S. requiring them to refrain

from "the use of any and all force or threats against Libya and from all violations of the sovereignty, territorial integrity, and the political independence of Libya."

March   4   Scotland Yard serves a subpoena on Pierre Salinger, chief foreign correspondent for ABC TV, demanding that he hand over all records relating to his interviews with the two Libyans.

March   17   The British Foreign Office advises all Britons to leave Libya.

March   The International Court of Justice hears Libya's case.

March   Gadaffi offers to meet U.S. President George Bush personally to supply proof that the Iranians and the Syrians were behind the bombing of Pan Am Flight 103. The PLO also offers to provide similar proof. President Bush refuses to meet Gadaffi.

March   27   British-based multinational conglomerate Lonrho sells a one-third share in its Metropole group of hotels to the Libyan Arab Foreign Investment Company for £77 million. The group includes hotels in London, Birmingham, Brighton, and Blackpool.

         Tiny Rowlands, chief executive of Lonrho, tells the *Daily Mail*: "To me Gadaffi is a super friend. This is not the only deal we will do with him. . . . Gadaffi and Lonrho are a super fit."

March   31   The U.N. Security Council adopts Resolution 748, imposing sanctions against Libya pending its compliance with Resolution 731. There are ten votes in favor with China, Morocco, Zimbabwe, India, and Cape Verde abstaining.

         The U.S. freezes the assets of forty-six multinational companies trading with Libya. They are involved in banking, investment, and petroleum. U.S. announces penalties for anyone found guilty of trading with Libya—fines of up to $250,000 and ten-year jail sentences for individuals, and $500,000 fines for companies.

April	1	Gadaffi threatens to cut off oil supplies to countries that support sanctions against Libya.
April	2	A mob attacks the Venezuelan Embassy in Libya. The Security Council had a Venezuelan chairman when sanctions were imposed. The Italian Embassy is also attacked.
April	8	Yasser Arafat narrowly escapes death when his plane crash lands during a sandstorm in southern Libya. His plane is missing for fifteen hours. The crew of three is killed. Carter, former president of the U.S., phones the White House and asks the U.S. to help find him.
April	11 and 15	Tiny Rowlands of Lonrho twice flies to Libya, conveying messages between Gadaffi and the West, trying to act as mediator.
April	13	President Mubarek flies to Tripoli to see Gadaffi, also acting as a mediator.
April		Libya loses its case in the International Court of Justice. The judges are not unanimous, voting 11–5.
April	14	Libya closes its airport, cuts off all telecommunications links with the outside world, and declares a Day of Mounring for those killed in the U.S. raid in 1986.
April	15	The U.N. sanctions against Libya come into force. Russia announces that it will be withdrawing all its twenty-five hundred citizens within a month.
April	17	Demonstrations in favor of Gadaffi in the Palestinian camps on the Gaza Strip and in Lebanon. Twenty-eight wounded.
April	19	The Libyan lawyer representing al Megrahi and Fhimah says his clients would surrender for trial if guaranteed a fair hearing. This remains the Libyan position, with Gadaffi saying at different times that the men were free to stand trial in Malta, Egypt, Sweden, or Switzerland.

April	27	*Time* magazine publishes a nine-page investigation suggesting that the U.S. and Britain are chasing the wrong quarry. They link the Pan Am bombing to a named drug dealer, to Abu Nidal and Ahmed Jibril, and the targeting of the six-man CIA unit traveling on the plane.
		The pretender to the Libyan throne, Prince al Hassan al Rida al Sanusi, dies in London at age sixty-five.
May	10	In an interview with Marie Colvin for the *Sunday Times*, Gadaffi admits his past links with the IRA—"We helped them because they told us they were revolutionaries like us." And he relates the case of the two Libyans to the Rodney King trial: "We cannot send our children to American justice. How can we trust American justice after the verdict in Los Angeles?"
May	14	In another interview, Gadaffi again insists that Libya has renounced terrorism.
June	9	Libya's former Ambassador to Tunis, Abdul Atti al Obeidi, provides British diplomats with background briefing on Libya's past dealings with the IRA at a two-hour meeting in Geneva. This is held in the presence of the U.N. Director General for Europe, Antoine Bianca.
August	9	Lonrho confirms that it has developed a joint company with the Libyans to expand its mining interests in Africa. These include the Ashanti gold mine in Ghana and Lonrho's cobalt and copper reserves in Zaire. The $300 million company has been established offshore with Lonrho holding forty-five percent and the Libyans fifty-five percent.
November	20	Gadaffi announces plans to distribute half of Libya's annual oil income directly to its people. Each family expected to receive $10,000 per year.
		Jalloud warns the People's Congress that

the U.N. ban on spare aviation parts is putting the lives of Libyan Arab Airways passengers at risk. "Every day there are dozens of flights on which passengers are in danger because of the lack of spare parts and maintenance. This is mass murder."

December 21 Just a few days later, on the fourth anniversary of the Locherbie bomb, a Libyan Arab Airways Boeing 727 crashes near Tripoli. There are reports that it may have collided with a military plane; 158 people killed.

December 22 Gadaffi declares three days of national mourning. Later, in a national TV broadcast, he suggests that either the IRA or "evil Western forces" could have been responsible for the Tripoli plane crash.

Part VI

The Desert Mystic

In the heat of the midday sun and at prayer times, all goes quiet, the shutters come down, but walk through its streets and markets as a light morning breeze wafts in from the Mediterranean, or at night when the air turns cool and people wear an extra layer of clothes, walking hand in hand, talking in groups, eating in restaurants, going to the cinema, and then Tripoli rustles and bustles ... date palms sway in the breeze, lights shine along the sea front, around the harbor, from the windows of new German-built apartment blocks, modern hotels, and the tall, impervious, pinkish walls of the fourteenth-century Moorish castle.

This is a shining, attractive, whitewalled capital city, with fine Italianate and Moorish houses in its center, open squares, broad streets, but also tiny, winding alleyways, where still a blind beggar, dressed in traditional robes and leaning on a stick, may stand in a doorway. (When I saw one such man, I stood some yards away and watched. Every passing Arab gave him alms.)

Gadaffi may say he decries the cult of personality and no doubt thinks he does—but by day or night, his symbols surround. Walk down one of the streets where one-man traders—shopkeepers, caterers, metalsmiths, light engineers, sheet-metal workers, or electricians have their shops and workshops, and there is his portrait, framed on a wall, or propped up behind a coffee jar. Out in the main square, commemorating the revolution, his portrait is picked out by spotlight; but it is modest in size, not like the vast, vulgar thirty-foot pictures of Saddam Hussein that one sees in Iraq.

281

The other symbols are there, too; the slogans wherever one goes, taken from *The Green Book* or Gadaffi's more recent pronouncements—PARTNERS NOT WAGE-WORKERS standing side by side with SPORT IS A PUBLIC ACTIVITY TO BE PLAYED NOT WATCHED and the mind-boggling THE WHALES AND US ARE WAITING FOR THEM, which I can only assume means that Gadaffi and all his committees have sworn to stand shoulder-to-shoulder with Greenpeace and the Friends of the Earth to defend whales against their common enemy (who would, of course, be the "imperialists").

This is not an unhappy country. Its people look healthy. They feel free, having no idea of Freedom's other meanings. They are gentle, courteous, and genuinely proud of Libya's achievements. Out in the desert, one can see mile upon mile of land reclaimed for orange, lemon, and olive groves; fields of potatoes, cabbage, lettuce, fennel, and root vegetables (I was there in April when these crops were ready for harvest, a month ahead of southern Italy or Greece); long rows of greenhouses; hedges of tall eucalyptus trees used as wind breaks, or mimosa, which grows wild and is considered a nuisance, and, where the reclaimed land meets the desert, scrub grazing for sheep, goats, and camels. (I noticed, too, a small herd of black and white Friesian cattle, presumably brought from the Netherlands, but adapting here to a hardier diet, their fur more wiry and their limbs stockier than one would see them in Western Europe.)

"Why don't you write about this?" said a Libyan, with an expansive gesture of his hand. "You may be ahead of us, but we are catching up with you. We are growing our own food now, bringing water to the desert, building our own tractors. . . ."

This is not wholly true. The Libyans do now have a tractor factory, but they also import tractors, trucks, cranes, and other vehicles from France, Germany, Korea, and, especially, Japan. While the rest of the world has been closing down its iron and steel works, to rationalize production, and develop other products like high-tensile plastics, the Libyans have built their own, their very first steel works, at Misurata, where Libyan factories produce the twelve-foot-diameter steel-and-concrete pipes needed for the greatest Libyan investment of all, the Great Manmade River. Gadaffi sometimes complains that the West is uninterested in his Great Manmade River, for it is one of the most remarkable civil engineering ventures in the history of mankind; a vast water duct being built at a cost of $35 billion to pipe water from huge underground lakes beneath the Sahara to the coastal towns and, eventually, to inland towns like Kufra. The first leg of the water duct, 350 miles in length, supplies Tripoli, and already two million cubic feet of water are being pumped through every day. By the time it is finished, the Great Manmade River will run for eleven hundred miles, providing Libya with a national water grid and enabling its government to reclaim even more desert.

Gadaffi's aim is that Libya should be self-sufficient, able to live without the outside world, produce all its own food and consumer goods so that if ever the oil and then the gas reserves run out, Libya will still be an advanced economy, providing its people with the highest standard of living in Africa and possibly, by then, outstripping many countries in Europe.

Already, Libya has factories producing medicines at Rabat and Tarhuna (though the West insists that these are for manufacturing chemical weapons, which Gadaffi denies). Others make paper, cardboard, fabrics, boxes, stationery, sheet-metal products, canned foods, their own cigarettes (which taste bitter), soft drinks—and even toilet paper. Predictably the toilet tissue wrappers bear the slogan PARTNERS NOT WAGE-WORKERS. No one can escape *The Green Book*, not even in the lavatory.

And yet what do the Libyans make of all this? How do they feel about the man who has made it possible, their leader, Col. Muammar Gadaffi?

Officially, Gadaffi has no executive duties to perform, no decisions to make. He is not responsible for anything, being merely head of state, Leader and Guide, as they call him. After Gadaffi threatened to resign several times in the early days of the revolution, and once left the country to live in Egypt with his wife and child, his colleagues in the Revolutionary Command Council realized that he was essentially a leader and thinker, rather than a nuts-and-bolts man. On April 6, 1974, they formally announced that Gadaffi had been "relieved of his political and administrative responsibilities" and would henceforth "undertake ideological work," while remaining head of state and commander-in-chief of the armed forces. His formal title is *Leader of the Revolution*.

But what of the Man himself, whom President Reagan described as "a barbarian" and "a mad dog"; whom President Sadat called "one hundred percent mad", saying that Gadaffi was "not quite a man", an Arabic form of abuse to describe him as a homosexual, and of whom former U.S. Secretary of State George Shultz said, "Why don't we give him AIDS?"

Surprisingly, I found that every Libyan that I met knew of the West's vilification of their Leader. None of this has been kept from them. They could tell me where, when, and what President Reagan had said—and why they thought he was wrong. One highly intelligent, well-read Libyan diplomat, who had lived in New York and still manages to get all the newly published American books that he wants to read sent through to him, said, as though this were something unknown in the West:

> Of course, the problem is that the Americans and the British have given far too much power to their security services. In America, the CIA has been allowed to operate independently of the government, without democratic control . . . and it's the same in Britain, where even your Members of Parliament have no idea what your MI5 and your MI6 get up to. They are still playing games like James Bond, but the world is changing, it's leaving you behind. . . . We thought things might get better when George Bush replaced Reagan, but we weren't too optimistic, for Bush was Reagan's Vice President and formerly director of the CIA. . . . As we say in our country, there's always tomorrow

Yes, yes, yes—the point is made, the comment heard; it may be part truth and part exaggeration, but does Gadaffi speak for his people? Does he have their support? Do they believe what he tells them? Do they identify with his crusade against the "evils" of the Christian West?

"He is our leader, and we respect our leader—just as we would expect you to respect your leaders."

But the nature of the respect is different, the word has different meanings. This is something I learned in Sicily, where "respect" has a semimythical connotation, both to the people and "the men of respect." Once respect is given, only death or dishonor can remove it, and there is this unspoken bond between Gadaffi and the Libyan people, who have, for centuries, accorded a very special, theological respect to their leaders. This was what enabled the Sanusi to establish their spiritual hold on the Bedouin through three generations, and now this same loyalty has its repository in Muammar Gadaffi, who was born of this land, knows its secrets, and, in a real, symbolic sense performs the role of a *marabout*, a phenomenon unique to Islam and the deserts of North Africa. There is no parallel to the *marabouts* in Christian religion, and as the Bedouin were illiterate and sought to avoid contact with foreigners, little of their history survives in written form. *Encyclopedia Britannica*, in a section based on the researches of the French writer L. Rinn, author of *Marabouts et Khouan* (1884), describes them as being, quite literally, "living saints." They were wandering hermits or monks, who traveled by foot across the desert; mystics appearing from nowhere, always honored guests in the Bedouin tents, for they were thoughtful and wise, able to dispense advice on family matters, to decide territorial disputes between neighbors, reciting verses from the Koran to an illiterate people who would otherwise never hear them spoken, and doing so in a way that showered *baraka*, divine blessing. *Marabouts* are not to be found anywhere else in Islam, for most Muslims are averse to the concept of "living saints," but in North Africa they have been a cult for centuries, with its followers particularly numerous among the Marabtin, the ancient tribes—of whom the Gadadfa were one—who could trace their history back to Andalusia, and before.

Evans-Pritchard talks of *marabouts* healing sick children and animals, praying for the rains to come, writing talismans and teaching the beliefs and law of Islam. "Such a man was also a *muhakkam*, one who arbitrated in their disputes and said the *fatiha* at their settlements and undertakings to make them binding. He could arbitrate among them because he was not of them . . . [but] a man who follows religion and not the rains. The Bedouin of Cyrenaica owe much to these holy men, for, ignorant and superstitious though they may have been, they taught the tribesmen to respect learning and religion and kept those twin lights burning, even if dimly, through centuries. The Bedouin do not forget them, or to say a prayer for them, when they pass their tombs. . . ."

Throughout North Africa, and especially in the Sirte Desert and Cyrenaica, these tombs—and there are hundreds of them—mark the places where *zawiyas* were established (see chapter 2), where the Bedouin would bury their dead and where they would meet with other tribes, either to feast or discuss tribal business. Often, the tombs would be no more than a pile of stones, and at the very most four small pillars of stone, supporting a cupola, for Muslims are opposed to grandiosity, in death as in life.

That Gadaffi should come from this tradition, born to desert Marabtin, educated in a *zawiya*, gives him a special status in Libyan, and especially Bedouin, eyes. Having led them in their revolution, established their system of society, and given them what *they* perceive to be freedom, he has the role of the *marabout*, or something close to it, for the rest of his natural days, with the title *Leader of the Revolution.*

Gadaffi does not have to submit himself for reelection. There is no need for him to explain himself. By and large, his opinions are respected (although he has, on occasion, changed courses in response to the views of the General People's Congress)—and he does not have to reveal himself any more than he wants to.

The West may well know more about Gadaffi than his own people do, for the Libyans value each other's privacy. Being passive by nature and living by values that are wholly understood, since ninety-six to ninety-eight percent of the population are Muslims, they tend to accept what they are told, providing this all happens within their accepted framework.

They may have seen him on television, or have his photograph framed on a wall, but most have never met Gadaffi. I have spoken to senior oil industry engineers, Britons and Americans who have worked in Libya for fifteen and twenty years, drilling for oil and developing its technology. None of them had ever seen Gadaffi. One of Libya's ambassadors, a senior official by any criteria, told me he had never spoken to Gadaffi, though he added proudly that twice he had been in the same room. A British photographer working for an American agency told me he spent six weeks crisscrossing Libya with an official escort, hoping to take photographs of Gadaffi. On two occasions he was specifically invited to be at Sebha and Cyrene at times when Gadaffi was expected. On neither occasion did Gadaffi arrive.

However, on the other hand, when Western pressure on Libya over the suspect chemical works at Rabat was at its height, Gadaffi himself drove up to the hotel where Western journalists were staying, walked in without an escort, went to the lounge, sat down, and ordered a cup of coffee. "I didn't think you'd be here," he said ingenuously, as he started to answer their questions.

So who is this man, this desert mystic, who has led a revolution in the name of Islam, given a nation a framework to live by, seized that nation's wealth for its people, sought to export *The Green Book* philosophy all around the globe, and chosen to defy the mightiest military power on earth?

The bare bones of his life are simply stated. Earlier chapters studied the background of his tribe, the culture that he overthrew, and the one that Gadaffi has since created. We know that his father Mohammad Abdel Salam ben Hamed ben Mohammad Gadaffi lived on until his late nineties, dying in 1985, and that father and son were close, which is not uncommon in the Arab world. We know, too, that his mother Aisha died in 1978, and that they continued to live in their Bedouin tent, for Gadaffi insisted that no one should ever have cause to say that Brother Muammar had shown preference to his parents when there were so many Libyans in desperate need of housing and medical attention. We know this, for Gadaffi continued to return there long after he became Leader of the Revolution, going back to the goatskin tent, sleeping on a mat, and living without tap water or electricity, just as he had as a child.

Likewise, we know that his three sisters also continued to live in the tents with their children, although the family is now dispersed, allegedly with Gadaffi's cousins, nephews, and brothers-in-law positioned around the country, holding army and civil posts that would be crucial in the event of an attempted countercoup. Since Gadaffi knows how revolutions are led, he has made sure that his own tribe can take control of Libya's ammunition dumps at short notice, i.e., by radio command. (Officially the tribal structure has been abolished, but it continues to function with the Gadadfa and Jalloud's tribe the Meghara providing many of the key officials within the Libyan state. The Meghara also come from the Sirte Desert, with neighboring grazing lands). Gadaffi's cousins Massoud Abdulhafiz, Ahmad Gaddalfadim, and Sayeed Gaddalfadam keep an eye on the departments dealing with external policy; another cousin, Khalifa Khanish, looks after Gadaffi's personal security, as he has done for over twenty years, while three surviving members of the original Revolutionary Command Council—Jalloud, Kharrubi, and Younis—control the Libyan equivalent of a civil service and military high command.

It is also known that Gadaffi's mother chose his first wife, Fatiha, daughter of a senior officer in King Idris's army, but that within a year Gadaffi divorced her (as Muslims may with a minimum of ceremony), preferring instead to marry Safiya, the raven-haired, striking-eyed nurse, who tended to his dressings when Gadaffi was struck down by appendicitis shortly after the revolution. President

Nasser is said to have witnessed their wedding, and although there have been many reports of Gadaffi's supposed dalliances, the marriage seems strong and good, with Safiya supporting her husband in public (which would be unthinkable in most Arab states). At different times, it has been suggested that Gadaffi has had a string of affairs with women, ranging from Imelda Marcos and the Austrian princess Ira von Furstenberg to an East German masseuse, a Yugoslav nurse, and an Austrian journalist Renate Possamig, who claimed that he showered her with golden gifts and begged her to become his third wife, which all sounds rather unlikely, though it made a good story at the time.

The Gadaffis have six sons, whom their father has said are all likely to become doctors. They have a daughter, also named Aisha, and probably wanted another, for it was an adopted daughter, Hana, who died in the American F111 bomber attack upon their home.

Throughout most of their marriage, the Gadaffis have lived within the army compound known as the Bab Aziziyah barracks, two miles from the center of Tripoli; that was where they were bombed, and although Gadaffi was reported to have moved away soon afterward, I have reason to believe they are still there, for this is where he works and receives visitors, the bombed house being but one building within a vast compound, six miles long and shaped like a teardrop, designed to give the Leader of the Revolution personal privacy and security. Although the compound has a helicopter pad, a range of satellite dishes pointing in all directions, and a hundred-foot tall communications tower that enables Gadaffi to keep in touch with the farthest outposts of the army, it is not like an army barracks at all, once one is inside its walls. I have been there myself, touring and photographing the house that was bombed.

This was an extraordinary experience, partly because one does not expect to see the site of an attempted assassination, preserved as of that moment, with bits of shrapnel and other debris, including the metal casing of American missiles complete with their serial numbers, but extraordinary, too, for the unexpected insight into the way Gadaffi lives, seeing how he furnishes his living room and bedroom, the colors he chose for his bathroom suite (mainly brown), and the separate suite for his children, with transfers of Snow White and the Seven Dwarfs and Donald Duck around the bath and over the basin, the choice of furnishings, the paintings, the marble floors and loose carpets, the children's schoolbooks, and the blood stained bed where Hana died, encased in glass. In his study, I sat in his chair, looked out through his window, held his red telephone, and looked around at the empty bookshelves.

The first surprises come before one gets this far, for the compound is surrounded by a fifteen-foot wall that is meant to be impenetrable. There are few entrances, and along the top of this wall heat sensors, remote-control cameras, and alarm systems are linked electronically to an internal master desk. At one entrance, I passed through three sets of doors, each vacuum-sealed like the door of a bank safe, leading from the first inner chamber to the next, with groups of men on guard, one manning the control desk, with telephones and microphones by his side. No doubt they were heavily armed, but, if so, their weapons were concealed. All this to protect the Leader of the Revolution and his family—but from what? To shield him from the People, from imperialist aggressors, or to give him privacy? Or, perhaps, the time to take control in the event of an attempted coup; time to either escape by helicopter—or issue commands over the radio and telecommunications systems that link him with the other main army command centers at Sebha, Kufra, Benghazi, and also, apparently, at Waddan in the Sirte Desert, where another command center has been established in an area closed to all visitors. Perhaps he would be safe here, for a battery of French-made Crotale antiaircraft missiles also protects this compound, together with tanks and antitank guns.

And yet, but for these defenses, it is not like an army barracks at all, more like a country club or a vacation camp, with houses spaciously positioned apart, orchards, lawns, vegetable gardens, two tennis courts, a soccer field, and plenty of trees and greenery to shield all the defensive hardware.

My invitation to go there came at a few minutes' notice on the night of April 14, 1990, when I was told that this would be my opportunity to hear Gadaffi speak as the finale to an evening of Saharan music, poetry, and speeches, staged to mark the fourth anniversary of the American bombing. Several thousand Libyans were gathered on the lawns and in the two large courtyards adjoining the house at right angles. Many were seated. Others were drinking orange juice or eating cream cakes, as they listened to the musicians beating drums made from hollowed gourds, shaking tambourines, and playing the delicate strings of the cithara. There was an excitement in the air, for Gadaffi rarely appears in public and tonight it was thought he would. His personal bodyguard, sometimes called the Green Angels or the Revolutionary Nuns, were guarding the stage, dressed in their olive-green uniforms, carrying rifles and trained to kill. The music continued for three or four hours, but the Leader didn't turn up; he seldom does—and someone else was given his speech to deliver instead, a fiery oration threatening revenge against the American imperialists, the devilish cowards, the sons of Satan, who dared not fight by day but sought to kill by night, murdering women and children as they slept.

Once again, the mystic had failed to materialize, and while the musicians played on and the warm air of the desert billowed in over the walls, I took this opportunity to walk around the ground floor of the house, the area now preserved as a museum, taking photographs as I went, walking through any door that I saw, since no one told me not to, finding myself on marble stairways and in corridors that had no windows. No one else was taking photographs, but neither did they mind that I was. Every few minutes, a Libyan would engage me in conversation, asking me about my Minolta camera, my lenses, where I came from, what America and Britain were really like, what I thought of their leader, and whether I enjoyed their music. None of them had ever met Gadaffi, nor even seen him, other than on a television screen. They were not surprised at his nonappearance. The Leader was a busy man. There was always tomorrow.

Externally, this seemed to be a rather ordinary flat-roofed, two-story building with a large upper veranda, built in what one might call the architecture of concrete brutalism; concrete walls two or three feet thick, curving stairwells opening out onto the lounge area without doors. The only rooms with doors were the bedrooms above. There was also a third floor, although one would never have thought so, and another door that led to Gadaffi's private study with its oak-paneled fitted bookcases, a leather-topped desk, and a wood-framed upholstered chair with armrests, carved in Louis XVI style though it probably came from a modern department store. I noticed that the Gadaffis have separate bedrooms, with his sporting a large, circular bed upholstered in brown velvet and hers with a stiffened mattress so that Safiya can rest her back in traction.

*　　*　　*

In every room, it was noticeable that the furniture was no better than one would find in any middle-income Western apartment block. The sofas and armchairs were large and comfortable, but not antique, and the "paintings" on the wall miserable reproductions of landscapes. If the reader begins to form the impression that this does not sound much like a flat-roofed, two story dwelling, then my point may be getting across: the inside bears no relation to the outside. I discovered that the building went back and back and back, with those internal corridors totally enclosed. I opened one door to find myself faced by a marble staircase, which I ascended alone to find myself in a large, red-ceramic-tiled, red-walled conference room, with a large crescent-shaped table that would have seated thirty people, and a garish painting of Gadaffi, predominantly in red and white, hanging above the chair, or was it a throne, where the Leader of the Revolution would have sat, bathed in spotlights, for there were lights trained upon this spot banked across the ceiling. Down another corridor, I came across a steel door set into a concrete wall which, I have no doubt, was the entrance to an elevator that would have taken Gadaffi down below to an underground concrete bunker—of the kind that the British security services built for themselves below Marsham Street, Westminster, in the mid-sixties.

But what does this tell us of Gadaffi the man? Rather a lot, I suppose, for here behind walls, sensors, and infrared cameras, protected by radar and missiles, lie these further layers of defense, beyond which he retreats if he has to—and where his family probably disappeared on the night that the bombers struck.

Here in this concrete redoubt, or whichever complex he chooses (for I am sure there are several), he is far from the People and yet, curiously, only two miles from the center of Tripoli and as totally in control of his world as was the Wizard of Oz. This is a strange kind of fantasy world, in which there are no strangers or passersby and no one to ask any questions, where he can spend most of his days in track suits (which is what he prefers), quickly changing into yachting jackets, tailored slacks, and silk shirts, or the flowing robes of the desert, if that is what he thinks an occasion demands; a world where he can read voraciously (Foyles of London send him all new books that they think he would like to read), listen to music (he has a sound system and prefers either Saharan music, Egyptian music, Beethoven sonatas, or Mozart), sometimes walking in the orchards or playing a game of tennis or volleyball. He is out of touch with the real world, yet does not miss a trick— for those satellite dishes bring the whole world to his fingertips.

It is a simple life, and yet it is not, for he lives in a world of satellite technology, the modern equivalent of the radio systems that obsessed him as a junior army officer, listening to everyone but accountable to no one, with no interest in wealth, drugs, or alcohol, few of the ordinary vices (so far as one can tell), as much a family man as any other, and totally removed from the day-to-day pressures that beset political leaders. A man who can quite literally appear from nowhere, and just as easily vanish.

A Singular Creation

F ew other political leaders, indeed none that I can think of, have endeavored to create a wholly new kind of society, fashioned around a personal creed. Such audacity is usually the preserve of the gods. Lenin and Mao Tse-Tung may have tried, with a borrowed idea, but too many mouths needed feeding and, already, their edifice crumbles. Gadaffi's chance lay within a barren landscape, a convenient location, a people with few aspirations—and oil.

Whatever the enormity of his actions (and who would deny that his abuse of power passes most understanding), there can be no denying his achievement. Nor can it be doubted that his motives were, in the main, admirable. Historically, his place may be more secure than that of many respected political leaders, for it was largely Libyan oil wealth that brought Nelson Mandela and his oppressed people to the brink of power in South Africa; which enabled the Palestinians (albeit with violence) to press their case for two decades until eventually they sat down at a conference table with the Israelis, and one day, perhaps, peace will come in Ireland, though bought at a hideous price. The Libyan checkbook has played its part in all this.

But will Gadaffi be judged by this, or by his attempt to use oil wealth to create his nonviolent society, where everyone follows the Leader? And is it really the kind of society that Gadaffi believes it to be?

"I have created a Utopia here in Libya," he says, "not an imaginary one that people write about in books, but a concrete Utopia."

But has he? Or is he merely a Caliban, doomed to be left alone while the world around him changes?

The Libya that Gadaffi portrays in his speeches, the society outlined in *The Green Book*, stands far removed from his real world, like an imaginary golden city on a distant mountain, but the image is maintained because the Leader constantly needs to rationalize rather than accept things as they are.

Yes, two million cubic meters of water flow through the pipes of the Great Manmade River every day, and by the time the project is finished in 1995 or 1996, this will have risen to five million, the fields will hum to the sound of tractors and the whistle of water sprinklers. Every Libyan will have a job, either working in a family business or within a cooperative. Every family will have a house, a garage, and a car. Most will possess televisions, videos, and washing machines. There will be food for all, free schooling, medical care, and dentistry. They will be able to travel abroad without restriction—and every year, under Gadaffi's latest plan, each Libyan family will receive an additional cash bonus from the state, roughly ten thousand dollars per family, as their share of the country's oil revenues. (The oil belongs to the People and therefore they should share in its income; that's the theory.)

It all sounds so wonderful ... but Libya is nothing like that. The country is in a mess. The Leader cannot be held accountable, for mystics are beyond all natural law.

Everywhere one goes in Libya, there is filth. This is not only through lack of conventional hygiene and an unwillingness to use lavatories, but because rubbish is left wherever anyone chooses to leave it.... There are vast piles of black plastic sacks, stinking with rotting garbage; abandoned furniture, beds, chairs, and old mattresses, and beside every highway, for miles on end, heaps of builders' rubble, burnt-out cars, derelict trucks and other vehicles, and, wherever one looks, dead cats and dogs rotting in the sun, infested with maggots.

This is a nation blessed with all the necessities of life that has not learned to live. I have seen this with my own eyes, and I have also spoken to thirty or forty other Britons and Americans who are still working in different parts of the country and whom I clearly cannot name, for their own sake. All are astonished when they see this for the first time, and yet, when one stops to think about it, can any nation make the transition from poverty to well-being without something going wrong? If it takes a century or more for a nation's foreign policy to evolve, or to acquire an agreeable code of common law, can one expect Libya to accomplish all Gadaffi's aims in just one generation—or its people to lose the habits they have lived by for centuries?

The country's underlying weakness lies in its economy. The Islamic anarcho-syndicalism of *The Green Book* does not work; it has failed Libya as much as Marxism failed the Soviet Union. The Libyans may be shielded from the harsher economic realities by their oil revenues, but at street level, where the value of the currency is tested, the truth is told: No one wants the Libyan dinar.

When the Libyan cargo/passenger vessel S.S. *Toletela* docks at the deep-water quay at Marsa in Malta, disgorging up to a thousand passengers, a queue quickly forms at the taxi rank. These are not people looking for taxis—but people selling dinars, exchanging them for Maltese pounds and U.S. dollars. The *bureaux de change* in Valletta do not want dinars; neither does anyone else, so the taxi rank bankers do well, buying dinars cheaply and then selling them to the next queue of passengers bound for Tripoli or Benghazi. This economic black market functions in reverse at the other end of the journey, for the Libyans demand that every new British or American worker arriving at the ports produces at least five hundred U.S. dollars to prove that he can support himself before his first paychecks are received.

We were warned before we went that we must have U.S. dollars. They want dollars, not sterling," one British engineer told me. "And then when we arrived we were told that our dollars would have to be changed into dinars at the official rate of 137.5 dinars for five hundred dollars, which bore little relation to the value of the U.S. dollar. Inside the country, there's a black economy and the dollar is all-powerful. The Libyans are desperate for dollars, and they will offer you as much as 1.2 or 1.6 dinars for the dollar, but you have to be careful. You can't trust them where money's concerned, and you run the risk of being stopped, jailed, or kicked out of the country, for what they call currency speculation, which is a criminal offense.

You can take as many dollars into the country as you like, but you are only supposed to exchange them at the official exchange rate. They check how many dollars you have when you arrive, and then when you leave you have to produce the dockets for any dollars you have changed at one of their banks to prove that you have changed them officially. It's okay to go in with dollars and leave with dollars, but the figures must add up and you must account for any dollars that you no longer have. . . . In the markets, and especially in the Gold Quarter, the traders all want dollars. There's a big trade in gold because Libyan girls like to wear it and own it. You might see a young girl walking down the street with her parents, wearing about three pounds in gold. . . . That would be great, in their eyes.

The result of this black market, and the fact that Libyan prices are high compared with those in Malta or other parts of the Mediterranean, is that foreign workers try to smuggle U.S. dollars into the country, either hidden in their shoes, sewn into the lining of their clothes, or concealed in their hand luggage. As Libyan customs inspection is often perfunctory, they usually get away with it—and then can get, at the unofficial rates, six hundred or maybe eight hundred dinars for each five hundred dollars, which enables them to hold their own.

Externally, this failure to manage their monetary policy has little effect upon Libya's revenus. Its oil and gas are sold for dollars, and its foreign contractors are likewise paid either in dollars or other foreign currencies through Libyan-owned, or part-owned, banks in Greece, Italy, Malta, Kuwait, and Bahrain, quite probably with money that has never entered Libya, but the existence of a thriving black-market economy is the clearest evidence of all that The Third Universal Theory is not working. The People have no confidence in the currency in their pockets.

This hunger for the U.S. dollar leads to the obvious question: why do the Libyans want it? The answer is further proof that there is something wrong with the fundamentals underpinning their society . . . for the money goes toward buying foreign consumer goods, clothes, cars, electrical appliances, videos, etc., which the younger Libyans acquire either on the black market, by driving across the border into Tunisia or Egypt, or by making weekend trips to Malta.

In his attempts to create a fair society, Gadaffi has frequently issued decrees that have had precisely the opposite effect to the one intended. Thinking he could keep the black market from flourishing, Gadaffi insisted in the early eighties that all shops should come under the control of the People's Committees. When that proved unpopular (because many Libyans aspire to be shopkeepers), he allowed the return of one-man businesses and family concerns in 1988–89, but hedged this concession by placing so many restrictions on imports that the shopkeepers cannot obtain the goods that people want ... and so there is this steady flow of Libyan vehicles to Tunisia and Egypt, returning with television sets, video recorders, video cameras, satellite dishes, sound systems, videotapes, compact discs, hair dryers, refrigerators, air conditioners, spare parts for German, French, and Italian cars and, especially, Western clothes like jeans, shirts, and jackets, which are difficult to obtain in Libya because of Gadaffi's controls. (The younger Libyans are desperate for Levi's jeans, and I have heard of several instances where younger British and American workers have been offered money for their jeans—there and then, in the street!)

An equally brisk trade is done by a new breed of Tunisian entrepreneurs, who have realized that Gadaffi's system of price subsidies means that some of their own country's goods are cheaper in Libya than they are in Tunisia. And so they, too, drive across the desert with television sets, video recorders, video cameras, etc., etc., which are sold from their car trunks in Tripoli, with the money being used to buy Tunisian sugar, coffee, olive oil, and tunafish for resale back home.

And then there is the other use for the dollar. ... Every weekend those Libyans who want it drive to Tunis, Cairo, or fly to Malta for women, gambling, and drink. Gadaffi himself may choose to live a virtuous, ascetic life, but there are still many Libyans who want to spend a night with a prostitute, gamble their dollars away at the tables, and drink the whiskey, brandy, and fine wines banned in their own country.

Of course, there are also prostitutes in Tripoli (although Gadaffi would probably deny it). They can be found touting for business in Mukhtar Street, with a steady queue of customers.

Its sexual and social patterns may often be as good a guide to the state of a nation's well-being as the health of its economy—and here, too, there is every indication that Gadaffi's dream of creating a society devoted to the ideals of Islam is far short of fruition. Libyan women are forbidden to marry non-Libyans, and when a young Libyan wants to take a wife he cannot go courting ... he has to visit a matchmaker, who is then employed to negotiate the terms of a dowry. Because a man can terminate a marriage under Muslim law by saying three times, "I divorce thee, I divorce thee, I divorce thee," a dowry is seen as a form of protection for the woman. A man will usually have to pay a dowry of twenty-five thousand to thirty thousand dinars, which gives the woman some money of her own to provide for herself if the marriage fails.

The Libyans justify this dowry system by saying that a divorced woman may never get the chance to marry again, for no Libyan will take a wife who has slept with another man—unless she is his brother's widow, for there is an equally firm tradition of widows remarrying within a family. In most situations, the bride is expected to be a virgin on her wedding night—and even to this day the father of the bridegroom has the honor of retrieving the bedsheet after their wedding night, and he will proudly show the bloody sheet to all his friends, as proof that his son has married a virgin. Sometimes he will dance through the streets, waving the sheet in the air, or wrapping it around his head, for the customs of the desert cannot be lost in one generation.

This is why there is such a demand for prostitutes and weekend trips to the fleshpots. Libya is a repressed society in which premarital sex is taboo, and young men have to save for their dowries. Many never make it and do not marry at all. Homosexuality is rife in Libya, although forbidden in the Koran.

It is in the basic, everyday business of the nation's economy that the failures of Gadaffi's vision are seen most starkly—for Libya is a country falling apart at the seams, and only held together through the employment of foreign workers. Gadaffi's dream is self-sufficiency, with fair shares for everyone, Libya for the Libyans— but its people have yet to grasp the concept of a work ethic. It is not that they are naturally lazy, but that centuries of living with the minimum of means have left them without the desire to work like Stakhanovites. They have no motivation, and live within a land still beset by sudden sandstorms, flash flooding, droughts, crop failure, plagues of locusts, and intense daily humidity at some times of the year, which makes even the simplest movements tiring. Decisions are never taken if they can possibly be avoided. Anything that can be left until tomorrow always is.

At the same time they combine this lassitude with a willingness to fulfill the Leader's wishes, so groups of soldiers man key sectors of the economy, factories, and oil fields that the Leader feels may be threatened by imperialist aggression; but because there are no aggressors, nor even the likelihood of one, the soldiers find armchairs, and sit there, fast asleep, their rifles across their knees, waiting to defend the fatherland. . . . Travel around Tripoli and you will see them, as astonishing in themselves as the dead cats and dogs, and the heaps of garbage.

Because the Libyans are reluctant to work, and can now choose not to perform the most menial tasks within the economy, over 700,000 Sudanese and 500,000 Egyptians do the dirtiest jobs for them, living in foreign workers' camps, which are ringed by metal fences and barbed wire, with the entrances also manned by soldiers with rifles, who check the workers in and out. "You should see how they treat the Sudanese," one British oil worker told me. "The Sudanese are the lowest of the low, employed to sweep away the sand, clean the sewers, and do all the messiest work in the hospitals . . . and the Libyans treat them with total contempt."

It's the same in the factories, the oil fields, and the Mediterranean ports; nothing would function but for the employment of foreign nationals, for it is they who handle all maintenance, provide the key personnel on the drilling platforms, and man the dredging craft that have the permanent task of keeping the ports free of the sand and silt that is always threatening to block Libya's waterways. Even when foreign tankers arrive to collect cargoes of oil and gas, it is foreign workers who travel out by motorboat or helicopter to monitor each operation and check the manifest.

In the factories, there is another problem—spare parts—for the machines are always breaking down. In the cardboard box factory, where, in theory, two hundred Libyans are employed to produce egg boxes, cigarette cartons, and the like, foreign workers have, at different times, been brought in from Egypt, Romania, and Britain to make its machines work. Each time they depart, production ceases again—for the machines, some of the most advanced in the world, imported from Switzerland and Denmark with a fully computer-controlled board mill, are invariably mishandled. One foreigner employed to work there told me:

It would make you weep. These are the finest machines of their kind that you will find anywhere. It's the same in all the Libyan factories. They only buy the best, and they bring it in from all over the world, but there seems to be something in their makeup that prevents them running anything properly.... If one of the machines breaks down, they will go and cannibalize another machine to get it working until, eventually, all the machines are out of action. The room in which the computers are kept is like a box room, with loose wires dangling and nothing connected where it should be.... It's the best equipment you could find, better than anything we've got in Britain, but lying idle because they don't know how to use it, and won't learn.

There was a big fire in this factory before we came here, so after the fire they bought a brand-new fire engine and recruited a fire crew to be on permanent stand-by. Soon after the fire engine arrived, one of the machines in the factory broke down, so they stripped the hose off the fire engine to mend the machine.... The fire engine is now completely useless, but every day they have a fire drill, driving around the factory site in all their uniforms, knowing that if they had another fire there would be nothing they could do about it.

The same sort of thing happened when they bought two brand-new buses, at a cost of sixty thousand pounds each, to transport the workers. As soon as the buses arrived, the Libyans started stripping them for spare parts—and they're now abandoned in a field, incapable of being driven.... outside in the yard we've got very expensive modern machinery just left out in the open because they haven't got a use for it, and a far greater stock of board than you would find in any Western factory, lying in the open without even tarpaulins to protect it. If the board gets damaged by rain, they just throw it away and buy some more.... They have absolutely no idea how to run a factory, and you can't tell them....

Although they pretend to be running their own economy, the Libyans continue to import foreign personnel because they know that without them, their system breaks down. The foreign workers are all well treated, but not exceptionally paid by European or American standards. There is a relatively narrow salary band in Libya, and this is reflected in the salaries paid to overseas workers. In the oil and gas fields, salaries of thirty thousand to forty thousand pounds are paid to some workers, but not many. More are paid in the twenty- to twenty-five-thousand range, with secretaries (British-trained secretaries are in high demand in Libya) paid around fifteen thousand pounds a year. These salaries may not be enormous, but if the workers stay out of Britain for a clear twelve months they are paid gross without any liability for tax—and the Britons and Americans working in Libya are provided with housing, food, and leisure facilities.

Like the Sudanese and Egyptians, they live in camps—but often complexes by the sea with private beaches, swimming pools, tennis courts, baseball fields, football fields, and, at Braygah, even their own golf course, and always a private room, sometimes a separate apartment. The Libyans treat them well. Although alcohol is officially prohibited, drinks are freely available—provided they follow the simple rule of never offering alcohol to a Muslim or consuming it in his or her presence. There are even known drinking clubs, where foreign workers meet socially, to which the Libyans turn a blind eye. In Tripoli, foreigners can also purchase spirits—whiskey, gin, or brandy—that arrive in the country in diplomatic bags and tend to cost around twenty-five pounds a bottle, or Flash, a locally produced crude alcohol, which is split down into thirds and mixed with fruit drinks. Drunk neat, it is said to send you blind.

"The Libyans drink a lot in their own homes, although they would never admit it," another expatriate worker told me.

There is a lot of drinking in the English, German, and Dutch communities, where people who have been working for the Libyans for years, in some cases twenty years or more, have been allowed to live with their families, but they are all kept well apart. . . . The Germans, the Swiss, the Dutch, and the Japanese are making fortunes out here, because everything is provided for them and they can save all the money they earn.

All this is a far cry from *The Green Book*, and its visions of a new society; it is also the Libya that nobody sees, for the Libyans themselves are forbidden to tell a foreigner anything about their society or the way it functions. No one can visit a factory making egg boxes, a complex housing foreign workers, the ports, or the oil platforms without a pass and an escort.

It is best not to be curious in Libya. "You have to be careful what you say, and you also have to be careful what you write in letters because letters are often opened up by the Post Office," another expatriate told me.

This seems to be done at random. It's the same with customs. Usually they will wave you through; but then sometimes they don't.... It is best to say nothing unless one is spoken to, and never, ever protest.... I always assume that someone is listening whenever I make a phone call, and take care to say nothing that might be misunderstood.

One night in a Malta bar, The Traffic Light, I was talking to an American. I will call him Jack. He was born in Sulphur, Louisiana, and has spent his whole life working in the oil industry. Now he has houses in Malta and Libya and still one in Texas, "though I don't reckon I can go back there now, after all these presidential orders.... That house in Texas is still costing me fourteen hundred dollars a month in outgoings, but one day I suppose the bank will have it, 'cause I don't reckon the government will let me go back."

That evening, Jack argued with his wife. Now the drink was talking and he told me about his brother, who died in a car crash in Jamaica, and had introduced him to his first prostitute, about the Texas oil fields, and his work in Libya as general manager for one of their oil companies, in charge of five drills, each employing eighty men—"and that includes the cooks and the roughnecks and five skilled engineers on each drill.... You have to have a full team to work a drill." He had worked on oil fields in India and Yemen, and spent seven years testing nuclear weapons underground in Nevada, until "an untimely and unnecessary divorce" left him homeless and starting all over again.

I have been out in Libya for eighteen months. There are now seven companies prospecting for oil.... I had one offshore drill that went down 19,944 feet without discovering oil, at a cost of $41 million, and there's a drill underway at the moment that's already cost $26 million and gone down nearly 13,000 feet without finding oil.... These are small sums of money by Libyan oil exploration standards. One drill costs $150,000 a day to operate, and presently $500 million a month is being spent in Libya, just looking for oil.... It's all costed, right down to the $5,600 a month that we spend on weather forecasts, for we lost $40 million when one offshore rig was blown away ... but if that oil is down there, we'll find it....

And they will, be sure they will, for Gadaffi is plowing his revenues back into finding new reserves, even though he knows that Libya has twenty years' production in reserve at present extraction rates, and maybe three hundred years' supply of gas.

The next morning, to check their accuracy, I put these figures to a geologist, another American also working in the oil fields in the Sirte Desert. I shall call him Don. He talks with a Texas accent, although he is now domiciled in Canada to avoid President Reagan's decree making it a criminal offense for any American to work in or engage in trade with Libya. This decree is still enforced. He is thirty-four years old and recently married for the second time.

They shouldn't have gone down to nearly twenty thousand," he said. "By twelve or thirteen thousand feet, they had enough information to know there was no oil to be found.... The world's reserves are dwindling, and most of the major producers now have less than nine years' supply. Libya is exceptional in having twenty years' supply, and their gas is now much more important, economically, than their oil. In Spain and Italy, Libyan gas is now being used to make calor gas, propane, butane, and naphtha ... but we're still looking for oil. We think it's there. So far we're looking near the coast, off shore, but there may be oil inland. There are still vast areas of desert that we haven't looked at. The oil companies haven't yet gone more than two hundred miles from the coast, to save the costs of laying new pipe—but that may be where the oil is. Wherever it is, we'll find it. Our expectations are high ... and they've got nothing to worry about, anyway, with all that uranium down in the south.

And so the revolution may continue as it began, with oil ... if it can survive the strains developing within, if its leader has humility enough to realize that his theories may be less than perfect, that the People do need help, and that today's enemies might be tomorrow's friends.

Postscript

Gadaffi is hardly a wicked man, no evil genius, and certainly no Saddam Hussein. He falls into none of the conventional molds into which the West usually enjoys casting its villains. His achievements have been understated, his character distorted, with Britain and America, and especially the Reagan government, relying too much upon low-level intelligence gathering in the Mediterranean basin and poor diplomatic advice. A conjunction of strange events, coinciding with Irangate and hostage-taking in Beirut, allowed the specter of Gadaffi to grow in the public mind, arising from the desert like some ethereal giant in an Arabian fairy tale. Gadaffi became a convenient bogeyman, the justification for the continued presence of the U.S. Sixth Fleet in the Mediterranean, but was the bogeyman ever more than a myth? Were Gadaffi's threats ever worse than his rhetoric? The West would do well to remember that a puny pugilist is still a puny pugilist even when he tries to enter the ring with the heavyweights. To carry the metaphor one stage further, if Gadaffi was boxing beyond his weight, as he surely was, why *did* America exaggerate his importance by deploying its military might against him upon flimsy and even false pretenses?

Gadaffi has never been a covert operator. His decisions to finance what were then perceived as left-wing movements in Africa, South America, the Middle East, and Northern Ireland were openly stated before the policies came into effect. This may have shocked the U.S. and British Ambassadors into a public walkout (see page 152), but there was nothing underhand.

Likewise, Gadaffi formally announced his decision to aid the IRA in Northern Ireland; said when he was going to cancel the program, and only resumed it again when Mrs. Thatcher colluded with President Reagan in the attempt to assassinate him. This policy was abandoned in 1989 after Gadaffi belatedly realized that the IRA was engaged in the murder of innocent civilians, but the weapons with which he supplied the IRA continue to be used against the British both in Ireland and on the mainland.

In recent years, Gadaffi has repeatedly renounced violence. Many of the causes that he funded twenty years ago are now respectable. Apartheid is coming to an end in South Africa. Democracy is spreading through South America. A constitutional settlement draws closer in the Middle East with more and more Arab states recognizing Israel's right to exist and the Jews themselves engaged in negotiation.

During Gadaffi's tenure of power, the world has become a smaller place, a global economy, with multinational manufacturers and bankers possessing the technology to operate as though neither night nor day nor natural boundaries any longer existed. One day, Libya will be brought back within the community of nations; the question is when—and will it be with Gadaffi still in charge? He is, after all, one of the world's younger leaders, despite his political longevity, and may well continue to outlast U.S. presidents and British prime ministers. There is little chance of the Libyans removing him, for they mostly seem to hold Gadaffi in genuine affection.

The reader will have noticed that I have made no further mention of Locherbie, largely restricting terrorism to the chronological sections where an appalling catalogue of hijackings, bombings, and carnage is detailed in sequence. This is not meant to minimize their horror, but to emphasize that there is little direct evidence linking Gadaffi to specific acts of terrorism.

Gadaffi has provided shelter for hijackers; funds for Carlos the Jackal, for Abu Nidal, and other freelance terrorist groups, plus training, arms, and finance for fellow-revolutionaries committed to aims similar to his own, but his finger has been far from the trigger, other than when he has ordered the assassination of emigres (as detailed in the chronological sections). These have been situations where Libyans have pursued other Libyans on foreign soil, and Gadaffi is by no means the only political leader to endeavor to shoot his enemies before they shoot him. This may be reprehensible, the sort of thing other governments engage in covertly, but it is not terrorism. The most that may be said of Gadaffi in that connection is that he made terrorism possible, without engaging in it. This allows him to plead that Libya's money was used to further the cause of the African National Congress, the Sandinistas or the Palestinians, without any control over whatever acts may have been committed in their name. In many parts of the world, this has made Gadaffi a hero for, whatever else he may be, Gadaffi is essentially an honest man. He is true to his faith and open in his objectives. It would be a mortal sin for a Muslim to lie.

So who was responsible for Locherbie? Unless the matter is properly tested in an international court of law, operating openly and fairly without being influenced by politics, we have no means of knowing whether the two accused Libyans are guilty of the charges against them. Likewise, there is no international process by which we may evaluate Libya's charges against the West, or establish the truth of the allegation—made by Yasser Arafat and others—that the Locherbie bomb was actually planted by Syrians and Iranians as an act of revenge for the shooting down of an Iranian airbus over the Persian Gulf by the U.S.S. *Vincennes* a few months before. Neither are we likely to learn whether it is true that the West knew of the Syrian and Iranian involvement, but chose to ignore it having received their tacit support in the conflict with Iraq.

Does the truth matter? The answer should always be yes, however murky the circumstances, but this leads us to the difficulty that has to be resolved internationally, by the United Nations, if not the two powers, Britain and the United States, that have chosen to involve the world as a whole in their long-running dispute with Gadaffi. The Libyans believe they are being persecuted by the British and the Americans, who cannot forgive them for being kicked out of Libya over twenty years ago. The Libyans remark that the Italians are mature enough in their political judgments and their sense of history to reach a modus vivendi, but the British, still sore after losing their empire and their status on the world stage, and the Americans, having suffered one humiliation after another in Asia and the Middle East, are unwilling to let bygones be bygones.

The author makes no comment on the Libyans' attitude, or whether the sins of one party outweigh the sins of another, other than to point out that Libya enjoys good relations with the other major European nations, exporting its gas and oil to the Mediterranean powers, including Israel, and importing whatever machinery, vehicles, or domestic products it needs from all parts of the world.

Through persuasion, or threats to remove their favored-nation trading status, America may be able to carry other U.N. states so far ... but, perhaps, no further once their interests and alliances become affected. The balance is a fine one. The British Conservative Party has removed the Prime Minister who got them into this mess. The United States has chosen a new President. Perhaps the time has come for the West to take Gadaffi at his word, to accept his renunciation of violence, and to learn to live with his own special brand of Islam.

Bibliography

Researching Libya's history, and particularly that of its tribal system, is difficult since much of the country was impassable to Western explorers until well into the twentieth century and the Bedouin kept no written records. A considerable literature was published during the Italian occupation, without being translated into English, which was another problem. In my researches I have therefore had to search far and wide for source material. Some of these books may only have a chapter on Libya, others more extensive sections.

Agee, Philip. *Inside the Company: CIA Diary.* (Stonehill Publishing Co., New York, 1975). Of no direct relevance, but does explain CIA thinking.

Allan, J.A., *Libya Since Independence.* (St. Martin's Press, New York, 1982). Academic essays dealing with economic and social aspects of Libya's development.

Alkhuli, Muhammad Ali. *The Need for Islam.* (Riyadh, Saudi Arabia, 1981). Explains Islam in a way that a non-Muslim can understand.

Bagnold, Ralph A. *Libyan Sands.* (Hodder & Stoughton, 1935). Classic travel book that describes Libyan landscape.

Bianco, Mirella. *Gadafi: Voice from the Desert.* (Published first in France by Editions Stock, 1974, and then in English translation by Longman, London, 1975). Thoroughly recommended; author managed to reach Gadaffi in the early days of the revolution, before Libya's isolation.

Blundy, David, and Andrew Lycett. *Qaddafi and the Libyan Revolution.* (George Weidenfeld & Nicholson, London, 1987). A serious study that should be read with caution. Relies too heavily on journalistic and CIA sources.

Blunsum, Terence L. *Libya: The Country and Its People*. (Queen Anne Press, London, 1968). Academic textbook that examines Libya in its early independence.

Carrington, Richard. *East from Tunis*. (Travel Book Club, London, c. 1957). Good descriptive detail.

Cooley, John K. *Libyan Sandstorm*. (Holt, Rinehart & Winston, New York, 1982). Journalistic account of the revolution, etc., without explaining historical background. Also relies heavily on journalistic and CIA sources.

Dawton, Anthony. *Libya: A Personal View of a Jamahiriya*. (Hakima P.R. Ltd., London, 1981). An uncritical view of the revolution, clearly financed by the Libyans—but with a fine selection of photographs.

De Gramont, Sanche. *The Strong Brown God: The Story of the Niger River*. (Granada, London, 1975). Useful for its study of the slave trade.

Dobson, Christopher, and Ronald Payne. *The Carlos Complex: A Pattern of Violence*. (Hodder & Stoughton, London, 1977). Predictable study of terrorism with some good sections on Gadaffi.

Epton, Nina. *Oasis Kingdom: The Libyan Story*. (Jarrolds, London, 1952). Flowery but useful study of Libya in the immediate postwar years.

Evans-Pritchard, E.E. *The Sanusi of Cyrenaica*. (Clarendon Press, Oxford, 1949). A reliable academic account of the Sanusi, examining their history and culture. Thoroughly recommended.

Fantoli, Amilcare. *The Tourist's Tripolitania*. (Triopoli, 1927). Suggests that the glories of ancient Rome are being reborn in Libya; written during the Fascist occupation.

First, Ruth. *Libya: The Elusive Revolution*. (Penguin Books, London, 1974). Looks at the early days of the revolution.

Forbes, Rosita. *The Secret of the Sahara: Kufara*. (Originally published 1921, republished by Penguin Books, London, 1937). Gives a clear impression of a world untouched by Western man.

Fox, Robert. *The Inner Sea: The Mediterranean and Its People*. (Sinclair-Stevenson Ltd., London, 1991). Useful for its historical context.

Gadaffi, Muammar. *The Green Book*. (English translation published in three parts between 1967 and 1981 by Martin Brian & O'Keefe Ltd., London).

———. *Discourses*. (Aedam Publishers, Malta and Tripoli, 1975)

———. *International Colloquium of Muammar Qathafi's Thought—The Green Book and The Third Universal Theory and The New Jamahiriyan System*. Report of the Conference in Venezuela. (World Center for Researches and Studies of *The Green Book*, Tripoli, c. 1981).

Habib, Dr. Henri. *Libya Past and Present*. (Aedam Publishing House Ltd., Malta and Tripoli, 1979). Almost indigestible, but packed with Libyan constitutional detail unavailable elsewhere; puts forth a pro-Libyan viewpoint.

Haynes, D.E.L. *Ancient Tripolitania*. (British Military Administration, 1947).

Holmboe, Knud. *Desert Encounter: An Adventurous Journey Through Italian Africa*. (First published in Denmark, 1931, under the title *Orkenen braender*. English translation pub. by George G. Harrap & Co. Ltd., London, 1936). Thorough account of the author's journey through Libya during the Fascist occupation. Recommended.

Jarvis, Maj. C.S. *Desert and Delta*. (John Murray, London, 1938). Useful for its description of the western desert.

———. *Heresies and Humours*. (Country Life, London, 1945). Some more good descriptive detail, especially of the wild life.

Keith, Agnes Newton. *Children of Allah: Between the Sea and the Sahara* (Michael Joseph, London, 1966). Interesting account of Bedouin customs.

Marchetti, Victor, and John D. Marks. *The CIA and the Cult of Intelligence*. (Dell, New York, 1983). Exposes the CIA's subversive activities in other countries. Indirectly, highly relevant—for the CIA has been implicated in numerous attempts to overthrow or assassinate Gadaffi.

Margoliouth, Prof. D.S. *Mohammedanism*. (Williams & Norgate, London, c. 1900).

Murabet, Mohammed. *Tripolitania: The Land and Its People*. (Progress Press, Malta, 1959). A slim book, but highly recommended for the background information on the el Gadadfa's life in the Sirte Desert.

Oliver, Roland and J.D. Fage. *A Short History of Africa*. (Penguin Books, London, 1962, et seq.). Useful general guide, though weak on historical background.

Ransley, Neville. *A Geography of the Maltese Islands*. (Progress Press Ltd., Malta, 1982). A good textbook that fills a gap, given the lack of published information on Libya's geography.

Rodinson, Maxine. *Israel and The Arabs*. (Penguin Books, London, 1968). Puts Libya's attitude in a wider context.

Rodwell, Rev. J.M. *The Koran, Translated from the Arabic*. (E.P. Dutton & Co., New York, 1909). There are other translations, but this is the one the author used when seeking to establish the origin of Libyan policy.

Sampson, Anthony. *The Seven Sisters: The Great Oil Companies and the World They Made*. (Hodder & Stoughton, London, 1975). A readable work that puts Libya's oil industry in a global context. Recommended.

Seale, Patrick, and Maureen McConville. *The Hilton Assignment*. (Maurice Temple Smith, London, 1973). Describes one of the earliest attempts to overthrow Gadaffi; essential reading for an understanding of the period.

Taheri, Amir. *Holy Terror: The Inside Story of Islamic Terrorism*. (Century Hutchinson, London, 1987). Looks at terrorism throughout the Islamic world, without explaining that Gadaffi has always opposed the fundamentalists.

Waddams, Frank. *The Libyan Oil Industry*. (Croom Helm, London, 1980). An academic study.

Wellard, James. *The Great Sahara*. (Hutchinson, London, 1964). Highly recommended history of the Sahara.

Williams, Gwyn. *Green Mountain: An Informal Guide to Cyrenaica and its Jebel Akhdar*. (Faber & Faber, London, 1963). Enjoyable description, written when it was still accessible to the casual traveler.

Willmore, J.S. *A Manual of the Spoken Arabic of Egypt*. (David Nutt, London, 1908). The author found this handbook indispensible, since Egyptian and Libyan spoken Arabic are very similar.

Wright, John. *Libya: A Modern History*. (Croom Helm, London, 1981). Useful, since the author was in Libya at the time of the revolution.

There were two other anonymous studies that also proved exceptionally useful: *Libya: A Brief Political and Economic Survey*, published by
the Royal Institute of Economic Affairs, 1958, and Amnesty International's *Libya: Prisoner Concerns in the Light of Recent Legal Reforms*
(1991), which insisted that Gadaffi was still holding political opponents
in prison.

INDEX

313